C-1893   CAREER EXAMINATION SERIES

This is your
PASSBOOK for...

Administrative Construction Project Manager

Test Preparation Study Guide
Questions & Answers

NATIONAL LEARNING CORPORATION®

COPYRIGHT NOTICE

This book is SOLELY intended for, is sold ONLY to, and its use is RESTRICTED to individual, bona fide applicants or candidates who qualify by virtue of having seriously filed applications for appropriate license, certificate, professional and/or promotional advancement, higher school matriculation, scholarship, or other legitimate requirements of education and/or governmental authorities.

This book is NOT intended for use, class instruction, tutoring, training, duplication, copying, reprinting, excerption, or adaptation, etc., by:

1) Other publishers
2) Proprietors and/or Instructors of "Coaching" and/or Preparatory Courses
3) Personnel and/or Training Divisions of commercial, industrial, and governmental organizations
4) Schools, colleges, or universities and/or their departments and staffs, including teachers and other personnel
5) Testing Agencies or Bureaus
6) Study groups which seek by the purchase of a single volume to copy and/or duplicate and/or adapt this material for use by the group as a whole without having purchased individual volumes for each of the members of the group
7) Et al.

Such persons would be in violation of appropriate Federal and State statutes.

PROVISION OF LICENSING AGREEMENTS – Recognized educational, commercial, industrial, and governmental institutions and organizations, and others legitimately engaged in educational pursuits, including training, testing, and measurement activities, may address request for a licensing agreement to the copyright owners, who will determine whether, and under what conditions, including fees and charges, the materials in this book may be used them. In other words, a licensing facility exists for the legitimate use of the material in this book on other than an individual basis. However, it is asseverated and affirmed here that the material in this book CANNOT be used without the receipt of the express permission of such a licensing agreement from the Publishers. Inquiries re licensing should be addressed to the company, attention rights and permissions department.

All rights reserved, including the right of reproduction in whole or in part, in any form or by any means, electronic or mechanical, including photocopying, recording, or by any information storage and retrieval system, without permission in writing from the Publisher.

Copyright © 2024 by
National Learning Corporation

212 Michael Drive, Syosset, NY 11791
(516) 921-8888 • www.passbooks.com
E-mail: info@passbooks.com

PUBLISHED IN THE UNITED STATES OF AMERICA

PASSBOOK® SERIES

THE *PASSBOOK® SERIES* has been created to prepare applicants and candidates for the ultimate academic battlefield – the examination room.

At some time in our lives, each and every one of us may be required to take an examination – for validation, matriculation, admission, qualification, registration, certification, or licensure.

Based on the assumption that every applicant or candidate has met the basic formal educational standards, has taken the required number of courses, and read the necessary texts, the *PASSBOOK® SERIES* furnishes the one special preparation which may assure passing with confidence, instead of failing with insecurity. Examination questions – together with answers – are furnished as the basic vehicle for study so that the mysteries of the examination and its compounding difficulties may be eliminated or diminished by a sure method.

This book is meant to help you pass your examination provided that you qualify and are serious in your objective.

The entire field is reviewed through the huge store of content information which is succinctly presented through a provocative and challenging approach – the question-and-answer method.

A climate of success is established by furnishing the correct answers at the end of each test.

You soon learn to recognize types of questions, forms of questions, and patterns of questioning. You may even begin to anticipate expected outcomes.

You perceive that many questions are repeated or adapted so that you can gain acute insights, which may enable you to score many sure points.

You learn how to confront new questions, or types of questions, and to attack them confidently and work out the correct answers.

You note objectives and emphases, and recognize pitfalls and dangers, so that you may make positive educational adjustments.

Moreover, you are kept fully informed in relation to new concepts, methods, practices, and directions in the field.

You discover that you are actually taking the examination all the time: you are preparing for the examination by "taking" an examination, not by reading extraneous and/or supererogatory textbooks.

In short, this PASSBOOK®, used directedly, should be an important factor in helping you to pass your test.

ADMINISTRATIVE CONSTRUCTION PROJECT MANAGER

DUTIES
Administrative Construction Project Managers under administrative direction, with extremely wide latitude for the exercise of independent judgment, initiative and action, perform extremely difficult, responsible and complex work in the capacity of directing that the execution of capital construction projects for a sizable and significant geographic locality or service area is timely and cost effective. They direct a large staff of construction professionals engaged in overseeing the execution of capital construction projects; exercise the full administrative and technical responsibilities for planning, organizing, and directing staff in the management of construction projects; direct the resolution of extraordinary construction problems; when designated, represent the agency head or his/her deputy in meetings with contractors and service delivery, regulatory, and oversight agencies or perform other assignments equivalent to that described herein; and all Administrative Construction Project Managers perform related work.

THE SCOPE OF THE EXAMINATION
The multiple choice In-Basket test is designed to assess candidates' abilities in the areas of problem solving and decision making; supervisory and management control including delegation, planning, organizing, and prioritizing; development of subordinates; written comprehension; written communication; mathematical and statistical analysis; standards of proper employee ethical conduct and other related areas.

HOW TO TAKE A TEST

I. YOU MUST PASS AN EXAMINATION

A. *WHAT EVERY CANDIDATE SHOULD KNOW*

Examination applicants often ask us for help in preparing for the written test. What can I study in advance? What kinds of questions will be asked? How will the test be given? How will the papers be graded?

As an applicant for a civil service examination, you may be wondering about some of these things. Our purpose here is to suggest effective methods of advance study and to describe civil service examinations.

Your chances for success on this examination can be increased if you know how to prepare. Those "pre-examination jitters" can be reduced if you know what to expect. You can even experience an adventure in good citizenship if you know why civil service exams are given.

B. *WHY ARE CIVIL SERVICE EXAMINATIONS GIVEN?*

Civil service examinations are important to you in two ways. As a citizen, you want public jobs filled by employees who know how to do their work. As a job seeker, you want a fair chance to compete for that job on an equal footing with other candidates. The best-known means of accomplishing this two-fold goal is the competitive examination.

Exams are widely publicized throughout the nation. They may be administered for jobs in federal, state, city, municipal, town or village governments or agencies.

Any citizen may apply, with some limitations, such as the age or residence of applicants. Your experience and education may be reviewed to see whether you meet the requirements for the particular examination. When these requirements exist, they are reasonable and applied consistently to all applicants. Thus, a competitive examination may cause you some uneasiness now, but it is your privilege and safeguard.

C. *HOW ARE CIVIL SERVICE EXAMS DEVELOPED?*

Examinations are carefully written by trained technicians who are specialists in the field known as "psychological measurement," in consultation with recognized authorities in the field of work that the test will cover. These experts recommend the subject matter areas or skills to be tested; only those knowledges or skills important to your success on the job are included. The most reliable books and source materials available are used as references. Together, the experts and technicians judge the difficulty level of the questions.

Test technicians know how to phrase questions so that the problem is clearly stated. Their ethics do not permit "trick" or "catch" questions. Questions may have been tried out on sample groups, or subjected to statistical analysis, to determine their usefulness.

Written tests are often used in combination with performance tests, ratings of training and experience, and oral interviews. All of these measures combine to form the best-known means of finding the right person for the right job.

II. HOW TO PASS THE WRITTEN TEST

A. NATURE OF THE EXAMINATION

To prepare intelligently for civil service examinations, you should know how they differ from school examinations you have taken. In school you were assigned certain definite pages to read or subjects to cover. The examination questions were quite detailed and usually emphasized memory. Civil service exams, on the other hand, try to discover your present ability to perform the duties of a position, plus your potentiality to learn these duties. In other words, a civil service exam attempts to predict how successful you will be. Questions cover such a broad area that they cannot be as minute and detailed as school exam questions.

In the public service similar kinds of work, or positions, are grouped together in one "class." This process is known as *position-classification*. All the positions in a class are paid according to the salary range for that class. One class title covers all of these positions, and they are all tested by the same examination.

B. FOUR BASIC STEPS

1) Study the announcement

How, then, can you know what subjects to study? Our best answer is: "Learn as much as possible about the class of positions for which you've applied." The exam will test the knowledge, skills and abilities needed to do the work.

Your most valuable source of information about the position you want is the official exam announcement. This announcement lists the training and experience qualifications. Check these standards and apply only if you come reasonably close to meeting them.

The brief description of the position in the examination announcement offers some clues to the subjects which will be tested. Think about the job itself. Review the duties in your mind. Can you perform them, or are there some in which you are rusty? Fill in the blank spots in your preparation.

Many jurisdictions preview the written test in the exam announcement by including a section called "Knowledge and Abilities Required," "Scope of the Examination," or some similar heading. Here you will find out specifically what fields will be tested.

2) Review your own background

Once you learn in general what the position is all about, and what you need to know to do the work, ask yourself which subjects you already know fairly well and which need improvement. You may wonder whether to concentrate on improving your strong areas or on building some background in your fields of weakness. When the announcement has specified "some knowledge" or "considerable knowledge," or has used adjectives like "beginning principles of..." or "advanced ... methods," you can get a clue as to the number and difficulty of questions to be asked in any given field. More questions, and hence broader coverage, would be included for those subjects which are more important in the work. Now weigh your strengths and weaknesses against the job requirements and prepare accordingly.

3) Determine the level of the position

Another way to tell how intensively you should prepare is to understand the level of the job for which you are applying. Is it the entering level? In other words, is this the position in which beginners in a field of work are hired? Or is it an intermediate or advanced level? Sometimes this is indicated by such words as "Junior" or "Senior" in the class title. Other jurisdictions use Roman numerals to designate the level – Clerk I, Clerk II, for example. The word "Supervisor" sometimes appears in the title. If the level is not indicated by the title, check the description of duties. Will you be working under very close supervision, or will you have responsibility for independent decisions in this work?

4) Choose appropriate study materials

Now that you know the subjects to be examined and the relative amount of each subject to be covered, you can choose suitable study materials. For beginning level jobs, or even advanced ones, if you have a pronounced weakness in some aspect of your training, read a modern, standard textbook in that field. Be sure it is up to date and has general coverage. Such books are normally available at your library, and the librarian will be glad to help you locate one. For entry-level positions, questions of appropriate difficulty are chosen – neither highly advanced questions, nor those too simple. Such questions require careful thought but not advanced training.

If the position for which you are applying is technical or advanced, you will read more advanced, specialized material. If you are already familiar with the basic principles of your field, elementary textbooks would waste your time. Concentrate on advanced textbooks and technical periodicals. Think through the concepts and review difficult problems in your field.

These are all general sources. You can get more ideas on your own initiative, following these leads. For example, training manuals and publications of the government agency which employs workers in your field can be useful, particularly for technical and professional positions. A letter or visit to the government department involved may result in more specific study suggestions, and certainly will provide you with a more definite idea of the exact nature of the position you are seeking.

III. KINDS OF TESTS

Tests are used for purposes other than measuring knowledge and ability to perform specified duties. For some positions, it is equally important to test ability to make adjustments to new situations or to profit from training. In others, basic mental abilities not dependent on information are essential. Questions which test these things may not appear as pertinent to the duties of the position as those which test for knowledge and information. Yet they are often highly important parts of a fair examination. For very general questions, it is almost impossible to help you direct your study efforts. What we can do is to point out some of the more common of these general abilities needed in public service positions and describe some typical questions.

1) General information

Broad, general information has been found useful for predicting job success in some kinds of work. This is tested in a variety of ways, from vocabulary lists to questions about current events. Basic background in some field of work, such as sociology or economics, may be sampled in a group of questions. Often these are principles which have become familiar to most persons through exposure rather than through formal training. It is difficult to advise you how to study for these questions; being alert to the world around you is our best suggestion.

2) Verbal ability

An example of an ability needed in many positions is verbal or language ability. Verbal ability is, in brief, the ability to use and understand words. Vocabulary and grammar tests are typical measures of this ability. Reading comprehension or paragraph interpretation questions are common in many kinds of civil service tests. You are given a paragraph of written material and asked to find its central meaning.

3) Numerical ability

Number skills can be tested by the familiar arithmetic problem, by checking paired lists of numbers to see which are alike and which are different, or by interpreting charts and graphs. In the latter test, a graph may be printed in the test booklet which you are asked to use as the basis for answering questions.

4) Observation

A popular test for law-enforcement positions is the observation test. A picture is shown to you for several minutes, then taken away. Questions about the picture test your ability to observe both details and larger elements.

5) Following directions

In many positions in the public service, the employee must be able to carry out written instructions dependably and accurately. You may be given a chart with several columns, each column listing a variety of information. The questions require you to carry out directions involving the information given in the chart.

6) Skills and aptitudes

Performance tests effectively measure some manual skills and aptitudes. When the skill is one in which you are trained, such as typing or shorthand, you can practice. These tests are often very much like those given in business school or high school courses. For many of the other skills and aptitudes, however, no short-time preparation can be made. Skills and abilities natural to you or that you have developed throughout your lifetime are being tested.

Many of the general questions just described provide all the data needed to answer the questions and ask you to use your reasoning ability to find the answers. Your best preparation for these tests, as well as for tests of facts and ideas, is to be at your physical and mental best. You, no doubt, have your own methods of getting into an exam-taking mood and keeping "in shape." The next section lists some ideas on this subject.

IV. KINDS OF QUESTIONS

Only rarely is the "essay" question, which you answer in narrative form, used in civil service tests. Civil service tests are usually of the short-answer type. Full instructions for answering these questions will be given to you at the examination. But in case this is your first experience with short-answer questions and separate answer sheets, here is what you need to know:

1) Multiple-choice Questions

Most popular of the short-answer questions is the "multiple choice" or "best answer" question. It can be used, for example, to test for factual knowledge, ability to solve problems or judgment in meeting situations found at work.

A multiple-choice question is normally one of three types—

- It can begin with an incomplete statement followed by several possible endings. You are to find the one ending which *best* completes the statement, although some of the others may not be entirely wrong.
- It can also be a complete statement in the form of a question which is answered by choosing one of the statements listed.

- It can be in the form of a problem – again you select the best answer.

Here is an example of a multiple-choice question with a discussion which should give you some clues as to the method for choosing the right answer:

When an employee has a complaint about his assignment, the action which will *best* help him overcome his difficulty is to
   A. discuss his difficulty with his coworkers
   B. take the problem to the head of the organization
   C. take the problem to the person who gave him the assignment
   D. say nothing to anyone about his complaint

In answering this question, you should study each of the choices to find which is best. Consider choice "A" – Certainly an employee may discuss his complaint with fellow employees, but no change or improvement can result, and the complaint remains unresolved. Choice "B" is a poor choice since the head of the organization probably does not know what assignment you have been given, and taking your problem to him is known as "going over the head" of the supervisor. The supervisor, or person who made the assignment, is the person who can clarify it or correct any injustice. Choice "C" is, therefore, correct. To say nothing, as in choice "D," is unwise. Supervisors have and interest in knowing the problems employees are facing, and the employee is seeking a solution to his problem.

2) True/False Questions

The "true/false" or "right/wrong" form of question is sometimes used. Here a complete statement is given. Your job is to decide whether the statement is right or wrong.

SAMPLE: A roaming cell-phone call to a nearby city costs less than a non-roaming call to a distant city.

This statement is wrong, or false, since roaming calls are more expensive.

This is not a complete list of all possible question forms, although most of the others are variations of these common types. You will always get complete directions for answering questions. Be sure you understand *how* to mark your answers – ask questions until you do.

V. RECORDING YOUR ANSWERS

Computer terminals are used more and more today for many different kinds of exams.
For an examination with very few applicants, you may be told to record your answers in the test booklet itself. Separate answer sheets are much more common. If this separate answer sheet is to be scored by machine – and this is often the case – it is highly important that you mark your answers correctly in order to get credit.
An electronic scoring machine is often used in civil service offices because of the speed with which papers can be scored. Machine-scored answer sheets must be marked with a pencil, which will be given to you. This pencil has a high graphite content which responds to the electronic scoring machine. As a matter of fact, stray dots may register as answers, so do not let your pencil rest on the answer sheet while you are pondering the correct answer. Also, if your pencil lead breaks or is otherwise defective, ask for another.

Since the answer sheet will be dropped in a slot in the scoring machine, be careful not to bend the corners or get the paper crumpled.

The answer sheet normally has five vertical columns of numbers, with 30 numbers to a column. These numbers correspond to the question numbers in your test booklet. After each number, going across the page are four or five pairs of dotted lines. These short dotted lines have small letters or numbers above them. The first two pairs may also have a "T" or "F" above the letters. This indicates that the first two pairs only are to be used if the questions are of the true-false type. If the questions are multiple choice, disregard the "T" and "F" and pay attention only to the small letters or numbers.

Answer your questions in the manner of the sample that follows:

32. The largest city in the United States is
    A. Washington, D.C.
    B. New York City
    C. Chicago
    D. Detroit
    E. San Francisco

1) Choose the answer you think is best. (New York City is the largest, so "B" is correct.)
2) Find the row of dotted lines numbered the same as the question you are answering. (Find row number 32)
3) Find the pair of dotted lines corresponding to the answer. (Find the pair of lines under the mark "B.")
4) Make a solid black mark between the dotted lines.

VI. BEFORE THE TEST

Common sense will help you find procedures to follow to get ready for an examination. Too many of us, however, overlook these sensible measures. Indeed, nervousness and fatigue have been found to be the most serious reasons why applicants fail to do their best on civil service tests. Here is a list of reminders:

- Begin your preparation early – Don't wait until the last minute to go scurrying around for books and materials or to find out what the position is all about.
- Prepare continuously – An hour a night for a week is better than an all-night cram session. This has been definitely established. What is more, a night a week for a month will return better dividends than crowding your study into a shorter period of time.
- Locate the place of the exam – You have been sent a notice telling you when and where to report for the examination. If the location is in a different town or otherwise unfamiliar to you, it would be well to inquire the best route and learn something about the building.
- Relax the night before the test – Allow your mind to rest. Do not study at all that night. Plan some mild recreation or diversion; then go to bed early and get a good night's sleep.
- Get up early enough to make a leisurely trip to the place for the test – This way unforeseen events, traffic snarls, unfamiliar buildings, etc. will not upset you.
- Dress comfortably – A written test is not a fashion show. You will be known by number and not by name, so wear something comfortable.

- Leave excess paraphernalia at home – Shopping bags and odd bundles will get in your way. You need bring only the items mentioned in the official notice you received; usually everything you need is provided. Do not bring reference books to the exam. They will only confuse those last minutes and be taken away from you when in the test room.
- Arrive somewhat ahead of time – If because of transportation schedules you must get there very early, bring a newspaper or magazine to take your mind off yourself while waiting.
- Locate the examination room – When you have found the proper room, you will be directed to the seat or part of the room where you will sit. Sometimes you are given a sheet of instructions to read while you are waiting. Do not fill out any forms until you are told to do so; just read them and be prepared.
- Relax and prepare to listen to the instructions
- If you have any physical problem that may keep you from doing your best, be sure to tell the test administrator. If you are sick or in poor health, you really cannot do your best on the exam. You can come back and take the test some other time.

VII. AT THE TEST

The day of the test is here and you have the test booklet in your hand. The temptation to get going is very strong. Caution! There is more to success than knowing the right answers. You must know how to identify your papers and understand variations in the type of short-answer question used in this particular examination. Follow these suggestions for maximum results from your efforts:

1) Cooperate with the monitor

The test administrator has a duty to create a situation in which you can be as much at ease as possible. He will give instructions, tell you when to begin, check to see that you are marking your answer sheet correctly, and so on. He is not there to guard you, although he will see that your competitors do not take unfair advantage. He wants to help you do your best.

2) Listen to all instructions

Don't jump the gun! Wait until you understand all directions. In most civil service tests you get more time than you need to answer the questions. So don't be in a hurry. Read each word of instructions until you clearly understand the meaning. Study the examples, listen to all announcements and follow directions. Ask questions if you do not understand what to do.

3) Identify your papers

Civil service exams are usually identified by number only. You will be assigned a number; you must not put your name on your test papers. Be sure to copy your number correctly. Since more than one exam may be given, copy your exact examination title.

4) Plan your time

Unless you are told that a test is a "speed" or "rate of work" test, speed itself is usually not important. Time enough to answer all the questions will be provided, but this does not mean that you have all day. An overall time limit has been set. Divide the total time (in minutes) by the number of questions to determine the approximate time you have for each question.

5) Do not linger over difficult questions

If you come across a difficult question, mark it with a paper clip (useful to have along) and come back to it when you have been through the booklet. One caution if you do this – be sure to skip a number on your answer sheet as well. Check often to be sure that you have not lost your place and that you are marking in the row numbered the same as the question you are answering.

6) Read the questions

Be sure you know what the question asks! Many capable people are unsuccessful because they failed to *read* the questions correctly.

7) Answer all questions

Unless you have been instructed that a penalty will be deducted for incorrect answers, it is better to guess than to omit a question.

8) Speed tests

It is often better NOT to guess on speed tests. It has been found that on timed tests people are tempted to spend the last few seconds before time is called in marking answers at random – without even reading them – in the hope of picking up a few extra points. To discourage this practice, the instructions may warn you that your score will be "corrected" for guessing. That is, a penalty will be applied. The incorrect answers will be deducted from the correct ones, or some other penalty formula will be used.

9) Review your answers

If you finish before time is called, go back to the questions you guessed or omitted to give them further thought. Review other answers if you have time.

10) Return your test materials

If you are ready to leave before others have finished or time is called, take ALL your materials to the monitor and leave quietly. Never take any test material with you. The monitor can discover whose papers are not complete, and taking a test booklet may be grounds for disqualification.

VIII. EXAMINATION TECHNIQUES

1) Read the general instructions carefully. These are usually printed on the first page of the exam booklet. As a rule, these instructions refer to the timing of the examination; the fact that you should not start work until the signal and must stop work at a signal, etc. If there are any *special* instructions, such as a choice of questions to be answered, make sure that you note this instruction carefully.

2) When you are ready to start work on the examination, that is as soon as the signal has been given, read the instructions to each question booklet, underline any key words or phrases, such as *least, best, outline, describe* and the like. In this way you will tend to answer as requested rather than discover on reviewing your paper that you *listed without describing*, that you selected the *worst* choice rather than the *best* choice, etc.

3) If the examination is of the objective or multiple-choice type – that is, each question will also give a series of possible answers: A, B, C or D, and you are called upon to select the best answer and write the letter next to that answer on your answer paper – it is advisable to start answering each question in turn. There may be anywhere from 50 to 100 such questions in the three or four hours allotted and you can see how much time would be taken if you read through all the questions before beginning to answer any. Furthermore, if you come across a question or group of questions which you know would be difficult to answer, it would undoubtedly affect your handling of all the other questions.

4) If the examination is of the essay type and contains but a few questions, it is a moot point as to whether you should read all the questions before starting to answer any one. Of course, if you are given a choice – say five out of seven and the like – then it is essential to read all the questions so you can eliminate the two that are most difficult. If, however, you are asked to answer all the questions, there may be danger in trying to answer the easiest one first because you may find that you will spend too much time on it. The best technique is to answer the first question, then proceed to the second, etc.

5) Time your answers. Before the exam begins, write down the time it started, then add the time allowed for the examination and write down the time it must be completed, then divide the time available somewhat as follows:
    - If 3-1/2 hours are allowed, that would be 210 minutes. If you have 80 objective-type questions, that would be an average of 2-1/2 minutes per question. Allow yourself no more than 2 minutes per question, or a total of 160 minutes, which will permit about 50 minutes to review.
    - If for the time allotment of 210 minutes there are 7 essay questions to answer, that would average about 30 minutes a question. Give yourself only 25 minutes per question so that you have about 35 minutes to review.

6) The most important instruction is to *read each question* and make sure you know what is wanted. The second most important instruction is to *time yourself properly* so that you answer every question. The third most important instruction is to *answer every question*. Guess if you have to but include something for each question. Remember that you will receive no credit for a blank and will probably receive some credit if you write something in answer to an essay question. If you guess a letter – say "B" for a multiple-choice question – you may have guessed right. If you leave a blank as an answer to a multiple-choice question, the examiners may respect your feelings but it will not add a point to your score. Some exams may penalize you for wrong answers, so in such cases *only*, you may not want to guess unless you have some basis for your answer.

7) Suggestions
    a. Objective-type questions
        1. Examine the question booklet for proper sequence of pages and questions
        2. Read all instructions carefully
        3. Skip any question which seems too difficult; return to it after all other questions have been answered
        4. Apportion your time properly; do not spend too much time on any single question or group of questions

5. Note and underline key words – *all, most, fewest, least, best, worst, same, opposite,* etc.
6. Pay particular attention to negatives
7. Note unusual option, e.g., unduly long, short, complex, different or similar in content to the body of the question
8. Observe the use of "hedging" words – *probably, may, most likely,* etc.
9. Make sure that your answer is put next to the same number as the question
10. Do not second-guess unless you have good reason to believe the second answer is definitely more correct
11. Cross out original answer if you decide another answer is more accurate; do not erase until you are ready to hand your paper in
12. Answer all questions; guess unless instructed otherwise
13. Leave time for review

b. Essay questions
 1. Read each question carefully
 2. Determine exactly what is wanted. Underline key words or phrases.
 3. Decide on outline or paragraph answer
 4. Include many different points and elements unless asked to develop any one or two points or elements
 5. Show impartiality by giving pros and cons unless directed to select one side only
 6. Make and write down any assumptions you find necessary to answer the questions
 7. Watch your English, grammar, punctuation and choice of words
 8. Time your answers; don't crowd material

8) Answering the essay question

Most essay questions can be answered by framing the specific response around several key words or ideas. Here are a few such key words or ideas:

M's: manpower, materials, methods, money, management
P's: purpose, program, policy, plan, procedure, practice, problems, pitfalls, personnel, public relations

   a. Six basic steps in handling problems:
    1. Preliminary plan and background development
    2. Collect information, data and facts
    3. Analyze and interpret information, data and facts
    4. Analyze and develop solutions as well as make recommendations
    5. Prepare report and sell recommendations
    6. Install recommendations and follow up effectiveness

   b. Pitfalls to avoid
    1. *Taking things for granted* – A statement of the situation does not necessarily imply that each of the elements is necessarily true; for example, a complaint may be invalid and biased so that all that can be taken for granted is that a complaint has been registered

2. *Considering only one side of a situation* – Wherever possible, indicate several alternatives and then point out the reasons you selected the best one
3. *Failing to indicate follow up* – Whenever your answer indicates action on your part, make certain that you will take proper follow-up action to see how successful your recommendations, procedures or actions turn out to be
4. *Taking too long in answering any single question* – Remember to time your answers properly

IX. AFTER THE TEST

Scoring procedures differ in detail among civil service jurisdictions although the general principles are the same. Whether the papers are hand-scored or graded by machine we have described, they are nearly always graded by number. That is, the person who marks the paper knows only the number – never the name – of the applicant. Not until all the papers have been graded will they be matched with names. If other tests, such as training and experience or oral interview ratings have been given, scores will be combined. Different parts of the examination usually have different weights. For example, the written test might count 60 percent of the final grade, and a rating of training and experience 40 percent. In many jurisdictions, veterans will have a certain number of points added to their grades.

After the final grade has been determined, the names are placed in grade order and an eligible list is established. There are various methods for resolving ties between those who get the same final grade – probably the most common is to place first the name of the person whose application was received first. Job offers are made from the eligible list in the order the names appear on it. You will be notified of your grade and your rank as soon as all these computations have been made. This will be done as rapidly as possible.

People who are found to meet the requirements in the announcement are called "eligibles." Their names are put on a list of eligible candidates. An eligible's chances of getting a job depend on how high he stands on this list and how fast agencies are filling jobs from the list.

When a job is to be filled from a list of eligibles, the agency asks for the names of people on the list of eligibles for that job. When the civil service commission receives this request, it sends to the agency the names of the three people highest on this list. Or, if the job to be filled has specialized requirements, the office sends the agency the names of the top three persons who meet these requirements from the general list.

The appointing officer makes a choice from among the three people whose names were sent to him. If the selected person accepts the appointment, the names of the others are put back on the list to be considered for future openings.

That is the rule in hiring from all kinds of eligible lists, whether they are for typist, carpenter, chemist, or something else. For every vacancy, the appointing officer has his choice of any one of the top three eligibles on the list. This explains why the person whose name is on top of the list sometimes does not get an appointment when some of the persons lower on the list do. If the appointing officer chooses the second or third eligible, the No. 1 eligible does not get a job at once, but stays on the list until he is appointed or the list is terminated.

X. HOW TO PASS THE INTERVIEW TEST

The examination for which you applied requires an oral interview test. You have already taken the written test and you are now being called for the interview test – the final part of the formal examination.

You may think that it is not possible to prepare for an interview test and that there are no procedures to follow during an interview. Our purpose is to point out some things you can do in advance that will help you and some good rules to follow and pitfalls to avoid while you are being interviewed.

What is an interview supposed to test?

The written examination is designed to test the technical knowledge and competence of the candidate; the oral is designed to evaluate intangible qualities, not readily measured otherwise, and to establish a list showing the relative fitness of each candidate – as measured against his competitors – for the position sought. Scoring is not on the basis of "right" and "wrong," but on a sliding scale of values ranging from "not passable" to "outstanding." As a matter of fact, it is possible to achieve a relatively low score without a single "incorrect" answer because of evident weakness in the qualities being measured.

Occasionally, an examination may consist entirely of an oral test – either an individual or a group oral. In such cases, information is sought concerning the technical knowledges and abilities of the candidate, since there has been no written examination for this purpose. More commonly, however, an oral test is used to supplement a written examination.

Who conducts interviews?

The composition of oral boards varies among different jurisdictions. In nearly all, a representative of the personnel department serves as chairman. One of the members of the board may be a representative of the department in which the candidate would work. In some cases, "outside experts" are used, and, frequently, a businessman or some other representative of the general public is asked to serve. Labor and management or other special groups may be represented. The aim is to secure the services of experts in the appropriate field.

However the board is composed, it is a good idea (and not at all improper or unethical) to ascertain in advance of the interview who the members are and what groups they represent. When you are introduced to them, you will have some idea of their backgrounds and interests, and at least you will not stutter and stammer over their names.

What should be done before the interview?

While knowledge about the board members is useful and takes some of the surprise element out of the interview, there is other preparation which is more substantive. It *is* possible to prepare for an oral interview – in several ways:

1) Keep a copy of your application and review it carefully before the interview

This may be the only document before the oral board, and the starting point of the interview. Know what education and experience you have listed there, and the sequence and dates of all of it. Sometimes the board will ask you to review the highlights of your experience for them; you should not have to hem and haw doing it.

2) Study the class specification and the examination announcement

Usually, the oral board has one or both of these to guide them. The qualities, characteristics or knowledges required by the position sought are stated in these documents. They offer valuable clues as to the nature of the oral interview. For example, if the job involves supervisory responsibilities, the announcement will usually indicate that knowledge of modern supervisory methods and the qualifications of the candidate as a supervisor will be tested. If so, you can expect such questions, frequently in the form of a hypothetical situation which you are expected to solve. NEVER go into an oral without knowledge of the duties and responsibilities of the job you seek.

3) Think through each qualification required

Try to visualize the kind of questions you would ask if you were a board member. How well could you answer them? Try especially to appraise your own knowledge and background in each area, *measured against the job sought*, and identify any areas in which you are weak. Be critical and realistic – do not flatter yourself.

4) Do some general reading in areas in which you feel you may be weak

For example, if the job involves supervision and your past experience has NOT, some general reading in supervisory methods and practices, particularly in the field of human relations, might be useful. Do NOT study agency procedures or detailed manuals. The oral board will be testing your understanding and capacity, not your memory.

5) Get a good night's sleep and watch your general health and mental attitude

You will want a clear head at the interview. Take care of a cold or any other minor ailment, and of course, no hangovers.

What should be done on the day of the interview?

Now comes the day of the interview itself. Give yourself plenty of time to get there. Plan to arrive somewhat ahead of the scheduled time, particularly if your appointment is in the fore part of the day. If a previous candidate fails to appear, the board might be ready for you a bit early. By early afternoon an oral board is almost invariably behind schedule if there are many candidates, and you may have to wait. Take along a book or magazine to read, or your application to review, but leave any extraneous material in the waiting room when you go in for your interview. In any event, relax and compose yourself.

The matter of dress is important. The board is forming impressions about you – from your experience, your manners, your attitude, and your appearance. Give your personal appearance careful attention. Dress your best, but not your flashiest. Choose conservative, appropriate clothing, and be sure it is immaculate. This is a business interview, and your appearance should indicate that you regard it as such. Besides, being well groomed and properly dressed will help boost your confidence.

Sooner or later, someone will call your name and escort you into the interview room. *This is it.* From here on you are on your own. It is too late for any more preparation. But remember, you asked for this opportunity to prove your fitness, and you are here because your request was granted.

What happens when you go in?

The usual sequence of events will be as follows: The clerk (who is often the board stenographer) will introduce you to the chairman of the oral board, who will introduce you to the other members of the board. Acknowledge the introductions before you sit down. Do not be surprised if you find a microphone facing you or a stenotypist sitting by. Oral interviews are usually recorded in the event of an appeal or other review.

Usually the chairman of the board will open the interview by reviewing the highlights of your education and work experience from your application – primarily for the benefit of the other members of the board, as well as to get the material into the record. Do not interrupt or comment unless there is an error or significant misinterpretation; if that is the case, do not hesitate. But do not quibble about insignificant matters. Also, he will usually ask you some question about your education, experience or your present job – partly to get you to start talking and to establish the interviewing "rapport." He may start the actual questioning, or turn it over to one of the other members. Frequently, each member undertakes the questioning on a particular area, one in which he is perhaps most competent, so you can expect each member to participate in the examination. Because time is limited, you may also expect some rather abrupt switches in the direction the questioning takes, so do not be upset by it. Normally, a board member will not pursue a single line of questioning unless he discovers a particular strength or weakness.

After each member has participated, the chairman will usually ask whether any member has any further questions, then will ask you if you have anything you wish to add. Unless you are expecting this question, it may floor you. Worse, it may start you off on an extended, extemporaneous speech. The board is not usually seeking more information. The question is principally to offer you a last opportunity to present further qualifications or to indicate that you have nothing to add. So, if you feel that a significant qualification or characteristic has been overlooked, it is proper to point it out in a sentence or so. Do not compliment the board on the thoroughness of their examination – they have been sketchy, and you know it. If you wish, merely say, "No thank you, I have nothing further to add." This is a point where you can "talk yourself out" of a good impression or fail to present an important bit of information. Remember, *you close the interview yourself*.

The chairman will then say, "That is all, Mr. _____, thank you." Do not be startled; the interview is over, and quicker than you think. Thank him, gather your belongings and take your leave. Save your sigh of relief for the other side of the door.

How to put your best foot forward

Throughout this entire process, you may feel that the board individually and collectively is trying to pierce your defenses, seek out your hidden weaknesses and embarrass and confuse you. Actually, this is not true. They are obliged to make an appraisal of your qualifications for the job you are seeking, and they want to see you in your best light. Remember, they must interview all candidates and a non-cooperative candidate may become a failure in spite of their best efforts to bring out his qualifications. Here are 15 suggestions that will help you:

1) Be natural – Keep your attitude confident, not cocky

If you are not confident that you can do the job, do not expect the board to be. Do not apologize for your weaknesses, try to bring out your strong points. The board is interested in a positive, not negative, presentation. Cockiness will antagonize any board member and make him wonder if you are covering up a weakness by a false show of strength.

2) Get comfortable, but don't lounge or sprawl

Sit erectly but not stiffly. A careless posture may lead the board to conclude that you are careless in other things, or at least that you are not impressed by the importance of the occasion. Either conclusion is natural, even if incorrect. Do not fuss with your clothing, a pencil or an ashtray. Your hands may occasionally be useful to emphasize a point; do not let them become a point of distraction.

3) Do not wisecrack or make small talk

This is a serious situation, and your attitude should show that you consider it as such. Further, the time of the board is limited – they do not want to waste it, and neither should you.

4) Do not exaggerate your experience or abilities

In the first place, from information in the application or other interviews and sources, the board may know more about you than you think. Secondly, you probably will not get away with it. An experienced board is rather adept at spotting such a situation, so do not take the chance.

5) If you know a board member, do not make a point of it, yet do not hide it

Certainly you are not fooling him, and probably not the other members of the board. Do not try to take advantage of your acquaintanceship – it will probably do you little good.

6) Do not dominate the interview

Let the board do that. They will give you the clues – do not assume that you have to do all the talking. Realize that the board has a number of questions to ask you, and do not try to take up all the interview time by showing off your extensive knowledge of the answer to the first one.

7) Be attentive

You only have 20 minutes or so, and you should keep your attention at its sharpest throughout. When a member is addressing a problem or question to you, give him your undivided attention. Address your reply principally to him, but do not exclude the other board members.

8) Do not interrupt

A board member may be stating a problem for you to analyze. He will ask you a question when the time comes. Let him state the problem, and wait for the question.

9) Make sure you understand the question

Do not try to answer until you are sure what the question is. If it is not clear, restate it in your own words or ask the board member to clarify it for you. However, do not haggle about minor elements.

10) Reply promptly but not hastily

A common entry on oral board rating sheets is "candidate responded readily," or "candidate hesitated in replies." Respond as promptly and quickly as you can, but do not jump to a hasty, ill-considered answer.

11) Do not be peremptory in your answers

A brief answer is proper – but do not fire your answer back. That is a losing game from your point of view. The board member can probably ask questions much faster than you can answer them.

12) Do not try to create the answer you think the board member wants

He is interested in what kind of mind you have and how it works – not in playing games. Furthermore, he can usually spot this practice and will actually grade you down on it.

13) Do not switch sides in your reply merely to agree with a board member

Frequently, a member will take a contrary position merely to draw you out and to see if you are willing and able to defend your point of view. Do not start a debate, yet do not surrender a good position. If a position is worth taking, it is worth defending.

14) Do not be afraid to admit an error in judgment if you are shown to be wrong
The board knows that you are forced to reply without any opportunity for careful consideration. Your answer may be demonstrably wrong. If so, admit it and get on with the interview.

15) Do not dwell at length on your present job
The opening question may relate to your present assignment. Answer the question but do not go into an extended discussion. You are being examined for a *new* job, not your present one. As a matter of fact, try to phrase ALL your answers in terms of the job for which you are being examined.

Basis of Rating
Probably you will forget most of these "do's" and "don'ts" when you walk into the oral interview room. Even remembering them all will not ensure you a passing grade. Perhaps you did not have the qualifications in the first place. But remembering them will help you to put your best foot forward, without treading on the toes of the board members.

Rumor and popular opinion to the contrary notwithstanding, an oral board wants you to make the best appearance possible. They know you are under pressure – but they also want to see how you respond to it as a guide to what your reaction would be under the pressures of the job you seek. They will be influenced by the degree of poise you display, the personal traits you show and the manner in which you respond.

ABOUT THIS BOOK

This book contains tests divided into Examination Sections. Go through each test, answering every question in the margin. We have also attached a sample answer sheet at the back of the book that can be removed and used. At the end of each test look at the answer key and check your answers. On the ones you got wrong, look at the right answer choice and learn. Do not fill in the answers first. Do not memorize the questions and answers, but understand the answer and principles involved. On your test, the questions will likely be different from the samples. Questions are changed and new ones added. If you understand these past questions you should have success with any changes that arise. Tests may consist of several types of questions. We have additional books on each subject should more study be advisable or necessary for you. Finally, the more you study, the better prepared you will be. This book is intended to be the last thing you study before you walk into the examination room. Prior study of relevant texts is also recommended. NLC publishes some of these in our Fundamental Series. Knowledge and good sense are important factors in passing your exam. Good luck also helps. So now study this Passbook, absorb the material contained within and take that knowledge into the examination. Then do your best to pass that exam.

EXAMINATION SECTION

THE "IN-BASKET" EXAMINATION

While the exact format of in-basket exercises will vary, they frequently involve each trainee in a group first individually assuming the role of a manager who is faced with a number of letters, memoirs, and notes to which he must respond in writing within a limited time period. For example, the trainee may be told that he has just returned from vacation and that he must leave on a trip in four hours, during which time he must respond in writing to all the items on his desk.

To further complicate the exercise, you, the trainee, may be told that you have just returned from vacation and must leave on a business trip in five hours. Also, it is a holiday and your secretary is home, and no one else is around the office to help you. There are more inquiries and problems to respond to than is possible in five hours and so you will have to determine the relative priority of the work to be done.

As you can see, the IN-BASKET EXERCISE demands good decision-making skills, rather than learning new facts or acquiring new skills. The time pressure factor may result in your finding out how well you perform under stress.

When these exercises are conducted in an oral format, and after each exercise is finished (time runs out), you may be asked to justify your decisions and actions to the examiner and the other participants when it is held as a group exercise, and then they in turn will evaluate your actions and critique it. The rating, of course, is done differently in competitive examinations.

The fact that this type of exercise can be given to groups of managerial trainees is considered an advantage to management, i.e., it is easier and cheaper to administer than other training methods. This training technique also tests managerial candidates for decision-making abilities, particularly due to the time constraints involved. This is considered a vital skill for most managerial candidates for decision-making abilities, particularly due to the time constraints involved. This is considered a vital skill for most managerial positions and, although other training techniques such as role playing can also provide stress, in-basket exercises do more so and are specifically designed for this purpose.

There are limitations, too. As with in-basket questions pertaining to case study examples, they are in large part hypothetical in nature, or static, in that the managerial candidate does not have to live or "die" with the consequences of a poor decision, except where he/she is rated poorly on an examination.

Some in-basket exercises provide guidelines or suggestions for solution. The candidate may be presented with a problem which requires a series of decisions and actions but is also presented with a number of alternate means of resolving the problem, from which he must choose the best option. Next, the problem may be further developed and you may be provided with a number of new choices to resolve this new, or expanded, problem. It may even be required a third time. Then comes the evaluation and critique.

So with this technique, the trainee receives information evaluating the consequences, good or bad, of his decisions at each decision point in the exercise.

In order to properly critique the trainee's decisions, the examiner must be highly skilled in conducting the exercise and in conducting the critique. At its extremes, the critique, as with performance evaluations, can be so general as to be meaningless or be so specific that the trainee becomes so overwhelmed as to render the whole training exercise pointless.

In-basket exercises are often used in on-the-job management group training programs, together with case studies.

EXAMINATION SECTION

Inbox Examination #1: **TEST 1**

Senior Technical Writer/Content Director, Interaxion

You are T. SMITH, the senior technical writer/content director for an eight-year-old business service provider, Interaxion. The primary services provided to its clients are Web hosting, security services, high-capacity Internet access, and information system audits. You and your staff of 4 writers and 2 assistants have recently completed a draft of customer use manuals for a new addition to the service line: a dedicated storage network for clients with large amounts of data. Within the next several months, Interaxion also intends to launch a new download hosting service that will help clients place large files and applications on their own dedicated servers for access.

Interaxion is a medium-sized company that aggressively competes with larger business-to-business service organizations, much of them sprung from existing computer or telecommunications companies. To hold its market share, Interaxion offers a level of service and individual client attention that goes beyond the norm.

The president and CEO of your company, Marlane Liddell, is the engine behind Interaxion's aggressive approach. She is anxious to make Interaxion into a one-stop destination for any and all business-to-business networking services, which explains the rapid schedule of new product/service rollouts—now occurring at a pace of nearly two per year. Many employees privately complain that the grueling pace of development and launch makes work more stressful and error-prone, but the business is growing steadily. While some errors do occur in implementing and documenting services, the departments are managed well enough to correct these mistakes before they cause a significant loss of up-time for clients—if they weren't managed this well, Interaxion would have real problems in customer relations.

As the head of the technical writing department, you are accountable to the Vice President of Customer Relations, Branch Stuckey. He's known as a calm, reasonable man who nevertheless keeps the pressure steady—if his memos or phone calls are not answered within a reasonable amount of time, he is sure to pay a personal visit to ask why. Both he and you share the vision of the technical writing department as the most important medium through which customers receive information about Interaxion's products and services.

You and your staff are responsible for writing the promotional materials and specifications that anchor every service's marketing campaign, and for writing easy-to-follow manuals for their use. You're also accountable for maintaining and updating the Interaxion Web site.

You and Stuckey have jointly decided that the clientele would be well-served by two additional projects. The first, a general technical glossary, is to be available both in print and from Interaxion's Web site, and will help customers to understand the increasingly complex jargon involved in implementing the company's services. You and Stuckey have set a deadline of six months for the launch of this glossary.

Another document you've decided will be helpful is a Frequently Asked Questions (FAQ)/Troubleshooting guide for each of the company's line of services. This will require close collaboration with both the Technical Support and Communications departments. This a project that is of particular interest to the president, who wants a progress report submitted at the end of each month.

As a matter of principle, you try to work no more than a standard 8-to-5 workday. The three-day focus for this exercise is the Monday-Wednesday span of the 23rd through the 25th. The items you find in your in-box are items 1 through 10 and a general information folder compiled by your trusted assistant, Fred. On Tuesday afternoon, a meeting is scheduled from 2 p.m. to 4. p.m. that will include the marketing staff and your department, to discuss reasons why the marketing campaign for Interaxion's security services is not doing well. Tina Niu, Vice President of Marketing, seems to believe it's because the promotional material is too technical and jargony. You met briefly with your staff on Friday to prepare a response to this, but were unsatisfied with the results. You'd like at least another two hours with your writers before meeting with the marketing department.

On the following pages are a list of important departments and personnel at Interaxion, a to-do list, messages, memos, and a planner covering the three-day period. Read the instructions below, then assume you have just arrived Monday morning to find these items in your in-basket.

1. *Look over the list of officers, the planner, the to-do list, and in-basket items quickly, to get an idea of the tasks to be done.*

2. *In the spaces provided in the left margin of the to-do list, indicate the priority of each item, and note how you would dispose of each. Priorities should be labeled in the following manner:*

    AB priorities = those that are both important and urgent
    A priorities = those that are important, but not particularly urgent (can be deferred)
    B priorities = those that are urgent, but not so important
    X priorities = neither urgent nor important

3. *After reading the in-basket items, do the following:*

    a. *First, decide which items can be delegated, and to whom. Use Form B, Delegated Calls and Correspondence, to list and prioritize these items.*
    b. *Next, prioritize the items to which you must respond personally on Form C, Personal Calls and Correspondence.*

4. *Take the planning guide and schedule the tasks you have in front of you. Be sure to allow some "flexible time" to handle any interruptions or crises.*

Interaxion

Important Departments/Personnel:

President/CEO: Marlane Liddell
VP Marketing: Tina Niu
  Marketing Director: Brian Paulsen
  General Sales Manager: Maxine Patton
VP Service Delivery: Owen Stark
  Director of Engineering: Anna Karpov
  Chief Information Architect: Juan Machuca
    (Various Project Managers)
VP Finance: Tom Wilson
  Treasurer: Mary Stravinsky
  Comptroller: Barbara Bernstein
    John Slingsby, Director of Cost Analysis
    Ruth Nielsen, Director of Budgeting and Accounting
VP Administration and Human Resources: Tariq Nayim
  Director of Human Resources: Amos Otis
  Director of Administration: Nancy Frank
VP Customer Relations: Branch Stuckey
  Director of Communications: Alvin Gehring
  Director of Technical Support: Hollis Holt
  Chief Technical Writer: T. SMITH
    Terry Appleton, Technical Writer
    Samir Naramayan, Technical Writer/Web Designer
    Jim Mason, Technical Writer
    Tracy Livingston, Associate Writer
      Fred Cummings, Assistant to **T. SMITH**
      Stacia Cocker, Office Assistant

Things to Do:

Priority   *Item*

_____   •attend meeting on downtime of hosting service. Some clients have fallen below the promised 99.999% uptime, and the company needs to devise ways to improve performance.

Disposition: _____

_____

_____

_____   •meet with technical writing staff for input on the promotion of security services.

Disposition: _____

_____

_____

_____   •meet with staff to outline promotional copy for download hosting service —now looks as if it will be rolled out in about 8 months.

Disposition: _____

_____

_____

_____   •see what's up with Mason's overtime.

Disposition: _____

_____

_____

Things to Do (cont'd):

_____   •contact people who sent in resumes for associate writing job--Sanchez looked best of all, but I'll interview Larkin, too. Reject Yancey and Crespin.

Disposition: _____

_____

_____

_____   •meet with writers to assign updates to manuals for each of the security services. Should take about an hour.

Disposition: _____

_____

_____

_____   •check on the progress of the technical glossary--Mason is falling way, way behind.

Disposition: _____

_____

_____

_____   •check with human resources and budgeting to ask about availability for part-time position, to compile the FAQ/Troubleshooting guide—even with new associate, not enough staff time to devote to this.

Disposition: _____

_____

_____

_____   •proofread/line-edit customer manual (8 hours work at least) for storage network operation, and send it to the printer. Must be done by you personally, and by Thursday morning! Several customers have already purchased network and are waiting.

Disposition: _____

_____

Item 1

NOTE TO: T. SMITH
DATE: 20th   TIME: 4:50 p.m.

WHILE YOU WERE OUT

M Janet Yancey

OF

PHONE ( )
  AREA CODE   NUMBER   EXTENSION

	Telephoned	✓	Please Call
	Called to See You		Will Call Again
	Wants to See You		Returned Your Call

Message: Anxious to speak w/ you about associate writer position.

Item 2

Memorandum

To: T. SMITH
CC: Hollis Holt, Director of Technical Support
From: Alvin Gehring, Director of Communications
Date: 20th
Re: Web site e-mail service

I've been contacted a few times in the past couple of weeks by customers who have visited our Web site and wanted to e-mail us a question. Apparently some of them have clicked on the "e-mail us" hypertext button from a product description page, and nothing has happened.

I know that this is probably a very small-scale problem, and that the more persistent customers will know to simply e-mail us using their own mail programs. But I can't help thinking we might be losing some potential customers without this direct link.

Can you look into this and see what the problem is? I'd like to find out as soon as possible.

Item 3

Memorandum

To: T. SMITH
CC:
From: Marlane Liddell, CEO and President
Date: 23rd
Re: Updates on troubleshooting guide and arrangement with Sturdevant

---

Just a note to remind you that I'll want to meet with you soon to talk about progress on the FAQ/Troubleshooting Guide.

I've also recently received a letter from Sturdevant Publishing about our arrangement with them. Their $6500 payment is figured into our revenues for the quarter, so we'll need to meet that contract deadline.

Let me know when you're available to meet—and when we do meet, make sure you're ready with the good news.

Item 4

NOTE TO: T. SMITH
DATE: 23rd   TIME: 9:00 a.m.

WHILE YOU WERE OUT

M Philip Larkin

OF

PHONE ( ) AREA CODE   NUMBER   EXTENSION

✓	Telephoned		Please Call
	Called to See You		Will Call Again
	Wants to See You		Returned Your Call

Message: Wants to know your decision about associate writer position.

Item 5

Memorandum

To: T. SMITH
CC: Terry Appleton, Samir Naramayan, Jim Mason, Technical Writers
From: Tracy Livingston, Associate Writer
Date: 23rd
Re: Security services/marketing

I hope this doesn't sound too compulsive, but I know we all worked very hard on the specs and promotional materials for security services, and I can't accept the idea that people aren't buying in because they don't understand our copy.

I conducted a little of my own market research over the weekend—interviewing purchasers from about a dozen clients who've bought other services from us, but went with another company for security. There were a few different reasons, but many clients seem to have placed the blame on some questionable architecture.

When pressed, a few said that they did find some parts of the promotional copy a little hard to follow—but added that it wasn't the factor that affected our buying decision.

We'll need to be careful about how we present this, so it doesn't appear we're shifting blame to Service Delivery. This can be one of the things we decide together when we meet (when are we meeting again? Isn't the meeting with Marketing tomorrow afternoon?).

Before we do meet, I hope you'll all take a look at some of the results of the interviews, enclosed here. It should take about a half-hour to get through them.

Item 6

NOTE TO: T. SMITH
DATE: 23rd   TIME: 8:24 a.m.

WHILE YOU WERE OUT

M: Jim Mason

OF:

PHONE: ( ) AREA CODE — NUMBER — EXTENSION

✓	Telephoned		Please Call
	Called to See You		Will Call Again
	Wants to See You		Returned Your Call

Message: Will come in at 10:30 a.m. today — had to take his wife to a rescheduled hospital appointment. Says he's sorry — the only time he could do it.

Item 7

Memorandum

To: All Department Heads
CC:
From: Marlane Liddell, President and CEO
Date: 23rd
Re: Meeting on hosting service downtime

A reminder: our meeting on resolving the hosting service downtime problem will be this Wednesday, the 25th, from 1 p.m. to 4 p.m.

Enclosed is a short examination of issues, compiled by Alvin Gehring Hollis Holt, and Owen Stark, that will need to be addressed if we are to improve the uptime of our Web hosting service. This is probably the most important problem facing our company today, and we'll all need to work together to resolve it as soon as possible.

Please take a look through the enclosed 30 pages to get an idea of what's holding us back, and try to have some ideas for resolution ready by the time we meet Wednesday.

Item 8

2642 Avenue of the Americas

New York, NY 00000

Sturdevant Publishing

November 10

T. SMITH
Chief Technical Writer
Interaxion
3445 Newton Ave.
Cambridge, MA 00000

Dear T. SMITH:

We at Sturdevant are pleased you've decided to contribute to our forthcoming publication, *The Encyclopedia of Technical Publishing*, to be compiled over the next 9 months and released early next year.

Last month, you agreed to send us a general profile of your company and a specific description of the different forms of writing (manuals, proposals, letters, specifications, etc.) performed by your department, along with a few recent samples of your work.

As you know, payment of $6500 to Interaxion was contingent on the delivery of this information by the end of the current month. We expect that you have every intention of honoring this contract, but we haven't heard from you recently and wanted to extend a reminder to you in any case.

Sincerely,

Bob Francis

Editorial Director

Memorandum

To: T. SMITH
CC: Jim Mason, Technical Writer; Barbara Bernstein, Comptroller
From: Ruth Nielsen, Director of Budgeting and Accounting
Date: 23rd
Re: Overtime

Our records show an unusual amount of overtime charged to the company by your department over the last month. In order to meet our budget targets for the quarter, you'll need to work with your employees to reduce the number of hours they work each week.

If you're unable to reduce these hours, it may be necessary to conduct an internal audit in order to verify their necessity. Of course this is simply adding time and expenditure to the situation, and we'd like to avoid it entirely.

Please let us know how this situation is resolved.

NOTE TO: T. SMITH
DATE: 23rd   TIME: 7:50 a.m.

WHILE YOU WERE OUT

M __Janet Yancey__

OF _____

PHONE ( ) _____
AREA CODE   NUMBER   EXTENSION

	Telephoned	✓	Please Call
	Called to See You	✓	Will Call Again
	Wants to See You		Returned Your Call

Message: Wants to speak w/ you ASAP about associate writer position — will keep calling.

General Information Folder:

1. Additional interdepartmental memos—about a dozen of them. Don't need a response but should be read for information. Should take about a half hour.

2. Eight news and trade newspapers and magazines—about two hours' worth of reading.

3. About 20 items of junk mail—should be reviewed. Will take about 30 minutes.

4. A detailed report—in addition to Liddell's 30-page report and Livingston's interviews—that need to be studied for possible action. It's a compilation of customer-satisfaction ratings for the company's other services, including their ratings of the documentation for each on a broad range of criteria, including readability, ease of understanding, and thoroughness. This should require about an hour.

DELEGATED CALLS AND CORRESPONDENCE

Priority   *Item*   *Delegated to:*

_____

_____

_____

_____

_____

_____

_____

_____

PERSONAL CALLS AND CORRESPONDENCE

Priority *Item* *Response:*

_____

_____

_____

_____

_____

_____

_____

_____

23 Monday	24 Tuesday	25 Wednesday
7 AM
8
9
10
11
12 PM
1
2
3
4
5
6 PM
7

KEY (CORRECT ANSWERS)

Discussion of Inbox Examination #1:

Senior Technical Writer/Content Director, Interaxion

One of the first things you should realize, when looking over all the information in front of you, is that there won't be enough time within the next three days for you to do the things on your list, as well as the tasks required by your in-box items. This is hardly surprising for a senior worker at a mid-sized company, but you'll have to decide quickly what can be either eliminated from your schedule, or postponed.

To-Do List:

In this case, the prime candidate for elimination is the three-hour meeting on the downtime of the company's hosting service. While the president is anxious about it, and wants input from people from all departments, there's really not much a technical writing staff can do about the problem. You should try to free up these three hours—speaking with the president personally and explaining what needs to be done by you and your staff in the next three days, and offering to send a representative to the meeting who will report back to you.

As chief technical writer, there are two situations that are both important and urgent: your meeting with marketing department to discuss the quality of your staff's promotional materials, and the huge task of editing the manual for Interaxion's storage network users. Since some customers have already purchased the network, they'll need the manual as soon as possible. The meeting with Marketing is on Tuesday, and you have two tasks to complete before then: read through the information supplied by Tracy Livingston, and call the afternoon meeting with the writers on Monday—they'll need to drop everything in the afternoon for this.

Once the most important and urgent items are taken care of, you should turn your attention to tasks that are important, but not as pressing. You'll need to meet with the staff for two further purposes: outlining promotional copy for the company's downloading hosting service (not that urgent, since the rollout isn't for another 8 months), and assigning updates for the manuals for security service users. Since your copy on the promotional materials for these services is being questioned by the marketing department, it's probably best to schedule this meeting after you've met with Marketing and these questions have been resolved. You'll also need to see if you can find a way to hire part-time help for compiling the FAQ/Troubleshooting guide, since this is of extreme importance to the president.

Urgent matters that aren't quite as significant as the others facing you right now are the progress of the technical glossary—not due out for another six months—and the related problem of Jim Mason's excessive overtime. His memo about taking his wife to the hospital hints that he might be going through some personal problems, and if they're affecting his work, this situation needs to be resolved soon.

Discussion (cont'd)

Delegated Calls and Correspondence:

Janet Yancey may insist on speaking with you personally, but it may simply be that she wants a yes or no answer regarding her hiring. For now, it should be enough to have your assistant send her a letter. Assuming Fred is informed about the progress of your arrangements with Sturdevant—and assuming the contract is being honored—he can also send a reply to them. The e-mail problem, presented in the memo from Hollis Holt, is best left to the expertise of your Web designer, Samir Naramayan.

Personal Calls and Correspondence:

It appears that the news on the progress of the FAQ/Troubleshooting guide is not that good, but you'll need to set up a meeting with the president anyway to tell her so. It might be a good time to state your case about needing more help. You should send a memo to set a meeting time, and to reassure her about the arrangement with Sturdevant.

Since you do intend to interview Philip Larkin about the associate writer position, you should probably call him personally to set this up—though some managers might leave this to an assistant. It's acceptable to include this in the "delegated" column as well.

The memo from the president is simply a re-statement of your obligation to attend the hosting service downtime meeting—and you've determined you can't do this. You should make every attempt to speak with the president personally, to explain why, and to see if sending your assistant is acceptable. You should also give the 30-page report to your assistant, Fred, to have him either outline it for you or see if any of it is relevant to the technical writing staff at all.

Jim Mason appears to be in some trouble, and he may need your help to resolve it—especially since his problems are being noticed by the budgeting department. Since it would be best to discuss it privately, out of the office, you might meet him somewhere for lunch and try to work things out. He'll have to find a way to get things done within a regular 40-hour week.

Planner:

Filling in the planner can be done in a number of ways—as long as everything on your to-do list and in your inbox gets taken care of, and in an appropriate sequence. The most difficult thing to schedule will probably be the meeting with the writers about promotional copy for the security services. It's a short-notice meeting, for one thing, and you'll need to look over Livingston's interviews first. The meeting must happen before the Tuesday meeting with marketing—and Since Jim Mason won't be in until 10:30 on Monday, it will have to take place after that. The tight window requires that the meeting happen Monday afternoon or Tuesday morning. Items such as progress on other projects can be discussed briefly, toward the end of scheduled meetings.

In addition, it wouldn't make sense to schedule the other meeting—regarding the updates to existing security service manuals—until after some of the questions raised by both the marketing department and Livingston's interviews have been resolved. This will have to take place some time on Wednesday.

Things to Do: 22

Priority | *Item*

___X___ •attend meeting on downtime of hosting service. Some clients have fallen below the promised 99.999% uptime, and the company needs to devise ways to improve performance.

Disposition: _Contact Marlane Liddell personally to explain why you can't make the meeting. Ask if you can send an assistant to take notes, promise to review them later and get back to her with ideas._

___AB___ •meet with technical writing staff for input on the promotion of security services.

Disposition: _Schedule meeting for Monday, the 23rd, after Mason gets in._

___A___ •meet with staff to outline promotional copy for download hosting service — now looks as if it will be rolled out in about 8 months.

Disposition: _Schedule after more urgent meetings—maybe combine with manual update meeting._

___B___ •see what's up with Mason's overtime.

Disposition: _Meet with him soon and privately, away from other writers._

___A___ •contact people who sent in resumes for associate writing job--Sanchez looked best of all, but I'll interview Larkin, too. Reject Yancey and Crespin.

Disposition: _Have Fred send letter to Yancey and Crespin; call Larkin and Sanchez personally to set up interviews_

Things to Do (cont'd):

___A___ •meet with writers to assign updates to manuals for each of the security services. Should take about an hour.

Disposition: ___Schedule meeting after all other concerns regarding security services documentation have been cleared up—no sooner than Wednesday.___

___B___ •check on the progress of the technical glossary--Mason is falling way, way behind.

Disposition: ___A quick check that can be slipped in at the end of another meeting—try for Monday or Wednesday.___

___A___ •check with human resources and budgeting to ask about availability for part-time position, to compile the FAQ/Troubleshooting guide—even with new associate, not enough staff time to devote to this.

Disposition: ___Contact them personally, during flex time, before scheduling meeting with Marlane Liddell.___

___AB___ •proofread/line-edit customer manual (8 hours work at least) for storage network operation, and send it to the printer. Must be done by you personally, and by Thursday morning! Several customers have already purchased network and are waiting.

Disposition: ___Try to fit in big time blocks to devote to this—give it your full attention.___

DELEGATED CALLS AND CORRESPONDENCE

Priority	Item	Delegated to:
X	#1—Yancey call	Fred
A	#2—Holt memo	Samir
X	#8—Sturdevant letter	Fred will write response
X	#10—Yancey call	Fred
_____		
_____		
_____		
_____		

PERSONAL CALLS AND CORRESPONDENCE

Priority	*Item*	*Response:*
A	#3—Liddell memo	Brief memo
A	#4—Larkin call	Phone call for interview
AB	#7—Liddell memo	Personal visit
A	#9—Nielsen memo	Meet w/ Mason and write memo

	23 Monday	24 Tuesday	25 Wednesday
7 AM			
8	flex-time: delegate, make calls, set up meeting	flex-time: reading, sorting work on storage network manual	read customer sat. report
9	reading: interdept. memos, trade publications		flex-time: schedule interviews
10			work on storage network manual
11			
12 PM		lunch, meeting w/ Mason	
1	flex-time: examine Livingston interviews	flex-time: sort through junk mail	meeting w. writers: •assign updates to manuals,
2	meeting w. writers:	meeting w/ Marketing	•outline download promo copy
3	•ideas for response to marketing,		work on storage network manual
4	•progress of tech. glossary,	work on storage network manual	
5	•FAQ/Troubleshooting guide		
6 PM			
7			

EXAMINATION SECTION
IN-BASKET

Senior Graphic Designer, Callens New Media

You are B. GARCIA, the senior graphic designer of Callens New Media, a small publisher of materials (newsletters, meeting planners, city guides, and more) for those who organize and attend trade conventions. You have a background both in art and in computer technology, and because the company is small, you play a dual role as both a project manager for the publications and a troubleshooter/technical support resource when there are problems with the publishing software or the company Web site, which you designed and now maintain.

Because of your company's size, its success has relied primarily on occupying this smaller niche in the business publishing market. Your boss, Reynold Callens, would like to draw upon your technological knowledge and expand services to include Web design and servicing, and eventually to include such things as hosting and downloading services for professional associations who conduct merchandising operations from their Web sites. In your last evaluation, you and your boss set an objective to produce a Web-based demonstration of the services that will be available to anyone who visits the company Web site. The deadline for completion of this project has been left open, but your boss is pressing you to show him results soon.

The organizational structure of the company is somewhat loose, due to its size, and could use some readjustment. There are no vice presidents; simply a few team leaders, each overseeing a few workers. Though each team leader reports directly to Reynold Callens, you are often approached by people from other departments for input on solutions, because you were one of the company's first employees and have more knowledge about clients and products, as well as some working knowledge of the earlier and simpler versions of the company's computer networks. Though you don't resent being thought of as a "catch-all" for projects or problems that don't fit neatly into the company's departmental structure, you believe your own responsibilities are keeping you busy enough. The added pressures from other departments is getting stressful for both you and your staff, whom you sense are becoming slightly indignant at the repeated encroachments on their time.

You and your staff bear much responsibility for the timeliness and completeness of the company's current operations. Your responsibilities include making sure the publications are proofread and camera-ready, making arrangements with the printers, arranging for distribution of your company's products to individual conferees, and offering the final say for photos, illustrations, or maps in every publication. Traditionally, you have been the one who communicates with customers directly about certain projects, answering questions or addressing concerns—though these are tasks which should logically fall to your production assistant, Craig Long.

The company's size also means that you have no office assistant. Any calls that come in are handled either by you or your staff of three—your associate graphic artist, Sally

Montrose, your technical writer/content provider, Stan Lee, or your production assistant, Craig Long. You hired all three of them, and you're generally pleased with their work so far—though you admit to having a hard time delegating tasks that can be handled by one or more of them. This is due, you admit, to your own reluctance to surrender control of details, and not with any problem you have with their work thus far.

The three-day focus is the Monday-Wednesday span of the 16th through the 18th—a period that coincides with the beginning of a convention in Cincinnati, to which Craig Long has been dispatched to oversee the distribution of materials to individual participants on Monday and early Tuesday. The items you find in your in-box are items 1 through 10 and a general information folder that you have compiled yourself, which contains items that you believe will need your attention, sooner or later.

On Tuesday afternoon from 1 p.m. to 3 p.m., you are meeting with your boss and an outside consultant, both to check on the progress of the demonstration and to discuss the resources that will be needed to make the proposed Web services available to clients. You'll need to supply an idea of manpower and work-hour needs for different types of sites—and you'll need to get input from your staff to do this, which you estimate will take an hour. Since Craig Long is in Cincinnati, the meeting will have to be a conference call.

On Wednesday morning from 9 a.m. to 11 a.m. you are meeting one-one-one with Callens to more clearly define two things: First, what your own personal responsibilities are, now that the company is growing and your title of "graphic designer" doesn't seem to quite encompass all the managerial tasks you've been taking on. Second, the extent and limit of what your team members are expected to do. You will need to go to this meeting armed with four proposed job descriptions: for yourself, which you will need to write before the meeting (anticipated time: 2 hours), and for Montrose, Lee, and Long, who have already been assigned to write their own. You'll need to meet together with them for an hour, to go over their written descriptions, before you present them to the boss.

You and your staff like to work a normal eight-hour day whenever possible. The day begins at 8 and ends at 5, so an hour-long lunch is the custom, though because of the recent pressures at the workplace it's often much shorter than that.

On the following pages are a list of important departments and personnel at Callens New Media, a to-do list, messages, memos, and a planner covering the three-day period. Read the instructions below, then assume you have just arrived Monday morning to find these items in your in-basket.

1. *Look over the list of officers, the planner, the to-do list, and in-basket items quickly, to get an idea of the tasks to be done.*

2. *In the spaces provided in the left margin of the to-do list, indicate the priority of each item, and note how you would dispose of each. Priorities should be labeled in the following manner:*

   AB priorities = those that are both important and urgent
   A priorities = those that are important, but not particularly urgent (can be deferred)
   B priorities = those that are urgent, but not so important
   X priorities = neither urgent nor important

3. *After reading the in-basket items, do the following:*

   a. *First, decide which items can be delegated, and to whom. Use Form B, Delegated Calls and Correspondence, to list and prioritize these items.*
   b. *Next, prioritize the items to which you must respond personally on Form C, Personal Calls and Correspondence.*

4. *Take the planning guide and schedule the tasks you have in front of you. Be sure to allow some "flexible time" to handle any interruptions, crises, or new issues or correspondence.*

Callens New Media

Important Departments/Personnel:

<u>Owner/CEO</u>: Reynold Callens

<u>Marketing and Sales Team</u>:
Marketing and Sales Director: Roland Brooks (team leader)
Sales Region 1: Tom Spencer
Sales Region 2: Lorna Stans

<u>Administrative Team</u>:
Accounting Officer: Terry Spath (team leader)
Budget and Accounting Assistant: Ed Stein
Information Architect: Gordon Wayne
Manager, Enterprise Systems: Frank Luntz
Director of Human Resources: Monica Torres

<u>Production/Customer Relations Team</u>:
Senior Graphic Designer: B. Garcia (team leader)
Associate Graphic Artist: Sally Montrose
Technical Writer/Content Provider: Stan Lee
Production Assistant: Craig Long

Things to Do:

<u>*Priority*</u>　　　　　　　　<u>*Item*</u>

_____　　• check and respond to e-mails, especially any from clients, hotels, or Craig Long in Cincinnati. Time required: half an hour

　　　　　　　　Disposition: _____

　　　　　　　　_____

　　　　　　　　_____

_____　　•write job description for Wednesday meeting. Would like to have this done before meeting with Callens on Tuesday, in order to be ready if there is time. Two hours.

　　　　　　　　Disposition: _____

　　　　　　　　_____

　　　　　　　　_____

_____　　•update the company Web site to add newly hired personnel, and to more accurately reflect the company's products and services. Estimated time: 3 hours—one hour design and layout, one hour writing content, one hour formatting/coding.

　　　　　　　　Disposition: _____

　　　　　　　　_____

　　　　　　　　_____

_____　　•deliver proofs for newsletter to local printer, for next month's radiologists' convention in Cleveland. Should take about a half hour.

　　　　　　　　Disposition: _____

　　　　　　　　_____

　　　　　　　　_____

Things to Do (cont'd):

_____ •respond to customer requests for information about upcoming projects and publications (requests for proofs, information about content, requests for edits, etc.). Should take about an hour and a half.

Disposition: _____

_____

_____

_____ •find illustrations, maps and photos for meeting planner, for next month's convention in Denver. Already been designed. Needs to be ready for printer within two weeks. Should take about two hours.

Disposition: _____

_____

_____

_____ • call temp agency, hotels to arrange for drops (hotel charges for doorman to make drops) for Philadelphia convention that begins this Thursday and runs through Sunday. Should take about an hour.

Disposition: _____

_____

_____

_____ •perform design and layout for a meeting planner and city guide for an upcoming convention in Nashville. Initial design must be done by you and should take about 8 hours total; you need to spend at least 3 hours on it before Thursday to stay on schedule.

Disposition: _____

_____

_____

General Information Folder:

1. Several articles in trade journals, flagged by Reynold Callens to be read by you and discussed with him at a later, unspecified date. Should take about an hour

2. About 30 items of junk mail—should be scanned. About an hour's worth of reading.

3. Additional interdepartmental memos—ten or so. Don't require a response but should be read for information. Should take about a half hour.

4. A written proposal from a software vendor detailing the newest features of the latest version of their desktop publishing suite. They are not your vendor but want you to switch to their line. You want to consider it. It's about an hour and a half of reading.

FORM B: DELEGATED CALLS AND CORRESPONDENCE

Priority　　　　　　　　*Item*　　　　　　　　　　　　*Delegated to:*

_____

_____

_____

_____

_____

_____

_____

_____

FORM C: PERSONAL CALLS AND CORRESPONDENCE

Priority   *Item*   *Response:*

_____

_____

_____

_____

_____

_____

_____

_____

Item 1

From: smontrose@cnm.com
Date: June 15, 7:22:39 PM EST
Subject: Monday
To: clong@cnm.com, bgarcia@cnm.com

Wanted to let you both know in advance that I'll be leaving the office tomorrow (Monday), after lunch. My son is sick and has an appointment with the doctor in the afternoon. I haven't forgotten our meeting—I'll be back first thing Tuesday morning.

Item 2

Memorandum

To: All Team Leaders
CC:
From: Reynold
Date: June 14
Re: The Future

I've been thinking a lot over the past month about the direction this company is taking, and I think you're all right, to a degree: We've outgrown the informal structure that was in place when we first started. Roles aren't as clearly defined as they need to be, and there is some overlap in responsibilities. I realize the potential for conflict here, and I'm grateful that you've all been able to bear these growing pains so graciously. You'd tell me if you were having any problems with each other, right?

Anyway, I think it's time we sat down together and had a serious talk about the future of this company—how it is structured, what each of our roles is going to be, an d where we out to be investing our resources in the coming years. It's a serious subject that deserves your serious consideration. I'm tentatively scheduling a leadership meeting for 1-4 on Wednesday. If there's some reason why that won't work—I know the Philadelphia convention begins the next day, but I'm assuming we're on top of that—then let me know. Otherwise, bring your best ideas.

--Reynold

Item 3

NOTE TO: B. Garcia
DATE: Friday, June 13th   TIME: 7:00 pm

WHILE YOU WERE OUT

M: Horst, concierge
OF: Cincinnati Hampden Court Hotel
PHONE: (513) 888-7777 EXTENSION: 55

[X] Telephoned
[ ] Please Call
[ ] Called to See You
[ ] Will Call Again
[ ] Wants to See You
[ ] Returned Your Call

Message: Materials haven't arrived yet for next week's convention — can't get hold of printer. Call back ASAP!
— Sally

Item 4

From: glesst@ana.org
Date: June 16, 8:07:12 AM EST
Subject: meeting
To: bgarcia@cnm.com

I have the advance proofs of the newsletter for our convention next month in Denver—thanks for sending them along so promptly. I have some questions. First, a general question about the style guide your staff uses (I'm curious about some of the choices you've made in indentation and layout—I think I might like a few changes to be made here). I also have a few corrections to make about the details of the convention and some of the bios that appear on the last page.

Thanks again—I hope I'll hear from you soon.

--Teresa Gless

Item 5

From: clong@cnm.com
Date: June 16, 8:07:12 AM EST
Subject: meeting
To: smontrose@cnm.com, bgarcia@cnm.com

I know we have to have a conference call today or tomorrow, but things are getting hairy here in Cincinnati and I'm going to need to stay on top of things nearly around the clock. I can be available today from 3-5 pm or tomorrow from 8-9 in the morning. Give me a call on the cell at either of those two times.

I'll be back in the office no later than 3 p.m. on Tuesday. See you both then.

Item 6

> 1947 Nautilus Ct.
> Mystic, CT 00000

June 8

Production Department
Callens New Media
7875 Shore Drive
Tampa, FL 00000

To Whom it May Concern:

I'm a Printing Technology Professional with many years of experience in the printing trade. As you will see from my attached resume, I have a plethora of skills which are directly related to the mission of a printing or marketing firm.

My skills in printing, graphic arts, web site design and customer service would be an excellent fit with any company utilizing the printing arts.

With over 12 years in commercial printing and 20 years of involvement with computers, it is my hope that your company could use a person with my expertise.

I am a very positive individual with excellent people skills and have previously been an inspiring force in team situations.

I'd like a chance to convince you that my skills and energy would be an asset to your firm. If needed, I can also provide a comprehensive portfolio that exhibits my greatest accomplishments in the last 10 years of my career, as well as letters of recommendation from previous employers.

> Sincerely,
>
> Fred G. Moose

Item 7

NOTE TO: B. Garcia
DATE: Friday, June 13th   TIME: 9:00 a.m.

WHILE YOU WERE OUT

M: Vivian Wu
OF: Hood Printing, Oregon
PHONE: (503) 555-2424

✓	Telephoned		Please Call
	Called to See You		Will Call Again
	Wants to See You		Returned Your Call

Message: Questions about sizing, res of photos for DHA convention in Portland next week, (25th?)

— Lorna

Item 8

NOTE TO: B. Garcia
DATE: Monday, June 16th   TIME: 8:11 am

WHILE YOU WERE OUT

MS. Merman
OF National League of Dental Hygienists
PHONE (212) 777-1234 203
AREA CODE / NUMBER / EXTENSION

X	Telephoned		Please Call
	Called to See You		Will Call Again
	Wants to See You		Returned Your Call

Message: Doesn't have confirmation that materials have arrived at hotel and are ready for distribution at Philadelphia Convention. Begins on Thurs., 19th.

—Sally

Item 9

Memorandum

To: B. GARCIA
CC: Reynold Callens, President
From: Roland Brooks, Director of Marketing and Sales
Date: June 13
Re: Marketing our new services

B.:

I'm going to be meeting with our sales staff next week about how to begin planting the seeds of interest in our new Web services to our clients—especially the national medical groups. The problem is, I'm not yet very knowledgeable about what these services are going to be and how, exactly, they are going to serve our clients. I'll be grateful if I could be brought up to speed on the technical details, but most especially I'll be interested in being able to explain, in layman's terms, what each of these proposed services is going to enable our clients to do.

Would it be possible to meet for an hour or so this week to talk about this? Thanks in advance.

Item 10

NOTE TO: B. Garcia
DATE: Monday, June 16th   TIME: 7:45 am

WHILE YOU WERE OUT

M: Horst, concierge
OF: Cincinnati Hampden Court Hotel
PHONE: (513) 888-7777   EXTENSION: 55

X	Telephoned		Please Call
	Called to See You		Will Call Again
	Wants to See You		Returned Your Call

Message: materials are there at front desk, but hasn't heard from anyone at CNM about distribution. Conferees calling to ask about it. Not his job! Call back ASAP!

— Sally

	16 Monday	20 17 Tuesday	18 Wednesday
7			
8			
9			
10			
11			
12			
1			
2			
3			
4			
5			
6			
7	16 Monday	17 Tuesday	18 Wednesday

KEY (CORRECT ANSWERS)

Discussion of Inbox Examination

Senior Graphic Designer, Callens New Media

There are 24 total work hours in these three days, and the four meetings listed in the introduction—with your staff, to discuss the requirements of the Web services demonstration; with Reynold Callens and the consultant; with the staff to go over job descriptions; and with Callens again—consume six of these hours, leaving you with 18 hours in which to handle everything else. It's not enough time—and so it's time for you to do what you've been reluctant to do so far: delegate.

To-Do List:

Since the convention in Cincinnati begins on the 16th, you should check your e-mails to see if any are concerned with it—and it turns out a couple of them are. This task should be done before any others, so that you can perform the necessary follow-up.

There are two other tasks on the To-Do List that are both important and urgent: the second (writing your job description, which you'd like to have ready in case Callens is ready to discuss it at Tuesday's meeting) and the seventh (arranging the details for the Philadelphia convention). The job description should be done as soon as possible on Monday. Ordinarily, the details of the Philadelphia convention should be delegated to Craig Long, your production assistant, but since the convention begins Thursday, and he won't return until Tuesday afternoon, you'd be better off taking care of it yourself, and soon.

There are several possibilities for delegation on the list. The third item—updating the company Web site—is a team effort that should involve all members. Design and layout should be Montrose's input, and it's Lee's job to write the content. Long can help them when he returns. Since you are the most technically proficient, you can handle the formatting and coding. You don't have three hours to spend on this—your commitment should not exceed one hour.

The fifth task—responding to customer requests—is specifically mentioned in the introduction as the kind of job you should be turning over to your production assistant, Craig Long. This isn't urgent and can be done by him when he returns from Cincinnati.

Another task that should be delegated to Lee or Montrose, or both, is the sixth item: finding graphic content for the Denver planner. It is a job well within their responsibilities.

The fourth task, delivering the Cleveland proofs, could be delegated to Long when he returns, but it's not a time-consuming job—it could probably be done on the way home from work, if you leave a little early.

The last task—three hours of design and layout for Nashville—is all yours. You will need to fit in your three hours somewhere during these three days.

Discussion (cont'd)

Delegated Calls and Correspondence:

Item 4, Teresa Gless's inquiry about the Denver materials' content, is best left to the person who wrote it. We can assume that was Stan Lee. Similarly, item 7 is a question about illustrations, and so should go to Sally Montrose.

It shouldn't be your job at all to answer an unsolicited letter of application to employment in your department. You should send item 6 straight to Monica Torres, human resources director.

You can admire Roland Brooks' enthusiasm for promoting the new Web services, but it should be obvious to anyone that the company hasn't even made the final decision about what these services will be. Instead of a one-on-one meeting with him, you should invite him to Tuesday's discussion with the consultant, or talk about it over lunch.

Personal Calls and Correspondence:

Nearly all of the in-box items that should be handled personally are both important and urgent. Items 1 and 5—emails from Long and Montrose about their availability for the conference call—simply require the quick response that the only possible time for the conference call about the work requirements for the demonstration is 8-9 Tuesday morning. You should remember this when filling out your planner.

Items 3 and 10 are your most urgent—the convention in Cincinnati is under way and the conferees don't have their newsletters or meeting planners yet. You need to get in touch with Long or the printer in Cincinnati to work this out immediately.

Item 8 presents a similar situation. Ordinarily, you should consider having Craig Long look into this, but since the convention begins Thursday, you probably ought to just take care of it.

The trickiest item, 2, takes a huge and unexpected chunk of important time away from your work this week. It's tricky because it's a memo from your boss, who should understand the irony of calling a meeting to eliminate role conflict and redundancies in the company—three hours after he has scheduled a one-on-one meeting with you to do basically the same thing.

You don't really have three hours to give for this meeting. You should suggest that most of your input on this issue will be presented during Wednesday's morning meeting, and that you'll still attend in the afternoon if he requires it—but you have a lot of work to do to keep things running smoothly. When filling out your planner, tentatively schedule things for 1-4 Wednesday that can, if needed, be put off.

Discussion (cont'd)

Planner:

There are many ways to fill out the planner, as long as the items on the to-do list and in your in-box are taken care of, and in a sequence that works. Fill in your four required meetings first. Here are some points to consider:

Montrose is out for Monday afternoon, which leaves only 8-9 Tuesday morning (the only other time Craig Long is available) for the staff conference call on the work requirements for the Web services demonstration.

You want your job description ready before Tuesday's meeting with Callens, in case he asks about it. Because you only have two hours total left to you on Tuesday morning, you should probably schedule this task for some time Monday.

Montrose is out Monday afternoon, and there are no meetings scheduled. This is a good time to work on the design and layout for the Nashville materials.

Flex-time is best scheduled at the margins of meetings, in case they begin early or run long.

As mentioned previously, you should try to convince Callens that your attendance at both Wednesday meetings is superfluous. Assume that he'll agree with you, but schedule tasks that can be postponed in case he insists.

Your input on the Web site updates—formatting and coding the changes made by your staff—should be done after you've given them a chance to provide the design and content. Try to schedule your work as late as possible during this time frame.

Things to Do:

Priority   *Item*

___A___   • check and respond to e-mails, especially any from clients, hotels, or Craig Long in Cincinnati. Time required: half an hour

Disposition: <u>Do this first, to head off any potential troubles in Cincinnati</u>

___AB___   •write job description for Wednesday meeting. Would like to have this done before meeting with Callens on Tuesday, in order to be ready if there is time. Two hours.

Disposition: <u>Given the way time is shaping up, this should be done some time Monday.</u>

___A___   •update the company Web site to add newly hired personnel, and to more accurately reflect the company's products and services. Estimated time: 3 hours — one hour design and layout, one hour writing content, one hour formatting/coding.

Disposition: <u>Take responsibility for formatting and coding, and delegate the rest to those who can do the work. Plan to spend an hour on it.</u>

___A___   •deliver proofs for newsletter to local printer, for next month's radiologists' convention in Cleveland. Should take about a half hour.

Disposition: <u>If you can make time, do this toward the end of one of your work days. If not, have Long do it.</u>

Things to Do (cont'd):

___B___ • respond to customer requests for information about upcoming projects and publications (requests for proofs, information about content, requests for edits, etc.). Should take about an hour and a half.

Disposition: Delegate this to Craig Long—it's why you hired him.

___A___ • Find illustrations, maps and photos for meeting planner, for next month's convention in Denver. Already been designed. Needs to be ready for printer within two weeks. Should take about two hours.

Disposition: Have your staff handle this—Lee and Montrose, or both.

___AB___ • call temp agency, hotels to arrange for drops (hotel charges for doorman to make drops) for Philadelphia convention that begins this Thursday and runs through Sunday. Should take about an hour.

Disposition: Since the convention is Thursday, and this has been your job in the past, you should simply handle this as soon as you can.

___B___ • perform design and layout for a meeting planner and city guide for an upcoming convention in Nashville. Initial design must be done by you and should take about 8 hours total; you need to spend at least 3 hours on it before Thursday to stay on schedule.

Disposition: Try to find a long interrupted period of time to do this work.

DELEGATED CALLS AND CORRESPONDENCE

Priority	Item	Delegated to:
A	4—Gless e-mail	Lee
X	6—Applicant cover letter	Torres
A	7—Hood Printing call	Montrose
X	9—Brooks memo	Callens, or lunch meeting

PERSONAL CALLS AND CORRESPONDENCE

Priority	Item	Response:
AB	1—Montrose e-mail	Brief reply: schedule conference call for 8-9 Tues. morning
A	2—Callens memo	Discuss w/him—try to cover this in Wed. morning meeting
AB	3—Cincinnati hotel call	Try to reach Long or the printer immediately
AB	5—Long e-mail	Brief reply: schedule conference call for 8-9 Tues. morning
AB	8—NLDH call	Check with the hotel and/or printer, then reply
AB	10—Cincinnati hotel call	Call Long or the printer immediately

	16 Monday	17 Tuesday	18 Wednesday
7			
8	flex-time: Cincinnati mess	demo meeting with staff	flex-time
	check additional e-mails		"
9	write job description for	flex-time	Callens meeting about job
	Tues. meeting	"	definitions
10	"	call temp. agencies, hotels,	"
	"	etc. for Philadelphia	"
11	read trade journal articles	scan junk mail	flex-time
	for Callens	"	"
12	lunch	lunch w/Brooks	lunch
	"		
1	design and layout, Nash-	demo meeting w/Callens,	respond to customer inqui-
	ville	consultant	ries (or delegate to Long)
2	"	"	"
	"	"	read software proposal
3	"	flex-time	"
	"	"	"
4	read dept. memos	job descriptions meeting	format and code Web site
	deliver Cleveland proofs	w/staff	updates
5			
6			
7			

EXAMINATION SECTION
TEST 1

DIRECTIONS: Each question or incomplete statement is followed by several suggested answers or completions. Select the one that BEST answers the question or completes the statement. *PRINT THE LETTER OF THE CORRECT ANSWER IN THE SPACE AT THE RIGHT.*

1. Management by exception (MBE) is   1.____

    A. designed to locate bottlenecks
    B. designed to pinpoint superior performance
    C. a form of index locating
    D. a form of variance reporting

2. In managerial terms, gap analysis is useful primarily in   2.____

    A. problem solving   B. setting standards
    C. inventory control   D. locating bottlenecks

3. ABC analysis involves   3.____

    A. problem solving   B. indexing
    C. brainstorming   D. inventory control

4. The Federal Discrimination in Employment Act as amended in 1978 prohibits job discrim-   4.____
   ination based on age for persons between the ages of

    A. 35 and 60   B. 40 and 65   C. 45 and 65   D. 40 and 70

5. Inspectors should be familiar with the contractor's CPM charts for a construction job pri-   5.____
   marily to determine if

    A. the job is on schedule
    B. the contractor is using the charts correctly
    C. material is on hand to keep the job on schedule
    D. there is a potential source of delay

6. The value engineering approach is frequently found in public works contracts. Value   6.____
   engineering is

    A. an effort to cut down or eliminate extra work payments
    B. a team approach to optimize the cost of the project
    C. to insure that material and equipment will perform as specified
    D. to insure that insurance costs on the project can be minimized

7. Historically, most costly claims have been either for   7.____

    A. unreasonable inspection requirements or unforeseen weather conditions
    B. unreasonable specification requirements or unreasonable completion time for the contract
    C. added costs due to inflation or unavailability of material
    D. delays or alleged changed conditions

57

8. A claim is a

   A. dispute that cannot be resolved
   B. dispute arising from ambiguity in the specifications
   C. dispute arising from the quality of the work
   D. recognition that the courts are the sole arbiters of a dispute

9. Disputes arising between a contractor and the owning agency are

   A. the result of inflexibility of either or both parties to the dispute
   B. mainly the result of shortcomings in the design
   C. the result of shortcomings in the specifications
   D. inevitable

Questions 10-13.

DIRECTIONS: Questions 10 through 13, inclusive, refers to the array of numbers listed below.

16, 7, 9, 5, 10, 8, 5, 1, 2

10. The mean of the numbers is

    A. 2   B. 5   C. 7   D. 8

11. The median of the numbers is

    A. 2   B. 5   C. 7   D. 8

12. The mode of the numbers is

    A. 2   B. 5   C. 7   D. 8

13. In statistical measurements, a subgroup that is representative of the entire group is a

    A. commutative group   B. sample
    C. central index   D. Abelian group

14. Productivity is the ratio of

    A. $\dfrac{\text{product costs}}{\text{labor costs}}$

    B. $\dfrac{\text{cost of final product}}{\text{cost of materials}}$

    C. $\dfrac{\text{outputs}}{\text{inputs}}$

    D. $\dfrac{\text{outputs cost}}{\text{time needed to product the output}}$

15. Downtime is the time a piece of equipment is

    A. idle waiting for other equipment to become available
    B. not being used for the purpose it was intended

C. being used inefficiently
D. unavailable for use

16. Index numbers

    A. relates to the cost of a product as material costs vary
    B. allows the user to find the variation from the norm
    C. are a way of comparing costs of different approaches to a problem
    D. a way of measuring and comparing changes over a period of time

17. The underlying idea behind Management by Objectives is to provide a mechanism for managers to

    A. coordinate personal and departmental plans with organizational goals
    B. motivate employees by having them participate in job decisions
    C. motivate employees by training them for the next higher position
    D. set objectives that are reasonable for the employees to attain, thus improving self-esteem among the employees

18. The ultimate objective of the project manager in planning and scheduling a project is to

    A. meet the completion dates of the project
    B. use the least amount of labor on the project
    C. use the least amount of material on the project
    D. prevent interference between the different trades

19. Scheduling with respect to the critical path method usually does not involve

    A. cost allocation
    B. starting and finishing time
    C. float for each activity
    D. project duration

20. When CPM is used on a construction project, updates are most commonly made

    A. weekly
    B. every two weeks
    C. monthly
    D. every two months

Questions 21-24.

DIRECTIONS: Questions 21 through 24 refer to the following network.

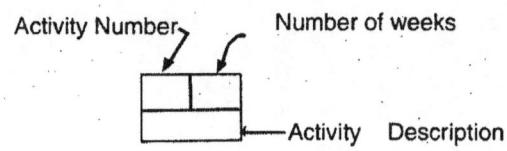

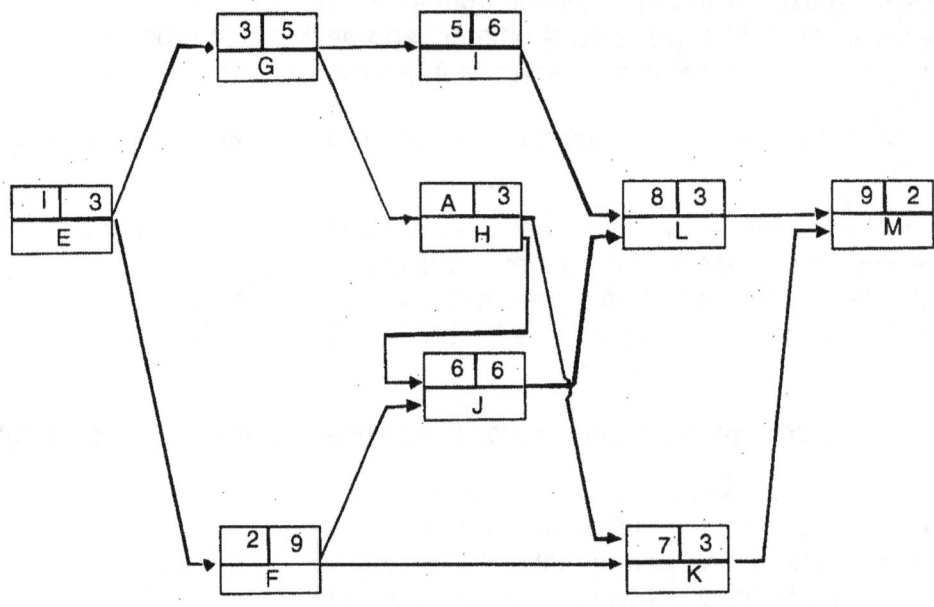

Activity Number	Activity Description	Duration in Weeks	Early Start	Early Finish	Late Start	Late Finish	Total Slack
1	E	3					
2	F	9					
3	G	5					
4	H	3					
5	I	6					
6	J	6					
7	K	3					
8	L	3					
9	M	2					

21. The critical path is

    A. E G H J L M   B. E G I L M
    C. E F J L M   D. E G H K M

22. The minimum time needed to complete the job is, in weeks,

    A. 19   B. 21   C. 22   D. 23

23. The slack time in J is, in weeks,

    A. 0   B. 1   C. 2   D. 3

24. The slack time in K is, in weeks,

    A. 4   B. 5   C. 6   D. 7

25. Of the following, the primary objective of CPM is to 25.____
    A. eliminate duplication of work
    B. overcome obstacles such as bad weather
    C. spot potential bottlenecks
    D. save on the cost of material

KEY (CORRECT ANSWERS)

1.	D	11.	C
2.	A	12.	B
3.	D	13.	B
4.	D	14.	C
5.	A	15.	D
6.	B	16.	D
7.	D	17.	A
8.	A	18.	A
9.	D	19.	A
10.	C	20.	C

21. C
22. D
23. A
24. C
25. C

TEST 2

DIRECTIONS: Each question or incomplete statement is followed by several suggested answers or completions. Select the one that BEST answers the question or completes the statement. *PRINT THE LETTER OF THE CORRECT ANSWER IN THE SPACE AT THE RIGHT.*

1. Gantt refers to

    A. bar charts
    B. milestone charts
    C. PERT networks
    D. Management by Objectives

    1.____

2. PERT is an abbreviation for

    A. Progress Evaluation in Real Time
    B. Preliminary Evaluation of Running Time
    C. Program Evaluation Review Techniques
    D. Program Estimation and Repair Times

    2.____

3. In project management terms, slack is equivalent to

    A. tare
    B. off time
    C. delay
    D. float

    3.____

4. The FIRST step in planning and programming a roadway pavement management system is to evaluate

    A. priorities for the work to be done
    B. the condition of your equipment
    C. the condition of the roads in the system
    D. the storage and maintenance facilities

    4.____

5. Managers accomplish their work in an ever changing environment by integrating three time-tested approaches. The one of the following that is NOT a time-tested approach is

    A. scientific adaptation
    B. scientific management
    C. behavior management
    D. management sciences

    5.____

6. The most effective managers manage for optimum results. This means that the manager is seeking to _____ a given situation.

    A. get the maximum results from
    B. get the most favorable results from
    C. get the most reasonable results from
    D. satisfy the conflicting interests in

    6.____

7. If a manager believes that an employee is irresponsible, the employee, in subtle response to the manager's assessment, will in fact prove to be irresponsible. This is an example of a(n)

    A. conditioned reflex
    B. self-fulfilling prophesy
    C. Freudian response
    D. automatic reaction

    7.____

8. Perhaps nothing distinguishes the younger generation from the older so much as the value placed on work. The older generation was generally raised to believe in the Protestant work ethic.
    This ethic holds primarily that

    8.____

A. people should try to get the highest salary possible
B. work should help people to advance
C. work should be well done if it is interesting
D. work is valuable in itself and the person who does it focuses on his work

9. The standard method currently in use in inspecting bituminous paving is to inspect each activity in detail as the paving work is being installed. In recent years some agencies use a different method of inspection known as a(n)

A. as-built quality control method
B. statistically controlled quality assurance method
C. data based history of previous contracts of this type
D. performance evaluation of the completed paving contract

10. Aggregates for use in bituminous pavements should be tested for grading,

A. abrasion, soundness, and specific gravity
B. type of rock, abrasion, and specific gravity
C. abrasion, soundness, and deleterious material
D. specific gravity, chemical composition of the aggregate, and deleterious material

11. Of the following, the one that is LEAST likely to be a test for asphalt is

A. specific gravity
B. flashpoint
C. viscosity
D. penetration

12. According to the AASHO, for bituminous pavements PSI is an abbreviation for _____ Index.

A. Present Serviceability
B. Pavement Smoothness
C. Pavement Serviceability
D. Present Smoothness

13. According to the AASHO, a bituminous pavement that is in extremely poor condition will have a PSI

A. above 5.5
B. above 3.5
C. below 3.5
D. below 1.5

14. The U.S. Federal Highway Administration defines asphalt maintenance as including work designed primarily for rejuvenation or protection of existing surfaces less than _____ inch minimum thickness.

A. 1/4
B. 1/2
C. 3/4
D. 1

15. The maintenance phase of a highway management system includes the establishment of a program and schedule of work based largely on budget considerations, the actual operations of crack filling, patching, etc. and

A. inspection of completed work
B. planning of future operations
C. upgrading existing pavements
D. acquisition and processing of data

16. In a bituminous asphalt pavement, the progressive separation of aggregate particles in a pavement from the surface downward or from the edges inward is the definition of

    A. alligatoring
    B. raveling
    C. scaling
    D. disintegration

17. The bituminous pavement condition for the purpose of overlay design includes ride quality, structural capacity, skid resistance, and

    A. durability
    B. age of the pavement
    C. CBR value
    D. surface distress

18. An asphalt mix is being transferred from an asphalt truck to the hopper of the paving machine. Blue smoke rises from the material being emptied into the hopper of the paving machine.
    Your conclusion should be that

    A. this is normal and is to be expected
    B. the mix is overheated
    C. the mix is too cold
    D. the mix is being transferred too rapidly

19. Polished aggregate in an asphalt pavement are aggregate particles that have been rounded and polished smooth by traffic. This is a

    A. *good* condition as it allows a smooth ride
    B. *good* condition as it preserves tires
    C. *poor* condition as it promotes skidding
    D. *poor* condition as it tends to break the bond between the asphalt and the aggregate

20. A slippery asphalt surface requires a skid-resistant surfacing material. Of the following, the cover that would be most appropriate is a(n)

    A. asphalt tack coat
    B. fog seal
    C. layer of sand rolled into the asphalt surface
    D. asphalt emulsion slurry seal

21. The maximum size of aggregate in a hot mix asphalt concrete surfacing and bases allowed by the Federal Highway Administration Grading A is _____ inch(es).

    A. 3/4   B. 1   C. 1 1/4   D. 1 1/2

22. Wet sand weighs 132 pounds per cubic foot and contains 8% noisture. The dry weight of a cubic foot of sand is _____ pounds.

    A. 122.2   B. 122.0   C. 121.7   D. 121.4

23. A very light spray application of 551h emulsified asphalt diluted with water is used on existing pavement as a seal to riinimize raveling and to enrich the surface of a dried-out pavement is known as a(n)

    A. prime coat
    B. tack coat
    C. fog seal
    D. emulsion seal

24. 90 kilometers per hour is equivalent to _____ miles per hour. 24.____

    A. 49 B. 54 C. 59 D. 64

25. In a table of pavement distress manifestations is a column broadly titled *Density of Pavement Distress*. 25.____
    This is equivalent to _____ of the defects.

    A. average depth
    B. average area
    C. extent of occurrence
    D. seriousness

KEY (CORRECT ANSWERS)

1. A		11. A	
2. A		12. A	
3. D		13. D	
4. C		14. C	
5. A		15. D	
6. B		16. B	
7. B		17. D	
8. D		18. B	
9. B		19. C	
10. C		20. D	

21. D
22. A
23. C
24. B
25. C

EXAMINATION SECTION
TEST 1

DIRECTIONS: Each question or incomplete statement is followed by several suggested answers of completions. Select the one that BEST answers the question or Complete the statement. *PRINT THE LETTER OF THE CORRECT ANSWER IN THE SPACE AT THE RIGHT.*

1. An accepted deadline for a project approaches. However, the project manager realizes only 85% of the work has been completed. The project manager then issues a change request.
   What should the change request authorize?

   A. Corrective action based on causes
   B. Escalation approval to use contingency funding
   C. Additional resources using the contingency fund
   D. Team overtime to meet schedule

   1.____

2. _____ is a valid tool or technique to assist the project manager to assure the success of the process improvement plan.

   A. Benchmarking
   B. Change control system
   C. Process analysis
   D. Configuration management system

   2.____

3. A project manager meets with the project team to review lessons learned from previous projects. In what activity is the team involved?

   A. Performance management
   B. Project team status meeting
   C. Scope identification
   D. Risk identification

   3.____

4. _____ process helps you to purchase goods from external suppliers.

   A. Quality management
   B. Procurement management
   C. Cost management
   D. Communication management

   4.____

5. Which of the following is not involved in procurement management?

   A. Review supplier performance against contract
   B. Identify and resolve supplier performance issues
   C. Communicate the status to management
   D. Manage a WBS

   5.____

6. _____ contract is advantageous to a buyer.

   A. Fixed price
   B. Cost reimbursable
   C. Time and material
   D. Fixed price plus incentive

   6.____

67

7. Which of the following contracts is advantageous to a seller?

    A. Fixed price
    B. Cost reimbursable
    C. Time and material
    D. Fixed price plus incentive

8. Tom is a manager of a project whose deliverable has many uncertainties associated with it. What kind of contract should he use during the procurement process?

    A. Fixed price
    B. Cost reimbursable
    C. Time and material
    D. Fixed price plus incentive

9. Cost plus _____ is not a cost-reimbursable contract.

    A. fixed fee
    B. fee
    C. fixed time
    D. incentive fee

10. _____ type of contract helps both the seller and buyer to save, if the performance criteria are exceeded.

    A. Cost plus fixed fee
    B. Cost plus fee
    C. Cost plus fixed time
    D. Cost plus incentive fee

11. A project manager with a construction company. She has to complete a project in a specified time, but does have enough time to send the job out for bids. What type of contract would save her time?

    A. Fixed price
    B. Cost reimbursable
    C. Time and material
    D. Fixed price plus incentive

12. The major type(s) of standard warranty (ies) that are used in the business environment is (are):

    A. express
    B. negotiated
    C. implied
    D. A and C

13. During contract management, the project manager must consider the

    A. acquisition process and contract administration
    B. contract administration and ecological environment
    C. ecological environment and acquisition process
    D. offer, acceptance and consideration

14. Which contract type places the most risk on the seller?

    A. Cost plus percentage fee
    B. Cost plus incentive fee
    C. Cost plus fixed fee
    D. Firm fixed price

15. Finalizing project close-out happens when a project manager

    A. archives the project records
    B. completes the contract
    C. complete lessons learned
    D. reassigns the team

16. Unit price contract is fair to both owner and contractor,

    A. as the actual volumes will be measured and paid as the work proceeds
    B. as the owner will provide bill of quantities
    C. as both are absorbing an equal amount of risk
    D. all of the above

17. Bill is the manager of a project that requires different areas of expertise. Which one of the following contracts should he sign?

    A. Fixed price
    B. Cost reimbursable
    C. Time and material
    D. Unit price

18. Which of the following contracts is commonly used in projects that involve pilot programs or harness new technologies?

    A. Fixed price
    B. Incentive
    C. Time and material
    D. Unit price

19. Procurement cycle involves all of the following steps EXCEPT

    A. supplier contract
    B. renewal
    C. sending a proposal
    D. information gathering

20. What would happen if a project manager does not take up a background review during the procurement process?

    A. Price might not be negotiated
    B. Credibility of the goods might not be validated
    C. Goods might not be shipped
    D. Both A and B

21. _____ is not a part of a procurement document.   21._____

   A. Buyer's commencement to the bid
   B. Summons by the financially responsible party
   C. Establishing terms and conditions of a contract
   D. Roles of responsibilities of internal team

22. Which of the following is NOT an example of a procurement document?   22._____

   A. Offers
   B. Contracts
   C. Project record archives
   D. Request for quotation

23. A project manager needs to follow _____ for a good procurement   23._____
    document to be drafted.

   A. clear definition of the responsibilities, rights and commitments of both parties
      in the contract
   B. clear definition of the nature and quality of the goods or services to be provided
   C. clear and easy to understand language
   D. all of the above

24. Which of the following is not a concern with respect to procurement management?   24._____

   A. Reassigning the team
   B. Not all goods and services that a business requires need to be purchased from
      outside
   C. You would need to have a good idea of what you exactly require and then go
      on to consider various options and alternatives
   D. You would need to consider different criteria, apart from just the cost, to finally
      decide on which supplier you would want to go with.

25. Source qualifications are a part of the _____ phase of Acquisition Process Cycle. 25._____

   A. post-award
   B. pre-award
   C. award
   D. origination

KEY (CORRECT ANSWERS)

1. A
2. C
3. D
4. B
5. D

6. A
7. B
8. B
9. C
10. D

11. C
12. D
13. A
14. D
15. B

16. C
17. D
18. B
19. C
20. B

21. D
22. C
23. D
24. A
25. C

TEST 2

DIRECTIONS: Each question or incomplete statement is followed by several suggested answers of completions. Select the one that BEST answers the question or Complete the statement. *PRINT THE LETTER OF THE CORRECT ANSWER IN THE SPACE AT THE RIGHT.*

1. Which of the following project tools details the project scope?　　　　　　　　　　　　1._____

   A. Project plan
   B. Gantt chart
   C. Milestone checklist
   D. Score cards

2. Which of the following is NOT a project tool?　　　　　　　　　　　　2._____

   A. Gantt chart
   B. Milestone checklist
   C. Score cards
   D. MS project

3. _____ is accompanied by project audits by a third party. As a result, non-compliance and action items are tracked.　　　　　　　　　　　　3._____

   A. Gantt chart
   B. Milestone checklist
   C. Project reviews
   D. Delivery reviews

4. An IT project manager, is involved in tracking his team's performance. Which tool would he use to gauge this performance?　　　　　　　　　　　　4._____

   A. Score cards
   B. Gantt chart
   C. Project management software
   D. Milestone checklist

5. What tool does a manager use to track the interdependencies of each project activity?　　　　　　　　　　　　5._____

   A. Project plan
   B. Gantt chart
   C. Project management software
   D. Milestone checklist

6. Which tool would be used for a manager to determine if he or she is on track in terms of project progress?　　　　　　　　　　　　6._____

   A. Project management software
   B. Delivery reviews
   C. Project reviews
   D. Milestone checklist

7. Which of the following tools is used for individual member promotion?

   A. Delivery reviews
   B. Score cards
   C. Project reviews
   D. Milestone checklist

8. Which of the following is NOT a project management process?

   A. Project planning
   B. Project initiation
   C. Project management software
   D. Closeout and evaluation

9. _____ is the phase in which the service provider proves the eligibility and ability of completing the project to the client.

   A. Pre-sale period
   B. Project execution
   C. Sign-off
   D. Closeout and evaluation

10. Controlling of the project could be done by following all of the following protocols EXCEPT

    A. communication plan
    B. quality assurance test plan
    C. test plan
    D. project plan

11. A manager wants his project to be successful and hence verifies the successful outcome of every activity leading to successful completion of the project. Which of the following activities would he use to do so?

    A. Control
    B. Test plan
    C. Project plan
    D. Validation

12. What happens during the closeout and evaluation phase?

    A. Evaluation of the entire project
    B. Hand over the implemented system
    C. Identifying mistakes and taking necessary action
    D. All of the above

13. A project manager, is conducting validation and verification functions. Which team's assistance would she need in order to do so?

    A. Quality assurance team
    B. Project team
    C. Client team
    D. Third-party vendor

14. Tracking the effort and cost of the project is done during _____.

    A. project execution
    B. control and validation
    C. closeout and evaluation
    D. communication plan

15. _____ is the entity created for governing the processes, practices, tools and other activities related to project management in an organization.

    A. Project management office
    B. Project management software
    C. Quality assurance
    D. None of the above

16. A project management office must be built with the following considerations EXCEPT

    A. process optimization
    B. productivity enhancement
    C. building the bottom line of their organization
    D. none of the above

17. An advantage of a project management office is that it

    A. helps cut down staff
    B. helps cut down resources
    C. refines the processes related to project management
    D. all of the above

18. A project management office could fail because of

    A. lack of executive management support
    B. incapability
    C. it adds figures to the bottom line of the company
    D. both A and B

19. _____ is used to analyze the difficulties that may arise due to the execution of the project.

    A. Project management office
    B. Project management triangle
    C. Both A and B
    D. None of the above

20. The three constraints in a project management triangle are _____.

    A. time, cost and scope
    B. time, resources and quality
    C. time, resources and people
    D. time, resources and cost

21. A project manager, is experiencing challenges related to project triangle and hence finds difficulty in achieving the project objectives. Which of the following skills would help her?

    A. Time management
    B. Effective communication
    C. Managing people
    D. All of the above

22. _____ is NOT a role of a project manager.

    A. Carrying out basic project tasks
    B. Keeping stakeholders informed on the project progress
    C. Defining project scope and assigning tasks to team members
    D. Setting objectives

23. Kathy is advising Nicole on the goals and challenges a project manager must consider. Which of the following should she discuss?

    A. Deadlines
    B. Client satisfaction
    C. No budget overrun
    D. All of the above

24. Team management deals with all of the following EXCEPT

    A. providing incentives and encouragement
    B. maintaining warm and friendly relationship with teammates
    C. meeting requirements of the client
    D. including them in project related decisions

25. _____ is vital to win client satisfaction.

    A. Finishing the work on scheduled time
    B. Ensuring that most standards are met
    C. Having a limited relationship with the client
    D. All of the above

KEY (CORRECT ANSWERS)

1. A
2. D
3. C
4. A
5. B

6. D
7. B
8. C
9. A
10. C

11. D
12. D
13. A
14. A
15. A

16. D
17. C
18. D
19. B
20. A

21. D
22. A
23. D
24. C
25. A

TEST 3

DIRECTIONS: Each question or incomplete statement is followed by several suggested answers of completions. Select the one that BEST answers the question or Complete the statement. *PRINT THE LETTER OF THE CORRECT ANSWER IN THE SPACE AT THE RIGHT.*

1. What type of strategy is followed by a manager before his workforce focuses on with performance?

    A. Activators
    B. Behaviors
    C. Consequences
    D. Deviators

    1._____

2. _____ define how the workforce performs or behaves within the activity or situation as a result of activators or consequences.

    A. Deviators
    B. Consequences
    C. Behaviors
    D. Activators

    2._____

3. _____ explain how the manager handles the workforce after the performance.

    A. Deviators
    B. Consequences
    C. Behaviors
    D. Activators

    3._____

4. Which of the following is found to have a great impact on workforce behavior?

    A. Deviators
    B. Consequences
    C. Behaviors
    D. Activators

    4._____

5. Nancy, an IT project manager, is keen to delegate her work. She is aware that a good manager's role is about delegating work effectively in order to complete the task. What should she consider before delegating?

    A. Delegating the work with clear instructions and expectations stated
    B. Providing enough moral support
    C. Identify individuals that are capable of carrying out a particular task
    D. All the above

    5._____

6. Which of the following is NOT a tool related to controlling and assuring quality?

    A. Check sheet
    B. Cause-and-effect diagram
    C. Activators
    D. Scatter diagram

    6._____

7. _____ are used for understanding business, implementation and organizational problems.

    A. Cause-and-effect diagrams
    B. Scatter diagrams
    C. Control charts
    D. Pareto charts

    7._____

8. Jim is replacing the earlier project manager in the middle of the project and hard-pressed with time. He has to work on a priority basis. Which of the following tools would he use to identify priorities?

   A. Cause-and-effect diagram
   B. Scatter diagram
   C. Control chart
   D. Pareto chart

Questions 9-11 refer to the following chart.

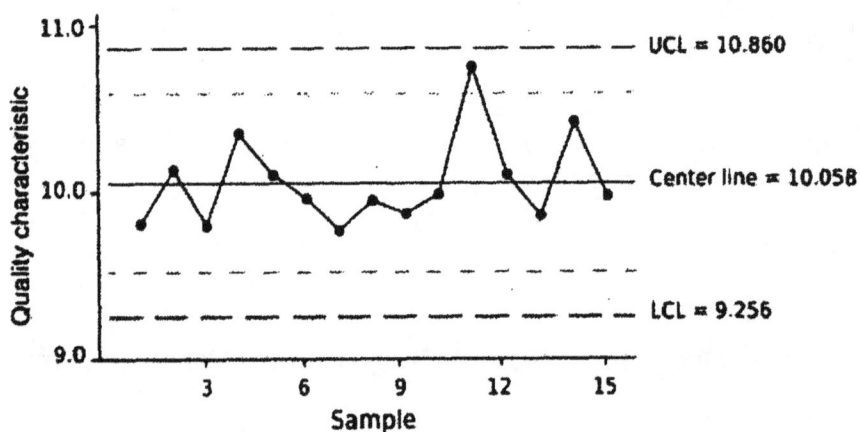

9. What type of tool is this?

   A. Control chart
   B. Flow chart
   C. Scatter diagram
   D. Pareto chart

10. The above-mentioned chart/tool is used for _____.

    A. identifying sets of priorities
    B. comparing two variables
    C. monitoring the performance of a process
    D. gathering and organizing data

11. The above chart/tool could be used to identify all of the following EXCEPT

    A. the stability of the process
    B. the common cause of variation
    C. the parameter(s) that have the highest impact on the specific concern
    D. conditions where the monitoring team needs to react

12. Which of the following tools would a project manager use to perform a trend analysis?

    A. Flow chart
    B. Scatter diagram
    C. Cause-and-effect diagram
    D. Pareto chart

13. _____ is/are a common and simple method used by project managers to arrive at an effective cause-and-effect diagram.

    A. Survey
    B. Brainstorming
    C. Informal discussions
    D. Formal presentations

14. Which of the following tools should a project manager use to gain a brief understanding of the project's critical path?

    A. Flow chart
    B. Pareto chart
    C. Histogram
    D. Check sheet

15. _____ is NOT a step involved in the benchmarking process.

    A. Planning
    B. Analysis of data
    C. Monitoring
    D. None of the above

16. As a project manager, where will you collect primary data when you collect information?

    i) Benchmarked company
    ii) Press
    iii) Publication
    iv) Website

    A. Only I
    B. Both I and II
    C. I, II, III and IV
    D. Both I and IV

17. Which of the following methods is recommended to conduct primary research?

    A. E-mail
    B. Referring to the website of other companies
    C. Telephone
    D. Face-to-face interviews

18. Analysis of data involves all of the following EXCEPT

    A. sharing data with all the stakeholders
    B. data presentation
    C. results projection
    D. classifying the performance gaps in processes

19. _____ is referred to as an enabler, which will help project managers to act wisely.

    A. Projection of results
    B. Performance gap identification
    C. Root cause of performance gaps
    D. Presentation of data

20. Which of the following needs to be done in order to monitor the quality of the project?

    A. Evaluating the progress made
    B. Reiterating the impact of change
    C. Making necessary adjustments
    D. All the above

Use the following cause-and-effect diagram to answer questions 21 through 23.

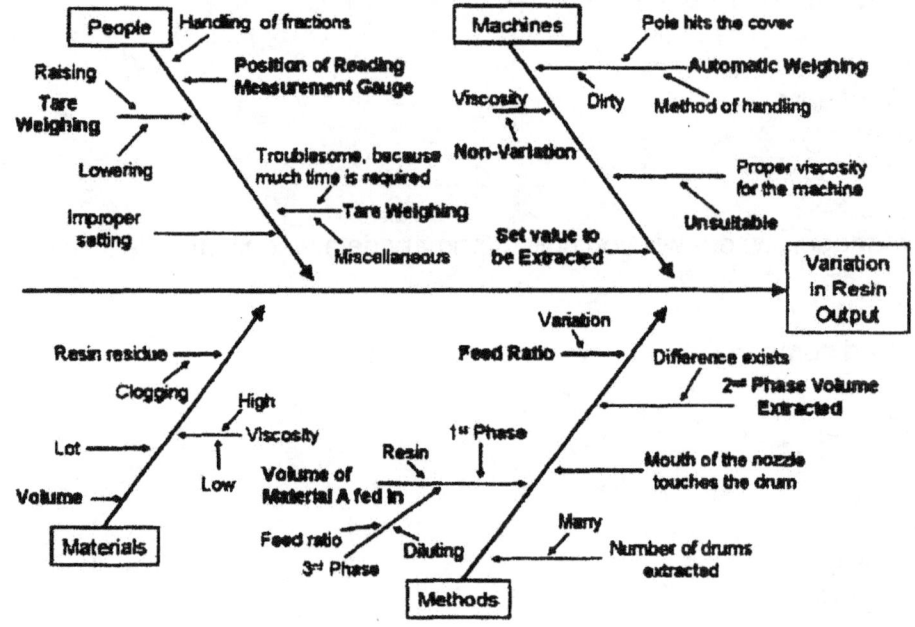

21. Which of the following is NOT represented in this diagram?

    A. Problem
    B. Major cause of the problem
    C. Contributing factors
    D. Possible causes of the problem

22. What is the effect with respect to the diagram?

    A. Materials
    B. Methods
    C. Variation in Resin Output
    D. People

23. As a project manager, what will you do to gain a better understanding of the problems and handling them?

    A. Investigations
    B. Surveys
    C. Interviews
    D. All the above

24. Kotter's change management process involves all the following steps EXCEPT

    A. building a team
    B. resource management
    C. creating a vision
    D. removing obstacles

25. _____ lets team members know why they are working on a change initiative.

    A. Removing obstacles
    B. Building a team
    C. Integrating the change
    D. Creating a vision

KEY (CORRECT ANSWERS)

1. A
2. C
3. B
4. B
5. D

6. C
7. A
8. D
9. A
10. C

11. C
12. B
13. B
14. A
15. D

16. C
17. B
18. A
19. C
20. D

21. B
22. C
23. D
24. B
25. D

TEST 4

DIRECTIONS: Each question or incomplete statement is followed by several suggested answers of completions. Select the one that best answers the question or Complete the statement. *PRINT THE LETTER OF THE CORRECT ANSWER IN THE SPACE AT THE RIGHT.*

1. Which of the following is NOT a communication blocker? 1._____
    A. Judging
    B. Accusing
    C. Globalizing
    D. Listening

2. Using words like "always" and "never" is an example of _____. 2._____
    A. judging
    B. accusing
    C. globalizing
    D. listening

3. What should you do as a project manager to eliminate communication blockers? 3._____
    A. Encourage others to avoid communication blockers by educating them
    B. Be aware of the various blockers and take steps to remove them
    C. Model to promote effective and empathetic communication
    D. All of the above

4. What would happen if there were no proper communication channel? 4._____
    A. Inefficient flow of information
    B. Clarity among employees on what is expected of them
    C. Sense of company mind/common vision among employees
    D. Clarity among employees on the happening within the company

5. As a project manager, you could use any one of the following types of language EXCEPT _____ for communicating with your team. 5._____
    A. formal
    B. insulting
    C. informal
    D. unofficial

6. A(n) _____ is/are NOT an example of formal communication. 6._____
    A. annual report
    B. business plan
    C. social gathering
    D. review meetings

7. _____ types of communication are used to communicate company policies, goals and procedures.
    A. Formal
    B. Informal
    C. Unofficial
    D. None of the above

8. _____ is NOT an example of informal communication.
    A. Survey
    B. Quality circle
    C. Team work
    D. Training program

9. "Grapevine" is an example of _____ communication.
    A. Formal
    B. Informal
    C. Unofficial
    D. None of the above

10. What question would you NOT consider as a project manager before choosing the right method to communicate?
    A. Who is the target audience?
    B. Will it lead to employee productivity?
    C. What kind of information would be helpful for clarity among employees?
    D. Which is the best way to threaten the employees?

11. Which of the following is not included in "The Five Ws of Communication Management"?
    A. What information would prompt employees to work out of fear?
    B. What information is essential for the project?
    C. What is the time required for the communication to happen effectively?
    D. Who requires information and what type of information is required?

12. _____ refers to developing a message.
    A. Decoding
    B. Encoding
    C. Transmission
    D. Feedback

13. _____ refers to interpreting the message.
    A. Decoding
    B. Encoding
    C. Transmission
    D. Feedback

14. Which of the following is not necessarily involved in a communication process?
    A. Sender
    B. Transmission
    C. Vision
    D. Receiver

15. _____ is NOT a sign of active listening.
    A. Making eye contact
    B. Asking questions to gain clarity
    C. Using gestures like nodding head
    D. Using gestures that distract the speaker

16. Madeline is a project manager and involved in conflict management. Which of the following should she use to manage a conflict?
    A. Identify actions that resolve conflicts
    B. Identify actions that would aggravate conflicts
    C. Consider different methods of resolving the conflict
    D. All the above

17. A managerial action that would NOT aggravate conflict is _____.
    A. poor communication
    B. assertive style of leadership
    C. ill-defined expectations
    D. authoritative style of leadership

18. An example of a managerial action that would NOT minimize a conflict is
    A. well-defined job descriptions
    B. participative approach
    C. submissive style of leadership
    D. fostering team spirit

19. Which of the following methods could you use as a project manager to handle conflicts?
    A. Flight
    B. Fake
    C. Fight
    D. All of the above

20. _____ is the term used when people run away from problems instead of confronting them and turn to avoidance as a means of handling conflict.
    A. Flight
    B. Fake
    C. Fight
    D. Fold

21. _____ is the term used when an individual is made to agree to a solution by means of browbeating.
    A. Flight
    B. Fake
    C. Fight
    D. Fold

22. Which of the following is NOT a step in conflict management?
    A. Choose the best solution that satisfy most people most of the time and implement this
    B. Engage in participatory dialogue and find a range of solutions that will be acceptable to all the parties concerned
    C. Eliminate those who promote mutual understanding and acceptance
    D. Identify the limiting resource or constraint that is generally at the root cause of the conflict

23. Which of the following is NOT a skill required for conflict resolution?
    A. Clarity in communication
    B. Aggressiveness
    C. Negotiation
    D. Listening

24. _____ is essential to be prepared for any problems that may arise when it is least expected.
    A. Conflict management
    B. Communication management
    C. Crisis management
    D. None of the above

25. Which of the following is NOT a type of crisis?
    A. Financial
    B. Technological
    C. Natural
    D. Negotiation

KEY (CORRECT ANSWERS)

1. D
2. C
3. D
4. A
5. B

6. C
7. A
8. A
9. C
10. D

11. A
12. B
13. A
14. C
15. D

16. D
17. B
18. C
19. D
20. A

21. D
22. C
23. B
24. C
25. D

EXAMINATION SECTION
TEST 1

DIRECTIONS: Each question or incomplete statement is followed by several suggested answers or completions. Select the one that BEST answers the question or completes the statement. *PRINT THE LETTER OF THE CORRECT ANSWER IN THE SPACE AT THE RIGHT.*

1. A management approach widely used today is based on the belief that decisions should be made and actions should be taken by managers closest to the organization's problems.
 This style of management is MOST appropriately called _____ management.
    A. scientific
    B. means-end
    C. decentralized
    D. internal process

    1._____

2. As contrasted with tall organization structures with narrow spans of control, flat organization structures with wide spans of control MOST usually provide
    A. fast communication and information flows
    B. more levels in the organizational hierarchy
    C. fewer workers reporting to supervisors
    D. lower motivation because of tighter control standards

    2._____

3. Use of the systems approach is MOST likely to lead to
    A. consideration of the impact on the whole organization of actions taken in any part of that organization
    B. the placing of restrictions on departmental activity
    C. use of mathematical models to suboptimize production
    D. consideration of the activities of each unit of an organization as a totality without regard to the remainder of the organization

    3._____

4. An administrator, with overall responsibility for all administrative operations in a large operating agency, is considering organizing the agency's personnel office around either of the following two alternative concepts:
 Alternative I: A corps of specialists for each branch of personnel subject matter, whose skills, counsel, or work products are coordinated only by the agency personnel officer
 Alternative II: A crew of so-called *personnel generalists*, who individually work with particular segments of the organization but deal with all subspecialties of the personnel function
 The one of the following which MOST tends to be a DRAWBACK of Alternative I, as compared with Alternative II, is that
    A. training and employee relations work call for education, interests, and talents that differ from those required for classification and compensation work
    B. personnel office staff may develop only superficial familiarity with the specialized areas to which they have been assigned

    4._____

C. supervisors may fail to get continuing overall personnel advice on an integrated basis
D. the personnel specialists are likely to become so interested in and identified with the operating view as to particular cases that they lose their professional objectivity and become merely advocates of what some supervisor wants

5. The matrix summary or decision matrix is a useful tool for making choices. Its effectiveness is MOST dependent upon the user's ability to
   A. write a computer program (Fortran or Cobol)
   B. assign weights representing the relative importance of the objectives
   C. solve a set of two equations with two unknowns
   D. work with matrix algebra

6. An organizational form which is set up only on an *ad hoc* basis to meet specific goals is said PRIMARILY to use
   A. clean break departmentation
   B. matrix or task force organization
   C. scalar specialization
   D. geographic or area-wide decentralization

7. The concept of job enlargement would LEAST properly be implemented by
   A. permitting workers to follow through on tasks or projects from start to finish
   B. delegating the maximum authority possible for decision-making to lower levels in the hierarchy
   C. maximizing the number of professional classes in the classification plan
   D. training employees to grow beyond whatever tasks they have been performing

8. As used in the area of admission, the principle of *unity of command* MOST specifically means that
   A. an individual should report to only one superior for any single activity
   B. individuals make better decisions than do committees
   C. in large organizations, chains of command are normally too long
   D. an individual should not supervise over five subordinates

9. The method of operations research, statistical decision-making, and linear programming have been referred to as the tool kit of the manager. Utilization of these tools is LEAST useful in the performance of which of the following functions?
   A. Elimination of the need for using judgment when making decisions
   B. Facilitation of decision-making without the need for sub-optimization
   C. Quantifying problems for management study
   D. Research and analysis of management operations

10. When acting in their respective managerial capacities, the chief executive officer and the office supervisor both perform the fundamental functions of management.
    Of the following differences between the two, the one which is generally considered to be the LEAST significant is the
    A. breadth of the objectives
    B. complexity of measuring actual efficiency of performance
    C. number of decisions made
    D. organizational relationships affected by actions taken

11. The ability of operations researchers to solve complicated problems rests on their use of models.
    These models can BEST be described as
    A. mathematical statements of the problem
    B. physical constructs that simulate a work layout
    C. toy-like representations of employees in work environments
    D. role-playing simulations

12. Of the following, it is MOST likely to be proper for the agency head to allow the agency personnel officer to make final selection of appointees from certified eligible lists where there are
    A. *small* numbers of employees to be hired in newly-developed professional fields
    B. *large* numbers of persons to be hired for key managerial positions
    C. *large* numbers of persons to be hired in very routine occupations where the individual discretion of operating officials is not vital
    D. *small* numbers of persons to be hired in highly specialized professional occupations which are vital to the agency's operations

13. Of the following, an operating agency personnel office is LEAST likely to be able to exert strong influence or control within the operating agency by
    A. interpreting to the operating agency head what is intended by the directives and rules emanating from the central personnel agency
    B. establishing the key objectives of those line divisions of the operating agency employing large numbers of staff and operating under the management-by-objectives approach
    C. formulating and proposing to the agency head the internal policies and procedures on personnel matters required within the operating agency
    D. exercising certain discretionary authority in the application of the agency head's general personnel policies to actual specific situations

14. PERT is a recently developed system used PRIMARILY to
    A. evaluate the quality of applicants' background
    B. analyze and control the timing aspects of a major project
    C. control the total expenditure of agency funds within a monthly or quarterly time period
    D. analyze and control the differential effect on costs of purchasing different quantities

15. Assume that an operating agency has among its vacant positions two positions, each of which encompasses mixed duties. Both require appointees to have considerable education and experience, but these requirements are essential only for the more difficult duties of these positions. In the place of these positions, an administrator creates two new positions, one in which the higher duties are concentrated and the other with the lesser functions requiring only minimum preparation.
Of the following, it is generally MOST appropriate to characterize the administrator's action as a(n)
    A. *undesirable* example of deliberate downgrading of standards and requirements
    B. *undesirable* manipulation of the classification system for non-merit purposes
    C. *desirable* broadening of the definition of a class of positions
    D. *desirable* example of job redesign

16. Of the following, the LEAST important stumbling block to the development of personnel mobility among governmental jurisdictions is the
    A. limitations on lateral entry above junior levels in many jurisdictions
    B. continued collection of filing fees for civil service tests by many governmental jurisdictions
    C. absence of reciprocal exchange of retirement benefit eligibility between governments
    D. disparities in salary scales between governments

17. Of the following, the MAJOR disadvantage of a personnel system that features the *selection out* (forced retirement) of those who have been passed over a number of times for promotion is that such a system
    A. wastes manpower which is perfectly competent at one level but unable to rise above that level
    B. wastes funds by requiring review boards
    C. leads to excessive recruiting of newcomers from outside the system
    D. may not be utilized in *closed* career systems with low maximum age limits for entrance

18. Of the following, the fields in which operating agency personnel offices generally exercise the MOST stringent controls over first line supervisors in the agency are
    A. methods analysis and work simplification
    B. selection and position classification
    C. vestibule training and Gantt chart
    D. suggestion systems and staff development

19. Of the following, computers are normally MOST effective in handling
    A. large masses of data requiring simple processing
    B. small amounts of data requiring constantly changing complex processing
    C. data for which reported values are often subject to inaccuracies
    D. large amounts of data requiring continual programming and reprocessing

5 (#1)

20. Contingency planning, which has long been used by the military and is assuming increasing importance in other organizations, may BEST be described as a process which utilizes
    A. alternative plans based on varying assumptions
    B. *crash programs* by organizations departmentalized along process lines
    C. plans which mandate substitution of equipment for manpower at predetermined operational levels
    D. plans that individually and accurately predict future events

21. In the management of inventory, two kinds of costs normally determine when to order and in what amounts.
    The one of the following choices which includes BOTH of these kinds of costs is _____ costs and _____ costs.
    A. carrying; storage
    B. personnel; order
    C. computer; order
    D. personnel; computer

22. At top management levels, the one of the following which is generally the MOST important executive skill is skill in
    A. budgeting procedures
    B. a technical discipline
    C. controlling actions in accordance with previously approved plans
    D. seeing the organization as a whole

23. Of the following, the BEST way to facilitate the successful operation of a committee is to set guidelines establishing its
    A. budget exclusive of personnel costs
    B. location
    C. schedule of meetings or conferences
    D. scope of purpose

24. Executive training programs that single out particular managers and groom them for promotion create the so-called organizational *crown princes*.
    Of the following, the MOST serious problem that arises in connection with this practice is that
    A. the managers chosen for promotion seldom turn out to be the best managers since the future potential of persons cannot be predicted
    B. not enough effort is made to remove organizational obstacles in the way of their development and achievement
    C. the resentment of the managers not selected for the program has an adverse effect on the motivation of those managers not selected
    D. performance appraisal and review are not carried out systematically enough

25. Of the following, the LEAST likely result of the use of the concept of job enlargement is that
    A. coordination will be simplified
    B. the individual's job will become less challenging
    C. worker satisfaction will increase
    D. fewer people will have to give attention to each piece of work

KEY (CORRECT ANSWERS)

1. C
2. A
3. A
4. C
5. B

6. B
7. C
8. A
9. A
10. C

11. A
12. C
13. B
14. B
15. D

16. B
17. A
18. B
19. A
20. A

21. A
22. D
23. D
24. C
25. B

TEST 2

DIRECTIONS: Each question or incomplete statement is followed by several suggested answers or completions. Select the one that BEST answers the question or completes the statement. *PRINT THE LETTER OF THE CORRECT ANSWER IN THE SPACE AT THE RIGHT.*

1. The one of the following which is MOST likely to be emphasized in the use of the brainstorming technique is the
    A. early consideration of cost factors of all ideas which may be suggested
    B. avoidance of impractical suggestions
    C. separation of the generation of ideas from their evaluation
    D. appraisal of suggestions concurrently with their initial presentation

    1.____

2. Of the following, the BEST method for assessing managerial performance is generally to
    A. compare the manager's accomplishments against clear, specific, agreed-upon goals
    B. compare the manager's traits with those of his peers on a predetermined objective
    C. measure the manager's behavior against a listing of itemized personal traits
    D. measure the manager's success according to the enumeration of the *satisfaction* principle

    2.____

3. As compared with recruitment from outside, selection from within the service must generally show GREATER concern for the
    A. prestige in which the public service as a whole is held by the public
    B. morale of the candidate group compromising the recruitment field
    C. cost of examining per candidate
    D. benefits of the use of standardized and validated tests

    3.____

4. Performance budgeting focuses PRIMARY attention upon which one of the following? The
    A. things to be acquired, such as supplies and equipment
    B. general character and relative importance of the work to be done or the service to be rendered
    C. list of personnel to be employed, by specific title
    D. separation of employee performance evaluations from employee compensation

    4.____

5. Of the following, the FIRST step in the installation and operation of a performance budgeting system generally should be the
    A. identification of program costs in relationship to the accounting system and operating structure
    B. identification of the specific end results of past programs in other jurisdictions

    5.____

C. identification of work programs that are meaningful for management purposes
D. establishment of organizational structures each containing only one work program

6. Of the following, the MOST important purpose of a system of quarterly allotments of appropriated funds generally is to enable the
   A. head of the judicial branch to determine the legality of agency requests for budget increases
   B. operating agencies of government to upgrade the quality of their services without increasing costs
   C. head of the executive branch to control the rate at which the operating agencies obligate and expend funds
   D. operating agencies of government to avoid payment for services which have not been properly rendered by employees

7. In the preparation of the agency's budget, the agency's central budget office has two responsibilities: program review and management improvement. Which one of the following questions concerning an operating agency's program is MOST closely related to the agency budget officer's program review responsibility?
   A. Can expenditures for supplies, materials, or equipment be reduced?
   B. Will improved work methods contribute to a more effective program?
   C. What is the relative importance of this program as compared to a higher level of program performance?
   D. Will a realignment of responsibilities contribute to a higher level of program performance?

8. Of the following, the method of evaluating relative rates of return normally and generally thought to be MOST useful in evaluating government operations is _____ analysis.
   A. cost-benefit
   B. budget variance
   C. investment capital
   D. budget planning program

9. The one of the following assumptions that is LEAST likely to be made by a democratic or permissive type of leader is that
   A. commitment to goals is seldom a result of monetary rewards alone
   B. people can learn not only to accept, but also to seek, responsibility
   C. the average person prefers security over advancement
   D. creativity may be found in most segments of the population

10. In attempting to motivate subordinates, a manager should PRINCIPALLY be aware of the fact that
    A. the psychological qualities of people, in general, are easily predictable
    B. fear, as a traditional form of motivation, has lost much of its former power to motivate people in our modern industrial society
    C. fear is still the most potent force in motivating the behavior of subordinates in the public service
    D. the worker has very little control over the quality and quantity of his output

11. Assume that the following figures represent the number of work-unit that were produced during a week by each of sixteen employees in a division:

    12 16 13 18
    21 12 16 13
    16 13 17 21
    13 15 18 20

    If all of the employees of the division who produced thirteen work-units during the week had instead produced fifteen work-units during that same week, then for that week the
    A. mean, median, and mode would all change
    B. mean and mode would change, but the median would remain the same
    C. mode and median would change, but the mean would remain the same
    D. mode, mean, and median would all still remain unchanged in value

12. An important law in motivation theory is called the *law of effect*. This law says that behavior which satisfies a person's needs tends to be repeated; behavior which does not satisfy a person's needs tends to be eliminated.
    The one of the following which is the BEST interpretation of this law is that
    A. productivity depends on personality traits
    B. diversity of goals leads to instability and motivation
    C. the greater the satisfaction, the more likely it is that the behavior will be reinforced
    D. extrinsic satisfaction is more important than intrinsic reward

13. Of the following, the MOST acceptable reason an administrator can give for taking advice from other employees in the organization only when he asks for it is that he wants to
    A. encourage creativity and high morale
    B. keep dysfunctional pressures and inconsistent recommendations to a minimum
    C. show his superiors and peers who is in charge
    D. show his subordinates who is in charge

14. A complete picture of the communication channels in an organization can BEST be revealed by
    A. observing the planned paperwork system
    B. recording the highly intermittent patterns of communication
    C. plotting the entire flow of information over a period of time
    D. monitoring the *grapevine*

Questions 15-16.

DIRECTIONS: Questions 15 and 16 are to be answered SOLELY on the basis of the following passage.

Management by objectives (MBO) may be defined as the process by which the superior and the subordinate managers of an organization jointly define its common goals, define each individual's major areas of responsibility in terms of the results expected of him and use these measures as guides for operating the unit and assessing the contribution of each of its members.

The MBO approach requires that after organizational goals are established and communicated, targets must be set for each individual position which are congruent with organizational goals. Periodic performance reviews and a final review using the objectives set as criteria are also basic to this approach.

Recent studies have shown that MBO programs are influenced by attitudes and perceptions of the boss, the company, the reward-punishment system, and the program itself. In addition, the manner in which the MBO program is carried out can influence the success of the program. A study done in the late sixties indicates that the best results are obtained when the manager sets goals which deal with significant problem areas in the organizational unit, or with the subordinate's personal deficiencies. These goals must be clear with regard to what is expected of the subordinate. The frequency of feedback is also important in the success of a management-by-objectives program. Generally, the greater the amount of feedback, the more successful the MBO program.

15. According to the above passage, the expected output for individual employees should be determined
    A. after a number of reviews of work performance
    B. after common organizational goals are defined
    C. before common organizational goals are defined
    D. on the basis of an employee's personal qualities

16. According to the above passage, the management-by-objectives approach requires
    A. less feedback than other types of management programs
    B. little review of on-the-job performance after the initial setting of goals
    C. general conformance between individual goals and organizational goals
    D. the setting of goals which deal with minor problem area in the organization

Questions 17-19.

DIRECTIONS: Questions 17 through 19 are to be answered SOLELY on the basis of the following passage.

During the last decade, a great deal of interest has been generated around the phenomenon of organizational development, or the process of developing human resources through conscious organization effort. Organizational development (OD) stresses improving interpersonal relationships and organizational skills, such as communication, to a much greater degree than individual training ever did.

The kind of training that an organization should emphasize depends upon the present and future structure of the organization. If future organizations are to be unstable, shifting coalitions, then individual skills and abilities, particularly those emphasizing innovativeness, creativity, flexibility, and the latest technological knowledge, are crucial, and individual training is most appropriate.

But if there is to be little change in organizational structure, then the main thrust of training should be group-oriented or organizational development. This approach seems better designed for overcoming hierarchical barriers, for developing a degree of interpersonal relationships which make communication along the chain of command possible, and for retaining a modicum of innovation and/or flexibility.

17. According to the above passage, group-oriented training is MOST useful in
    A. developing a communications system that will facilitate understanding through the chain of command
    B. highly flexible and mobile organizations
    C. preventing the crossing of hierarchical barriers within an organization
    D. saving energy otherwise wasted on developing methods of dealing with rigid hierarchies

17._____

18. The one of the following conclusions which can be drawn MOST appropriately from the above passage is that
    A. behavioral research supports the use of organizational development training method rather than individualized training
    B. it is easier to provide individualized training in specific skills than to set up sensitivity training programs
    C. organizational development eliminates innovative or flexible activity
    D. the nature of an organization greatly influences which training methods will be most effective

18._____

19. According to the above passage, the one of the following which is LEAST important for large-scale organizations geared to rapid and abrupt change is
    A. current technological information
    B. development of a high degree of interpersonal relationships
    C. development of individual skills and abilities
    D. emphasis on creativity

19._____

Questions 20-25.

DIRECTIONS: Each of Questions 20 through 25 consist of a statement which contains one word that is incorrectly used because it is not in keeping with the meaning that the quotation is evidently intended to convey. Determine which word is INCORRECTLY used. Select from the choices lettered A, B, C, and D the word which, when substituted for the incorrectly used word, would BEST help to convey the meaning of the statement.

20. One of the considerations likely to affect the currency of classification, particularly in professional and managerial occupations, is the impact of the incumbent's capacities on the job. Some work is highly susceptible to change as the result of the special talents or interests of the classifier. Organization should never be so rigid as not to capitalize on the innovative or unusual proclivities of its key employees. While a machine operator may not be able, even subtly, to change the character or level of his job, the design engineer, the attorney, or the organization and methods analyst might readily do so. Reliance on his judgment and the scope of his assignments may both grow as the result of his skill, insight, and capacity.

    A. unlikely B. incumbent C. directly D. scope

21. The supply of services by the state is not governed by market price. The aim is to supply such services to all who need them and to treat all consumers equally. This objective especially compels the civil servant to maintain a role f strict impartiality, based on the principle of equality of individual citizens vis-à-vis their government. However, there is a clear difference between being neutral and impartial. If the requirement is construed to mean that all civil servants should be political eunuchs, devoid of the drive and motivation essential to dynamic administration, then the concept of impartiality is being seriously utilized. Modern governments should not be stopped from demanding that their hirelings have not only the technical but the emotional qualifications necessary for whole-hearted effort.

    A. determined B. rule C. stable D. misapplied

22. The manager was barely listening. Recently, at the divisional level, several new fronts of troubles had erupted, including a requirement to increase production yet hold down operating costs and somehow raise quality standards. Though the three objectives were basically obsolete, top departmental management was insisting on the simultaneous attainment of them, an insistence not helping the manager's ulcer, an old enemy within. Thus, the manager could not find time for interest in individuals—only in statistics which regiment of individuals, like unconsidered Army privates, added up to.

    A. quantity B. battalion C. incompatible D. quiet

23. When a large volume of data flows directly between operators and first-line supervisors, senior executives tend to be out of the mainstream of work. Summary reports can increase their remoteness. An executive needs to know the volume, quality, and cost of completed work, and exceptional problems. In addition, he may desire information on key operating conditions. Summary reports on these matters are, therefore, essential features of a communications network and make delegation without loss of control possible.

    A. unimportant B. quantity C. offset D. incomplete

24. Of major significance in management is harmony between the overall objectives of the organization and the managerial objectives within that organization. In addition, harmony among goals of managers is impossible; they should not be at cross-purposes. Each manager's goal should supplement and assist the goals of his colleagues. Likewise, the objectives of individuals or non-management members should be harmonized with those of the manager. When this is accomplished, genuine teamwork is the result, and human relations are aided materially. The integration of managers' and individuals' goals aids in achieving greater work satisfaction at all levels.
    A. competition   B. dominate   C. incremental   D. vital

25. Change constantly challenges the manager. Some of this change is evolutionary, some revolutionary, some recognizable, some non-recognizable. Both forces within an enterprise and forces outside the enterprise cause managers to act and react in initiating changes in their immediate working environment. Change invalidates existing operations. Goals are not being accomplished in the best manner, problems develop, and frequently because of the lack of time, only patched-up solutions are followed. The result is that the mode of management is profound in nature and temporary in effectiveness. A complete overhaul of managerial operations should take place. It appears quite likely that we are just beginning to see the real effects of change in our society; the pace probably will accelerate in ways that few really understand or know how to handle.
    A. confirms   B. decline   C. instituting   D. superficial

KEY (CORRECT ANSWERS)

1.	C	11.	B
2.	A	12.	C
3.	B	13.	B
4.	B	14.	C
5.	C	15.	B
6.	C	16.	C
7.	C	17.	A
8.	A	18.	D
9.	C	19.	B
10.	B	20.	B

21. D
22. C
23. C
24. D
25. D

EXAMINATION SECTION
TEST 1

DIRECTIONS: Each question or incomplete statement is followed by several suggested answers or completions. Select the one that BEST answers the question or completes the statement. *PRINT THE LETTER OF THE CORRECT ANSWER IN THE SPACE AT THE RIGHT.*

1. The PRIMARY purpose of program analysis as it is used in government is to
    A. replace political judgments with rational programs and policies
    B. help decision-makers to sharpen their judgments about program choices
    C. analyze the impact of past programs on the quality of public services
    D. reduce costs by eliminating waste in public programs and services

2. While there is no complete method for program analysis that is agreed to by all the experts and is relevant to all types of problems, the MOST important element in program analysis involves the
    A. development of alternatives and the definition of objectives or criteria
    B. collection of information and the construction of a mathematical model
    C. design of experiments and procedures to validate results
    D. collection of expert opinion and the combination of their views

3. Electronic data processing is a particularly valuable tool of analysis in situations where the analyst has a processing problem involving
    A. *small* input, *few* operations, and *small* output
    B. *large* input, *many* operations, and *small* output
    C. *large* input, *few* operations, and *large* output
    D. *small* input, *many* operations, and *small* output

4. In order for an analyst to use electronic data processing to solve an analytic problem, the problem must be clearly defined.
    The BEST way to prepare material for such definition in electronic data processing is to
    A. discuss the problem with computer programmers in a meeting
    B. prepare a flow diagram outlining the steps in the analysis
    C. write a memorandum with a list of the relevant program issues
    D. write a computer program using FORTRAN, BASIC, or another language

5. The "growth rate" referred to in current political and economic discussion refers to change from year to year in a country's
    A. investments   B. population
    C. gross national product   D. sale of goods

6. Interactive or conversational programming is important to the program analyst ESPECIALLY for
   A. preparing analyses leading to management information systems
   B. communicating among analysts in different places
   C. using canned programs in statistical analysis
   D. testing trial solutions in rapid sequence

7. Program analysts often calls for recommendation of a choice between competing program possibilities that differ in the timing of major costs. Analysts using the present value technique by setting an interest or discount rate are in effect arguing that, other things being equal,
   A. it is inadvisable to defer the start of projects because of rising costs
   B. projects should be completed within a short time period to save money
   C. expenditures should be made out of tax revenues to avoid payment of interest
   D. postponing expenditures is advantageous at some measurable rate

8. Of the following, the formula which is MOST appropriately used to estimate the net need for a given type of service is that net need equals
   A. current clients – anticipate losses + anticipated gains
   B. $\dfrac{\text{current supply}}{\text{standard}}$ + current clients
   C. (client population x standard) – current supply
   D. current supply – anticipated losses + anticipated gains

9. The purpose of feasibility analysis is to protect the analyst from naïve alternatives and, MOST generally, to
   A. identify and quantify technological constraints
   B. carry out a preliminary stage of analysis
   C. anticipate potential blocks to implementation
   D. line up the support of political leadership

Questions 10-11.

DIRECTIONS: Questions 10 and 11 are to be answered on the basis of the following chart. In a hypothetical problem involving four criteria and four alternatives, the following data have been assembled.

Cost Criterion	Effectiveness Criterion	Timing Criterion	Feasibility Criterion
Alternative A $500,000	50 units	3 months	probably feasible
Alternative B $300,000	100 units	6 months	probably feasible
Alternative C $400,000	50 units	12 months	probably infeasible
Alternative D $200,000	75 units	3 months	probably infeasible

10. On the basis of the above data, it appears that the one alternative which is dominated by another alternative is Alternative
    A. A   B. B   C. C   D. D

11. If the feasibility constraint is absolute and fixed, then the critical trade-off is between lower cost
    A. on the one hand and faster timing and higher effectiveness on the other
    B. and higher effectiveness on one hand and faster timing on the other
    C. and faster timing on the one hand and higher effectiveness on the other
    D. on the one hand and higher effectiveness on the other

12. A classification of an agency's activities in a program structure is MOST useful if it highlights
    A. trade-offs that might not otherwise be considered
    B. ways to improve the efficiency of each activity
    C. the true organizational structure of an agency
    D. bases for insuring that expenditures stay within limits

13. CPM, like PERT, is a useful tool for scheduling large-scale, complex processes. In CPM, the critical path is the
    A. path composed of important links
    B. path composed of uncertain links
    C. longest path through the network
    D. shortest path through the network

14. Classical evaluative research calls for the use of control groups. However, there are practical difficulties in collecting data on individuals to be used as "controls" in program evaluations.
    Researchers may attempt to overcome these difficulties by
    A. using control groups that have no choice such as prison inmates or inmates of other public institutions or facilities
    B. developing better measures of the inputs, processes, and outputs relevant to public programs and services
    C. using experimental demonstration projects with participants in the different projects serving as comparison groups for one another
    D. abandoning attempts at formal evaluation in favor of more qualitative approaches employing a journalistic style of analysis

15. During the course of an analysis of the remaining "life" of a certain city's landfill for refuse disposal, there was a great deal of debate about the impact of changing rates of garbage generation on the amount of landfill needed and about what rates of garbage generation to expect over the next decade. Faced with the need to attempt to resolve this debate, an analyst would construct a simple model of the refuse disposal system and
    A. project landfill needs without considering refuse generation in the future
    B. conduct a detailed household survey in order to estimate future garbage generation rates
    C. ask the experts to continue to debate the issue until the argument is won by one view
    D. do a sensitivity analysis to test the impact of alternative assumptions about refuse generation

16. The limitations of traditional surveys have fostered the development and use of panels.
A panel is a
   A. group of respondents that serves as a continuous source of survey information
   B. group of advisors expert in the design and implementation of surveys
   C. representative sample of respondents at a single point in time
   D. post-survey discussion group composed of former respondents

17. The difference between sensitivity analysis and risk analysis is that risk analysis
   A. is applicable only to profit and loss situations where the concept of risk is operable
   B. includes an estimate of probabilities of different values of input factors
   C. is applicable to physical problems while sensitivity analysis is applicable to social ones
   D. requires a computer simulation while sensitivity analysis does not

18. A decision tree, although initially applied to business problems, is a graphic device which is useful to public analysts in
   A. scheduling complex processes
   B. doing long-range forecasting
   C. formulating the structure of alternatives
   D. solving production-inventory problems

19. The purpose of a management information system in an agency is to
   A. structure data relevant to managerial decision-making
   B. put all of an agency's data in machine-processing form
   C. simplify the record-keeping operations in an agency
   D. keep an ongoing record of management's activities

20.

[Chart: Number of responses to alarms vs. Time, showing two rising lines labeled "total alarms" (upper) and "false alarms" (lower)]

Assume that an analyst is presented with the above chart for a fire department and supplied also with information indicating a stable size firefighting staff over this time.
The analyst could REASONABLY conclude regarding productivity that
   A. productivity over this time period was essentially stable for this firefighting force because the number of responses to real fires during this period was stable, as was the work force
   B. productivity was essentially increasing for this force because the number of total responses was increasing relative to a stable force

C. productivity was declining because a greater proportion of the total work effort was wasted effort in responding to false alarms
D. it is impossible to make a judgment about the productivity of the firefighting staff without a judgment about the value of a response to a false alarm

21. In the design of a productivity program for the sanitary department, the BEST measure of productivity would be
    A. tons of refuse collected annually
    B. number of collections made per week
    C. tons of refuse collected per truck shift
    D. number of trucks used per shift

22. The cohort-survival method for estimating future population has been widely employed.
    In this method,
    A. migration is assumed to be constant over time
    B. net migration within cohorts is assumed to be zero
    C. migration is included as a multiplier factor
    D. net migration within cohorts is assumed to be constant

23. Cost-effectiveness and cost-benefit analysis represent a systematic approach to balancing potential losses against potential gains as a prelude to public action.
    In addition to limitations based on difficulties of measurement and inadequacies in data that are typical of systematic program analysis, cost-benefit analysis suffers from a serious conceptual flaw in that
    A. the definition of benefit or cost does not typically distinguish to whom benefits or costs accrue
    B. a full-scale cost benefit analysis takes too long to do, is too expensive, and needs too much data
    C. it has been shown that such analyses are more suitable for defense or water resources problems
    D. such analyses are not useful in any problem involving capital and operating costs or benefits

24. If you were asked to develop a total cost estimate for one year for a program involving both a capital improvement and operating costs, the BEST way to estimate the capital cost component would be to
    A. divide the estimated cost of the capital improvement by the projected operating costs over the life of the improvement
    B. multiply the annual operating cost by the projected life of the capital improvement
    C. divide the amortized cost of the capital improvement by the projected life of the improvement
    D. multiply the portion of the capital improvement to be completed within the year by the cost of the improvement

25. In comparing the costs of two or more alternative programs, it is important to consider all relevant costs.
    The MOST important principle in defining "relevant cost" is that
    A. only marginal or incremental cost should be considered in the estimate
    B. only recurring costs should be considered for each alternative
    C. estimates should include the sunk costs for each alternative
    D. cost estimates need to be as precise as in budget preparation

25._____

26. Different techniques for projecting future costs may be suitable in different situations. Assume that it is necessary to estimate the future costs of maintaining garbage collection vehicles.
    Under which of the following conditions would it be advisable to develop a cost-estimating equation rather than to use unadjusted current data?
    A. When it is expected that more complex equipment will replace simpler equipment
    B. Whether or not it is expected that the nature of future garbage collection will change
    C. When the current unadjusted data still has to be verified
    D. When the nature of future garbage collection equipment is unknown

26._____

27. The following data has been collected on the costs of two pilot programs, each representing a different approach to the same problem.

	Total Cost	Fixed Cost	Variable Cost	Average Unit Cost	Number of Users
Program A	$45,000	$20,000	$50 per user	$90 Per User	500
Program B	$42,000	$7,000	$100 Per User	$120 Per User	350

Assume that the pilot programs are extended city-wide and other factors are constant.
Using the above data, what would a cost analysis conclude about the relative costs of the two programs?
Program
   A. B would be less costly with fewer than 300 users and Program A would be less costly with more than 300 users
   B. B would be less costly with fewer than 260 users and Program A would be less costly with more than 260 users
   C. A would be less costly without regard to the size of the program
   D. B would be less costly without regard to the size of the program

27._____

Questions 28-30.

DIRECTIONS: Questions 28 through 30 are to be answered on the basis of the following data assembled for a cost-benefit analysis.

	Cost	Benefit
No program	0	0
Alternative W	$3,000	$6,000
Alternative X	$10,000	$17,000
Alternative Y	$17,000	$25,000
Alternative Z	$30,000	$32,000

7 (#1)

28. From the point of view of pushing public expenditure to the point where marginal benefit equals or exceeds marginal cost, the BEST alternative is Alternative
    A. W B. X C. Y D. Z

    28._____

29. From the point of view of selecting the alternative with the best cost-benefit ratio, the BEST alternative is Alternative
    A. W B. X C. Y D. Z

    29._____

30. From the point of view of selecting the alternative with the best measure of net benefit, the BEST alternative is Alternative
    A. W B. X C. Y D. Z

    30._____

Questions 31-35.

DIRECTIONS: The set of answers listed below applies to Questions 31 through 35. Each answer is a type of statistical test.

    A. Analysis of variance
    B. Pearson Product-Moment Correlation (r)
    C. t-test
    D. x^2 test (Chi-squared)

Pick the test which is MOST appropriate to the situation described. An answer may be used more than once.

31. A comparison between two correlated means obtained from a small sample.
    The CORRECT answer is:
    A. A B. B C. C D. D

    31._____

32. A comparison of three or more means.
    The CORRECT answer is:
    A. A B. B C. C D. D

    32._____

33. A comparison of the divergence of observed frequencies with those expected on the hypothesis of equal probability of occurrence.
    The CORRECT answer is:
    A. A B. B C. C D. D

    33._____

34. A comparison of the divergence of observed frequencies with those expected on the hypothesis of a normal distribution.
    The CORRECT answer is:
    A. A B. B C. C D. D

    34._____

35. A comparison between two uncorrelated means obtained from small samples.
    The CORRECT answer is:
    A. A B. B C. C D. D

    35._____

36. There are many different models for evaluative research.
A time-series design is an example of a _____ experimental design.
   A. field   B. true   C. quasi-   D. pre-

37. In policy research, as in all kinds of research, it is important to develop research hypotheses early.
The MAIN purpose of a research hypothesis is to
   A. include the kind of statistical procedures to be used in the research
   B. provide a ready answer in case data is not available for doing research
   C. serve as a guide to the kind of data that must be collected in order to answer the research question
   D. clarify what is known and what is not known in the research problem

38. While descriptive and causal research are not completely separable, there has been a distinct effort to move in the direction of causal research.
Such an effort is epitomized by the use of
   A. predictive models and measures of deviation from predictions
   B. option and attitudinal surveys in local neighborhoods
   C. community studies and area profiles of localities
   D. individual case histories and group case studies

39. The one of the following which BEST describes a periodic report is that it
   A. provides a record of accomplishments for a given time span and a comparison with similar time spans in the past
   B. covers the progress made in a project that has been postponed
   C. integrates, summarizes, and perhaps interprets published data on technical or scientific material
   D. describes a decision, advocates a policy or action, and presents facts in support of the writer's position

40. The PRIMARY purpose of including pictorial illustrations in a formal report is usually to
   A. amplify information which has been adequately treated verbally
   B. present detail that are difficult to describe verbally
   C. provide the reader with a pleasant, momentary distraction
   D. present supplementary information incidental to the main ideas developed in the report

KEY (CORRECT ANSWERS)

1.	B	11.	B	21.	C	31.	C
2.	A	12.	A	22.	B	32.	A
3.	B	13.	C	23.	A	33.	D
4.	B	14.	C	24.	C	34.	D
5.	C	15.	D	25.	A	35.	C
6.	D	16.	A	26.	A	36.	C
7.	D	17.	B	27.	B	37.	C
8.	C	18.	C	28.	C	38.	A
9.	C	19.	A	29.	A	39.	A
10.	C	20.	D	30.	C	40.	B

TEST 2

DIRECTIONS: Each question or incomplete statement is followed by several suggested answers or completions. Select the one that BEST answers the question or completes the statement. *PRINT THE LETTER OF THE CORRECT ANSWER IN THE SPACE AT THE RIGHT.*

1. A measurement procedure is considered to be RELIABLE to the extent that 1.____
   A. independent applications under similar conditions yield consistent results
   B. independent applications under different conditions yield similar results
   C. scores reflect true differences among individuals or situations
   D. scores reflect true differences in the same individual over time

2. Different scales of measurement are distinguished by the feasibility of various empirical operations. 2.____
   An ordinal scale of measurement
   A. is not as useful as a ratio or interval scale
   B. is useful in rank-ordering or priority setting
   C. provides the data for addition or subtraction
   D. provides the data for computation of means

3. A widely used approach to sampling is systematic sampling, i.e., selecting every Kth element in a listing. 3.____
   Even with a random start, a DISADVANTAGE in this approach is that
   A. the listing used may contain a cyclical pattern
   B. it is too similar to a simple random sample
   C. the system does not insure a probability sample
   D. it yield an unpredictable sample size

4. A rule of thumb sometimes used in sample size selection it to set sample size equal to five percent of the population size. 4.____
   Other things being equal, this rule
   A. tends to oversample small populations
   B. tends to oversample large populations
   C. provides an accurate rule for sampling
   D. is a relatively inexpensive basis for sampling

5. With regard to a stratified random sample, it may be APPROPRIATE to sample the various strata in different proportions in order to 5.____
   A. approximate the characteristics of a true random sample
   B. establish classes that are internally heterogenous in each case
   C. avoid the necessity of subdividing the cases within each stratum
   D. adequately cover important strata that have small numbers of cases

6. One possible response to the "unknown" or "no answer" category in a tabulation of survey information is to "allocate" the unknown responses, i.e., to estimate the missing data on the basis of other known information about the respondents. 6.____

This technique is APPROPRIATE when the unknown category
- A. is very small and is randomly distributed within all subgroups of respondents
- B. is very large and is randomly distributed within all subgroups of respondents
- C. reflects an interviewing failure and a subgroup in the sample ends to produce more unknowns
- D. is a legitimate category and a subgroup in the sample tends to produce more unknowns

7. In presenting cross-tabulated data showing the relationship between two variables, it is MOST meaningful to compute percentages
   - A. in both directions in all instances
   - B. of each cell in relation to the grand total
   - C. in the direction of the smaller number of cells
   - D. in the direction of the causal factor

8. In portraying data based on a sampling operation, it is MOST meaningful and comprehensible to the reader to present
   - A. percentages for the sample and the universe
   - B. percentages by themselves
   - C. percentages and the base figures
   - D. numbers by themselves

9. A new bridge spanning a river is expected to carry 60,000 cars a day on a rainy day and 80,000 cars a day on other kinds of days.
   If there is a $5 toll and one chance in four of a rainy day, the expected value of a day's revenue is
   A. $175,000   B. $375,000   C. $475,000   D. $700,000

10. The analyst who is asked to estimate the probability of a relatively rare event occurring cannot use the classical frequency measures of probability but rather should
    - A. use a random-numbers table to pick a probability
    - B. project historical data into the future
    - C. indicate that no probabilistic judgment is possible
    - D. make the best possible judgment as to the subjective probability

11. A useful source of census data for computing annual indicators is the
    - A. Public Use Sample
    - B. Continuing Population Survey
    - C. Census of Population
    - D. Census of Governments

12. An analyst presented with a set of household records showing age, ethnicity, income, and family status and wishing to study the inter-relationship of all of these variables simultaneously will probably equal
    - A. one four-way cross-tabulation
    - B. four three-way cross-tabulation
    - C. six two-way cross-tabulations
    - D. four single tabulations

13. Downward communication, from high management to lower levels in an organization, will often not be fully accepted at the lowest levels of an organization unless high-level management
    A. communicates through several levels of mid-level management, where the message can be properly modified and interpreted
    B. communicates directly with the level of the organization it wishes to reach, bypassing any intermediate levels
    C. first establishes an atmosphere in which upward communication is encouraged and listened to
    D. establishes penalties for non-compliance with its communications

13.____

14. A top-level manager sometimes has an inaccurate view of the actual lower-level operations of his agency, particularly of those operations which are not running well.
    Of the following, the MOST frequent cause of this is the
    A. general unconcern of top-level management with the way an agency actually operates
    B. tendency of the people at the lowest level in an agency to lie about their actual performance
    C. unwillingness of top-level management to deal with unfavorable information when it is presented
    D. tendency of mid-level management to edit bad news and unpleasant information from reports directed to top management

14.____

15. In the conduct of productivity analyses, work measurement is a USEFUL technique for
    A. substantiating executive decisions
    B. designing a research study
    C. developing performance yardsticks
    D. preparing a manual of procedure

15.____

16. Issue analysis is closely identified with the "fire-fighting" function of management. As such, issue analysis is a(n)
    A. systematic assessment over time of an agency's strategic options
    B. annual review of the issues that have come up during the past year
    C. basis for a set of procedures to be followed in an emergency
    D. analysis of a specific policy question often performed in a crisis environment

16.____

17. The transportation agency in a large city wishes to study the impact of fare increases on ridership in buses. Ridership data for peak hours has been assembled for the same time period for three geographic subareas (A, B, and C) with approximately the same socio-economic characteristics, residential density, and distance from the central business district (CBD). Subarea A had experienced a moderate fare increase on its bus line; Subarea B had had no fare increase; and Subarea C had experienced a major fare increase during the time period

17.____

In the design of this study, the analysis should be framed:
  A. Ridership = f (fare level)
  B. Ridership = f (fare level), distance from CBD)
  C. Fare level = f (ridership)
  D. Ridership = f (fare level, socio-economic characteristics, residential density)

18. What organizational concept is illustrated when a group is organized on an *ad hoc* basis to accomplish a specific goal?
    A. Functional Teamwork   B. Line/staff
    C. Task Force   D. Command

19. The concept of "demand" provides an appropriate theoretical basis for estimating the needs for public services or programs where the service will be on a _____ basis and _____ life-sustaining necessities.
    A. fee; involves   B. free; involves
    C. free; does not involve   D. fee; does not involve

20. Analysts should be wary of relying exclusively on traditional service standards (e.g., one acre of playground per 1,000 population).
    Such standards are often DEFICIENT because they tend to overstate
    A. the consumer view and understate behavior and values of producers
    B. the producer view and understate behavior and values of users or consumers
    C. local conditions and understate national conditions
    D. behavioral factors and understate practical effects

21. The BEST measure of the performance of a manpower program would be
    A. percentage reduction in unemployment by impacted population groups
    B. number of trainees placed in jobs at the beginning of the training program
    C. percentage of students completing a training program
    D. cost per student of the training program and the job placement effort

22. Indices are single figures that measure multi-dimensional concepts.
    The critical judgment in the construction of an index involves
    A. the trade-off between accuracy and simplicity
    B. determination of enough data to do the measurement
    C. avoidance of all possible error
    D. developing a theoretical basis for it

23. Evaluation of public programs is complicated by the reality that programs tend to reflect negotiated compromises among conflicting objectives.
    The absence of clear, unitary objectives PARTICULARLY complicates the
    A. assessment of program input or effort
    B. development of effectiveness criteria
    C. design of new programs to replace the old
    D. diagnosis of a program's processes

24. The BASIC purpose of the "Super-Agencies" is to
    A. reduce the number of departments and agencies in the city government
    B. reduce the number of high-level administrators
    C. coordinate agencies reporting to the mayor and supervise agencies in related fields
    D. supervise departments and agencies in unrelated fields

25. In most municipal budgeting systems involving capital and operating budgets, the leasing or renting of facilities is usually shown in
    A. the operating budget
    B. the capital budget
    C. a separate schedule
    D. either budget

26. New York City's budgeting procedure is unusual in that budget appropriations are considered in two parts, as follows:
    A. Capital budget and income budget
    B. Expense budget and income budget
    C. Revenue budget and expense budget
    D. Expense budget and capital budget

27. The "growth rate" referred to in current political and economic discussion refers to change from year to year in a country's
    A. gross national product
    B. population
    C. available labor force
    D. capital goods investment

Questions 28-29.

DIRECTIONS: Questions 28 and 29 are to be answered on the basis of the following illustration. Assume that the figures in the chart are cubes.

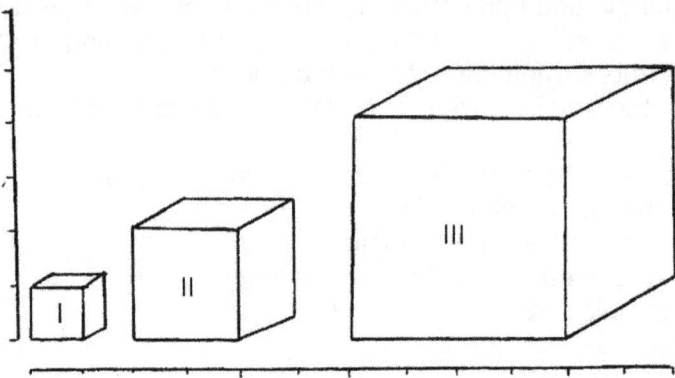

28. In the illustration above, how many times GREATER is the quantity represented by Figure III than the quantity represented by Figure II?
    A. 2   B. 4   C. 8   D. 16

29. The above illustration illustrates a progression in quantity BEST described as
    A. arithmetic   B. geometric   C. discrete   D. linear

Questions 30-35.

DIRECTIONS: Questions 30 through 35 are to be answered on the basis of the following chart.

In a national study of poverty trends, the following data have been assembled by interpretation.

	Persons Below Poverty, By Residence			
	Number (millions)		Percent	
Item	U.S.	Metropolitan Areas	U.S.	Metropolitan Areas
2010				
Total	38.8	17.0	22.0	15.3
Under 25 years	20.0	8.8	25.3	18.1
65 years & over	5.5	2.5	35.2	26.9
Black	9.9	5.0	55.1	42.8
Other	28.3	11.8	18.1	12.0
2020				
Total	24.3	12.3	12.2	9.5
Under 25 years	12.2	6.4	13.2	10.4
65 years & over	4.8	2.3	25.3	20.2
Black	7.2	3.9	32.3	24.4
Other	16.7	8.2	9.5	7.3

30. If no other source of data were available, which of the following groups would you expect to have the HIGHEST rate of poverty?
    A. Others over 65
    B. Others under 65
    C. Blacks over 65
    D. Blacks under 65

31. Between 2010 and 2020, the percentage of poor in the United States who were Black
    A. increased from 25.5% to 29.6%
    B. decreased from 55.1% to 32.3%
    C. decreased from 9.9% to 7.2%
    D. stayed the same

32. The data in the second column of the table indicate that, in the metropolitan areas, the number of poor declined by 4.7 million or 36.2% between 2010 and 2020. Yet, the fourth column shows a corresponding decline from 15.3% to 9.5%, or only 5.8%.
    This apparent discrepancy reflects the fact that
    A. metropolitan areas are growing while the number of poor is contracting
    B. two columns in question are based on different sources of information
    C. difference between two percentages is not the same as the percent change in total numbers
    D. tables have inherent errors and must be carefully checked

33. The percentages in each of the last two columns of the table for 2010 and 2020 don't add up to 100%. This is for the reason that
    A. rounding off each entry to the nearest decimal place caused an error in the total such that the total is not equal to 100%
    B. these columns show the percentage of Blacks, aged, etc. who are poor rather than the percentage of poor who are Black, aged, etc.
    C. there was an error in the construction of the table which was not noticed until the table was already in print
    D. there is double counting in the entries in the table; some people ae counted more than once

34. Data such as that presented in the table on persons below poverty level are shown to a single decimal place because
    A. data in every table should always be shown to a single decimal place
    B. it is the minimal number of decimal places needed to distinguish among table entries
    C. there was no room for more decimal places in the table without crowding
    D. the more accurately a figure is shown the better it is for the user

35. In comparing the poverty of the young (under 25 years) with that of the older population (65 years and over) in 2010 and 2020, one could REASONABLY conclude that
    A. more young people than old people were poor but older people had a higher rate of poverty
    B. more older people than young people were poor but young people had a higher rate of poverty
    C. there is a greater degree of poverty among the younger population than among the older people

Questions 36-37.

DIRECTIONS: Questions 36 and 37 are to be answered ONLY on the basis of the information given in the following passage.

Two approaches are available in developing criteria for the evaluation of plans. One approach, designated Approach A, is a review and analysis of characteristics that differentiate successful plans from unsuccessful plans. These criteria are descriptive in nature and serve as a checklist against which the plan under consideration may be judged. These characteristics have been observed by many different students of planning, and there is considerable agreement concerning the characteristics necessary for a plan to be successful.

A second approach to the development of criteria for judging plans, designated Approach B is the determination of the degree to which the plan under consideration is economic. The word "economic" is used here in its broadest sense, i.e., effective in its utilization of resources. In order to determine the economic worth of a plan, it is necessary to use a technique that permits the description of any plan in economic terms and to utilize this technique to the extent that it becomes a "way of thinking" about plans.

36. According to <u>Approach B</u>, the MOST successful plan is generally one which
    A. costs least to implement
    B. gives most value for resources expended
    C. uses the least expensive resources
    D. utilizes the greatest number of resources

36.____

37. According to <u>Approach A</u>, a successful plan is one which is
    A. descriptive in nature
    B. lowest in cost
    C. similar to other successful plans
    D. agreed upon by many students of planning

37.____

Questions 38-40.

DIRECTIONS: Questions 38 through 40 are to be answered ONLY on the basis of the information provided in the following passage.

The primary purpose of control reports is to supply information intended to serve as the basis for corrective action if needed. At the same time, the significance of control reports must be kept in proper perspective. Control reports are only a part of the planning-management information system. Control information includes non-financial as well as financial data that measure performance and isolate variances from standard. Control information also provides feedback so that planning information may be updated and corrected. Whenever possible, control reports should be designed so that they provide feedback for the planning process as well as provide information of immediate value to the control process.

Since the culmination of the control process is the taking of necessary corrective action to bring performance in line with standards, it follows that control information must be directed to the person who is organizationally responsible for taking the required action. Usually the same information, though in a somewhat abbreviated form, is given to the responsible manager's superior. A district sales manager needs a complete daily record of the performance of each of his salesmen; yet, the report forwarded to the regional sales manager summarizes only the performance of each sales district in his region. In preparing reports for higher echelons of management, summary statements and recommendations for action should appear on the first page; substantiating data, usually the information presented to the person directly responsible for the operation, may be include if needed.

38. A control report serves its primary purpose as part of the process which leads DIRECTLY to
    A. better planning for future action
    B. increasing the performance of district salesmen
    C. the establishment of proper performance standards
    D. taking corrective action when performance is poor

38.____

39. The one of the following which would be the BEST description of a control report is that a control report is a form of
    A. planning   B. communication
    C. direction   D. organization

39.____

40. If control reports are to be effective, the one of the following which is LEAST essential to the effectiveness of control reporting is a system of
    A. communication
    B. standards
    C. authority
    D. work simplification

40.____

KEY (CORRECT ANSWERS)

1. A	11. B	21. A	31. B
2. B	12. A	22. A	32. C
3. A	13. C	23. B	33. B
4. B	14. D	24. C	34. D
5. D	15. C	25. A	35. A
6. C	16. D	26. D	36. B
7. D	17. A	27. A	37. C
8. C	18. C	28. C	38. D
9. B	19. D	29. B	39. B
10. D	20. B	30. C	40. D

EXAMINATION SECTION
TEST 1

DIRECTIONS: Each question or incomplete statement is followed by several suggested answers or completions. Select the one that *BEST* answers the question or completes the statement. *PRINT THE LETTER OF THE CORRECT ANSWER IN THE SPACE AT THE RIGHT.*

1. An analyst is writing a report dealing with the distribution of deaths caused by various types of cardiovascular diseases. He decides to facilitate the reader's grasp of the information presented by including in the report a device that permits comparison of parts to each other, and to the whole at the same time.
   Of the following, the *MOST* appropriate and efficient device he should use for this purpose is the

   A. graph
   B. pie diagram
   C. flow sheet
   D. line chart with one series

2. In carrying out a cost-effectiveness analysis, the analyst should follow certain guidelines. The *MOST* important of these guidelines involves the

   A. utilization of both the fixed utility approach and the fixed budget approach
   B. proper structuring of the problem and design of the analysis
   C. necessity of building a model that is highly formal and mathematical
   D. provision for implicit treatment of uncertainty

3. In a decision which involves fairness -- such as assigning new office equipment to workers when the agency does not receive enough new office equipment for the entire group -- the *PRIMARY* determinant of the decision's effectiveness will be the

   A. systematic or traditional approach which is emphasized in reaching the decision
   B. random nature of the assignment
   C. feedback a decisionmaker receives concerning the decision
   D. acceptance of the decision by the persons who have to execute it

4. In order to give line personnel some insight into staff problems and vice versa it has been suggested that line and staff assignments within a particular city agency be rotated. Which of the following criticisms would be *MOST* valid for opposing such a proposal?

   A. Generally speaking, line and staff personnel have different perspectives on organizational structures which makes rotation in assignments extremely difficult.
   B. Since their educational backgrounds are often quite diverse, staff personnel are often at a disadvantage when serving in line assignments.
   C. Line personnel frequently resent having to perform the more difficult tasks that staff assignments entail.
   D. Serving in a rotating assignment may not necessarily provide the personnel with any significant degree of insight as anticipated.

5. Which one of the following approaches to criticism of a subordinate or associate is *generally* the *MOST* appropriate and effective?
   Criticize

   A. by making a comparison with a more exemplary employee

B. the act, not the person
C. in a humorous vein
D. in general rather than specific terms

6. Assume that two policy units have been formed to study the impact of Federal programs in the city. The two units operate in an essentially similar manner, except for their communications procedures. In unit A any member may communicate and exchange information with any other member of the unit; in unit B a member may only communicate information with the unit supervisor.
In evaluating the effect that these communications procedures have on the level of productivity, it will *generally* be found that

   A. unit A's level of productivity will be greater than unit B's level of productivity for simple problems
   B. unit B's level of productivity will be greater than unit A's level of productivity for simple problems
   C. initial levels of profuctivity are higher in unit A than unit B for complex problems
   D. initial levels of productivity are higher in unit B than in unit A for complex problems

7. In the process of communicating an idea, the following five distinct steps are generally involved:
   I. Selection of a media and transmission of the message
   II. Decoding of a message, i.e., meaning is extracted from the message
   III. Message is received
   IV. Idea is organized into a series of symbols designed to give meaning
   V. Action is taken and/or feedback is given

   In what logical, sequential order should these steps be arranged for effective two-way communications to take place?

   A. V, I, II, III, IV
   B. II, I, III, IV, V
   C. IV, I, III, II, V
   D. I, III, IV, II, V

8. Informal employee groups that share certain norms and strive for member satisfaction through the achievement of group goals are known as work groups.
Which of the following statements can *generally* be considered as being *FALSE* in describing work groups in a moderate size organization?

   A. Formation of work groups is ubiquitous and inevitable.
   B. Work groups strongly influence the overall behavior and performance of their members.
   C. An organization can reap positive and negative consequences as a result of work groups.
   D. Elimination of work groups can be easily achieved by management pressure.

9. Under the management approach known as *management by objectives* which of the following criteria is *generally* used to determine whether the manager has been successful?

   A. Activities performed
   B. Results achieved
   C. Production schedules completed
   D. Financial savings accomplished

10. Of the following, the MOST accurate statement relative to job attitudes is that they

 A. cannot be influenced by only one person
 B. are always the result of work groups
 C. have no relationship to productivity
 D. are strongly influenced by work situation

11. Assume that measures to overcome a budget deficit, including attrition and a hiring freeze, have significantly decreased the work-output of a city agency. The agency administrator desires to develop a plan to restore production to its former level by increasing the work-load and responsibility of the agency's employees.
In order to obtain *maximum* employee cooperation and *minimize* employee resistance, it would be MOST advisable for the

 A. administrator of the agency to personally describe to the employees the new work changes that they are to follow
 B. employees to decide what the optimal changes in the work load should be
 C. management representatives to consult with employee representatives on these matters
 D. immediate supervisor of the employees to decide on the work changes to be implemented

12. Eliciting the support and cooperation of others often requires a great deal of persuasion. Which one of the following persuasive techniques or practices is generally the LEAST desirable for you, an analyst, to use?

 A. Establish your expertness and authority
 B. Present your arguments without emotion
 C. In presenting your arguments, express yourself in the manner to which you are accustomed
 D. Try to find a face-saving way for your opponent to change his/her mind

13. The following illustration depicts the structure of a municipal agency.

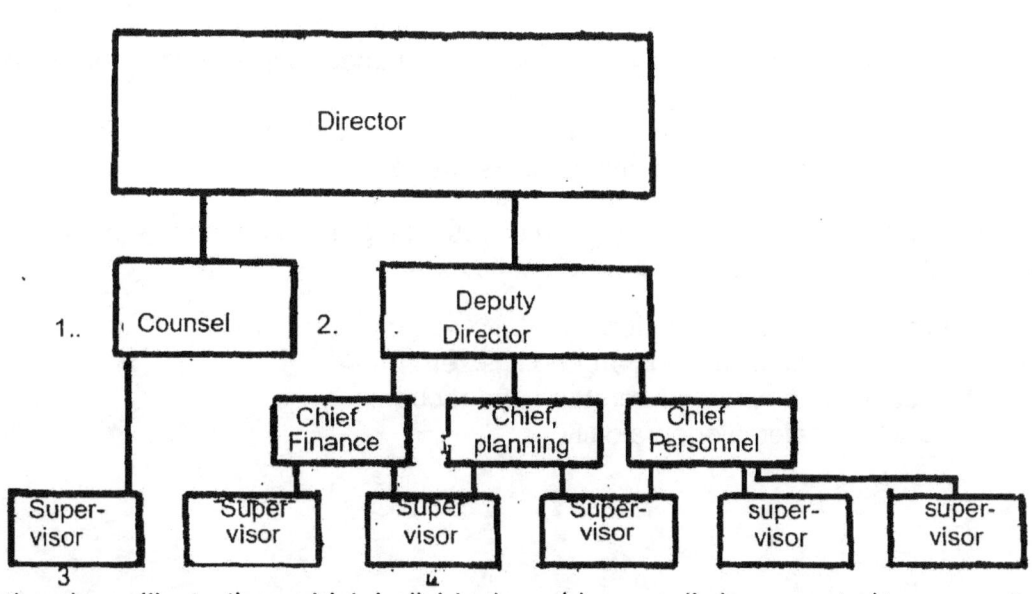

In the above illustration, which individual would generally be expected to encounter the MOST difficulty in carrying out his organizational functions?

 A. 1 B. 2 C. 3 D. 4

14. An agency in which a free flow of communication exists is an agency in which no barriers or structures are erected to control or bar the flow of information and messages between and among management and staff, horizontally or vertically.
Of the following, the GREATEST disadvantage that would be most likely to occur in an agency in which such a free flow of communication exists, is that

    A. it would be difficult to determine which information is important and which is irrelevant
    B. there would be a lesser degree of staff-employee participation and cooperation in communicating
    C. more restrictive controls would be placed on managerial employees
    D. important communications would tend to be eliminated, and and trivial communications over-emphasized

15. Feedback is generally considered an essential factor in oral communication MAINLY because

    A. it enables the speaker to know whether he is understood
    B. the speed of communication is accelerated
    C. it eliminates the necessity of the speaker to use gestures and facial expressions when speaking
    D. the listener is unable to immediately respond to the speaker until the latter is finished

16. Assume that two employees are working on a joint project and they have a difference of opinion on the methodology to be used. Each employee not only listens to the other's opinion on methodology but projects him-self into the other's position.
This type of listening is usually considered

    A. ineffective, mainly because it will be impossible for the employees to reach a satisfactory agreement
    B. effective, mainly because each employee will then be more critical of the other's argument
    C. ineffective, mainly because each worker will unconsciously and unintentionally accept the other's viewpoint
    D. effective, mainly because each speaker can understand the other's viewpoint and can then respond intelligently to his remarks

17. The arithmetic mean is commonly used in describing data. Which one of the following statements is NOT true about the arithmetic mean?

    A. It is a measure of dispersion.
    B. The sum of the deviations around it is zero.
    C. It is easy to compute, understand and recognize.
    D. It may be treated alegebraically.

Questions 18 - 20.

DIRECTIONS: Answer Questions 18 through 20 on the basis of the following data. Assume that you are using these data in assessing the impact of Federal and State income taxes on New York City residents, and comparing it to the effect of Federal and State taxes in other areas.

EFFECT OF DEDUCTIBILITY (i.e., deductibility of taxes levied by other jurisdictions in calculating the net base of the tax in the taxing jurisdiction.)

Net income before personal exemption	Effective rate of tax				
	Federal (assuming no state tax)	State		Combined Federal and State	
		New York*	Minnesota (assuming no federal tax)	New York	Minnesota
	(1)	(2)	(3)	(4)	(5)
$20,000	25.0	4.1	6.9	27.6	27.9
50,000	42.2	5.4	9.1	44.0	43.9
100,000	56.0	5.9	9.8	57.5	57.1
200,000	69.2	6.1	10.1	69.9	69.5
1,500,000	88.0	6.3	10.5	89.3	88.9

*New York has no deductibility; the Federal government has deductibility.

18. In which of the following columns is the tax rate shown to be the LEAST progressive?

    A. 1   B. 2   C. 4   D. 5

19. Which of the following statements is TRUE about the reasons why Columns 1 and 2 do not equal Column 4 for each salary level?

    A. Personal deductions are taken into account in Column 4 but not in Columns 1 and 2.
    B. Federal deducibility of state taxes only is taken into account in Column 4 but not in Columns 1 and 2.
    C. Reciprocal deductibility is taken into account in Column 4 but not in Columns 1 and 2.
    D. State deductibility of federal taxes only is taken into account in Column 4 but not in Columns 1 and 2.

20. The EFFECT of the State's introducing deductibility, given that the Federal government maintains deductibility, is to

    A. increase Federal and State income
    B. decrease Federal and State income
    C. decrease Federal income and increase State income
    D. increase Federal income and decrease State income

21. Assume that you have been made project coordinator for a study concerning the implementation of casino gambling in the city. You have assigned each of the professional staff members simple tasks in specialized areas for the duration of the project. For you to make such job assignments would *generally* be

    A. *desirable;* the performance of simple tasks will motivate individuals to work diligently
    B. *desirable;* specialized tasks induce a sense of accomplishment to individuals
    C. *undesirable;* specialized tasks are more difficult to learn
    D. *undesirable;* specialized tasks may lead to a loss of feeling of accomplishment

22. Assume that you have been asked to submit a proposal for the reorganization of a unit that is charged with performing difficult nonroutine work. Frequently decisions must be made quickly and concurrence obtained from high-level agency heads.
    Given the above conditions, of the following it would be *MOST* logical to structure the organization

    A. on the basis of a relatively wide span of control
    B. on the basis of a relatively narrow span of control
    C. with many organizational levels with a wide span of control
    D. with more emphasis on line than staff units

23. Assume that a study has indicated that a recently created city *superagency* has had formal communication difficulties among various component agencies. It appears that jurisdictional overlapping among those agencies has caused frequent rerouting and unnecessary duplication of communications within the organization. Which one of the following proposals would *MOST* effectively deal with the communications problem encountered by this *superagency?*

    A. Create a central communications office to handle all communications for this *superagency.*
    B. Duplicate and distribute all communications to each component within this *superagency.*
    C. Reduce the overlapping areas of jurisdiction among the component agencies
    D. Decentralize the *superagency* on a *borough* basis to expedite mail delivery

24. The utilization of input-output concepts in connection with the application of the systems concept to government raises the problem of the quantification of objectives and performance (the value of the public benefit). The one of the following which is *MOST* easily *quantifiable* is

    A. education
    B. police service
    C. subway car maintenance
    D. the effectiveness of a welfare administrator

25. When an analyst tries to conceive of a city management problem as a *systems* problem, he is, first of all, confronted with establishing the boundaries of the system. Of the following, the city problem which can *most likely* be conceived of within a system whose boundaries are roughly equivalent to those of the city is

    A. taxation
    B. welfare
    C. fire protection
    D. transportation

25.____

KEY (CORRECT ANSWERS)

1.	B	11.	C
2.	B	12.	B
3.	D	13.	D
4.	D	14.	A
5.	B	15.	A
6.	C	16.	D
7.	C	17.	A
8.	D	18.	B
9.	B	19.	B
10.	D	20.	D

21. D
22. B
23. C
24. C
25. C

TEST 2

DIRECTIONS: Each question or incomplete statement is followed by several suggested answers or completions. Select the one that *BEST* answers the question or completes the statement. *PRINT THE LETTER OF THE CORRECT ANSWER IN THE SPACE AT THE RIGHT.*

1. When installing a new *system,* an analyst may choose among several types of installation plans - the *all-at-once type,* the *piecemeal type,* or the *parallel type* each suited to a particular problem or degree of complexity in the system.
   The one of the following situations in which the *parallel type* would be *MOST* appropriate is a situation

   A. in which a minimum installation cost is required
   B. involving a small volume of transactions
   C. in which the change is not radical or does not involve new machines
   D. involving large installation projects and intricate processing

2. Many decision situations involve a great deal of uncertainty about the future, which is difficult to take into account in the analysis of alternatives. One technique developed for treating such uncertainty is designed to measure the possible effects on alternatives under analysis resulting from variations in uncertain elements. The analyst uses several *expected values* for uncertain parameters in an attempt to ascertain how the results vary (i.e., the relative ranking of the alternatives under consideration) in light of variations in the uncertain parameters. The analyst attempts to determine the alternative (or feasible combination of alternatives) likely to achieve a specified objective, gain or utility at the lowest cost. The one of the following which *BEST* describes the above technique is:

   A. Contingency analysis employing the fixed-budget approach
   B. Contingency analysis employing the fixed-benefits approach
   C. Sensitivity analysis employing the fixed-budget approach
   D. Sensitivity analysis employing the fixed-benefits approach

3. In general, the analytical techniques of management science are of the *LEAST* value when

   A. the effects of a small number of controlled variables must be considered
   B. the number of relevant uncontrolled variables is small
   C. relevant causes and effects are factual in nature and can be stated and measured numerically or symbolically
   D. There are reasons to believe that past relationships will continue to hold in the future

4. During the installation period of a new system, tight controls must be maintained over every phase of the operation. To do this, an analyst may set up a *warning system* within the system which forecasts potential bottle-necks and affords sufficient clues for correcting any problems, errors or fall-downs.
   The one of the following control devices or techniques which would be *most likely* to involve extra effort during the installation, and slow down the processing time is

A. paper flow controls - log sheets, numerical controls, etc. (a system of logging input and output)
B. timing controls - to inform the analyst about the proper time interval between certain activities with-in the systems
C. program check points - a periodic review of processing to date at each check point
D. accounting control totals, to accumulate invoice numbers as the first and last steps in the system and compare the totals

5. Which of the following types of work measurement techniques would be MOST appropriate for obtaining details of a particular job for cost analysis purposes, such as the operating costs of various types of duplicating machines?

   A. Work sampling
   B. Predetermined time standards
   C. The time study (stop-watch timing)
   D. Historical

6. It is anticipated that a certain cancer detection program will be capable of detecting many cases at an early stage and that society will be thus enabled to cure twice as many cases as it cures currently. The benefits to society include the reduction in cost of hospitalization, etc., that would have been incurred otherwise.
   Benefits such as a reduction in the cost of hospitalization are *most usually* called

   A. direct benefits
   B. secondary benefits
   C. intergenerational benefits
   D. external benefits

7. The results of departmental and agency programs can be measured in terms of EFFECTIVENESS or BENEFITS. Thus, careful budget preparation will permit the calculation of costs which can then be compared, or equated, to these results. Which one of the following statements pertaining to cost-effectiveness measurements is MOST valid?

   A. In cost-effectiveness measurements, a dollar value is assigned to the output.
   B. The measurement is expressed in terms of quality of output for a given cost.
   C. Cost effectiveness ratios express the relationship between the costs of programs
   D. A cost-effectiveness measurement will show the number of outputs which can be achieved for the expenditure of a given amount of money.

8. Assume that you have been asked to evaluate personnel programs in four city agencies The statistical test that would be MOST appropriate for testing the significance of the differences in the mean number of days absent (normality may be assumed) during the year 2004 in four different agencies is the

   A. one-way analysis of variance
   B. standard deviation
   C. regression analysis
   D. Chi-square test (x^2-test)

9. Assume that you have been asked to evaluate differences in the children just enrolled in two youth programs. In reviewing the relevant published material you find that in one particular study involving two groups, N = 9 and N = 13, there is a significant difference in the mean scores of the two groups on a characteristic which you believe to be normally distributed.
The statistical test *most likely* used in this study to determine the significance of the difference in the means of the two groups on this characteristic is the

   A. Chi-square test (x2-test)
   B. Pearson Product-Moment correlation (r)
   C. t-test
   D. two-way analysis of variance

10. In statistics, three common measures of central tendency are the mean, median and mode.
For which of the following conditions would the median generally be the BEST choice to use? When the

   A. distribution of scores is skewed
   B. scores are distributed symmetrically around a central point
   C. standard deviation must also be calculated
   D. most frequently occurring value is required

11. Nonparametric statistical tests are *usually* employed when

   A. large samples are used
   B. a very powerful or exact test is needed
   C. data cannot be expressed in ranks
   D. a normally distributed population cannot be assumed

12. Assume that in a report presented to you by an employee under your supervision, a coefficient of correlation of +1.73 is reported between the age at which one first smokes cigarettes and the age at which one first smokes marijuana.
You should *most reasonably* interpret this figure to mean there is a

   A. strong positive correlation
   B. weak positive correlation
   C. weak negative correlation
   D. typographical error

13. One of the major research techniques most often used in studies of organizational behavior problems is the survey. An analyst who utilizes the survey technique should be aware that its *MAJOR* drawback is

   A. the lack of depth obtained from the two major data-collection tolls used in surveys: the mailed question-naire and the personal interview
   B. its impracticality in assessing or estimating the present state of affairs with regard to a variable that changes over time for a large group of subjects
   C. the restriction of this technique to a single, or very few, units of analysis
   D. its absence of dependence upon the collection of empirical data

14. In order for an analyst to understand and interpret statistical data he/she must understand which types of data tend to approximate the normal probability curve, i.e., are normally distributed.
Which of the following types of data falls into this category?
Frequency of

   A. educational test scores for students of a given age, plotted against test score
   B. filing of income tax returns for citizens of a given age, plotted against date of filing
   C. deaths due to childhood disease plotted against age
   D. deaths due to degenerative diseases, plotted against age

14.____

15. Which of the following terms describes a line or curve formed by plotting employees salaries that increase yearly by a fixed percentage over the previous year? (In answering the question, assume that time is on the horizontal axis (abscissa) and salary is on the vertical axis (ordinate) - both axes are marked linearly.)

   A. Linear (increasing at a constant rate)
   B. Positively accelerating (increasing at an increasing rate)
   C. Negatively accelerating (increasing at a decreasing rate)
   D. Negatively decelerating (decreasing at a decreasing rate)

15.____

Questions 16 - 17

DIRECTIONS: Answer Questions 16 and 17 on the basis of the following groups, both of which depict the same information in different ways.

The x and y axes in graphs A and B are not necessarily drawn in the same scale. The points along the curves on both graphs represent corresponding points, and are the upper limits of class intervals.

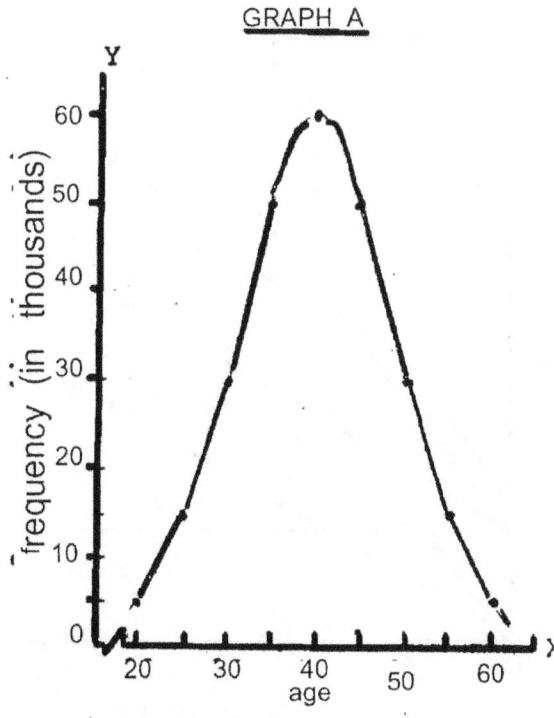
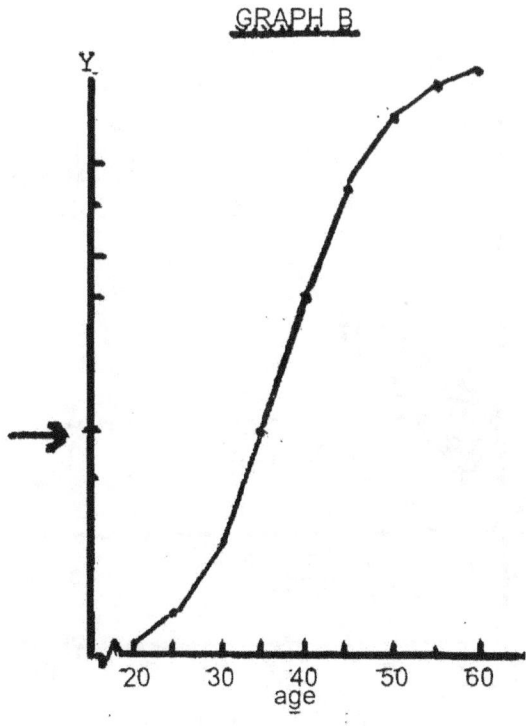

16. The ordinate (y-axis) in graph B is

    A. frequency
    B. cumulative frequency
    C. average frequency
    D. log frequency

17. The arrow on the y-axis in graph B indicates a particular number. That number is, *most nearly*

    A. 100   B. 50,000   C. 100,000   D. 150,000

Questions 18 - 19

DIRECTIONS: Answer Questions 18 and 19 on the basis of the graphs that appear on the following page.

18. In Graph I, the vertical distance between lines E and T within the crosshatched area represents the

    A. savings to the city if work of less than 50 miles is performed by the city
    B. loss to the city if work of less than 50 miles is performed by the city
    C. savings to the city if work of more than 50 miles is performed by the city
    D. loss to the city if work of more than 50 miles is performed by the city

19. Graph II is identical to Graph I except that contractor costs have been eliminated. Total costs (line E) are the sum of fixed costs (line F) and variable costs. Variable costs are represented by line

    A. A   B. B   C. C   D. D

ROAD REPAIR COSTS IF PERFORMED BY CITY STAFF OR AN OUTSIDE CONTRACTOR

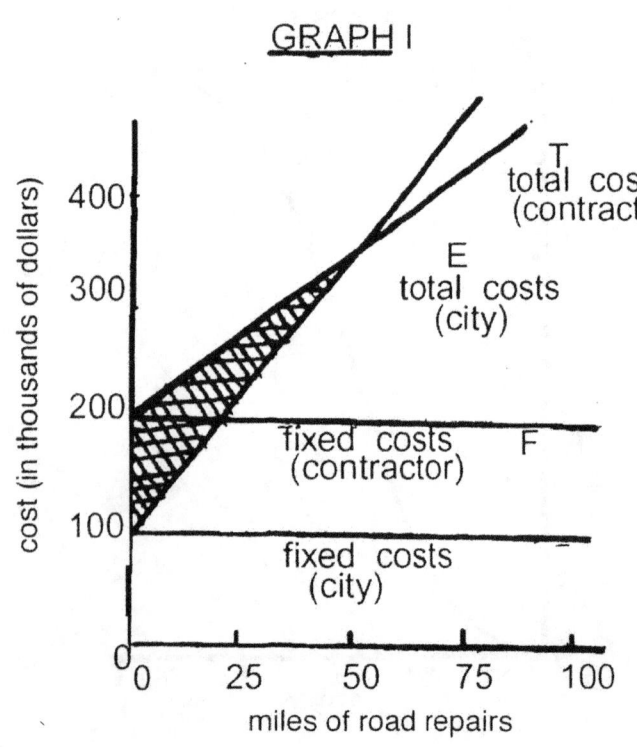
GRAPH I

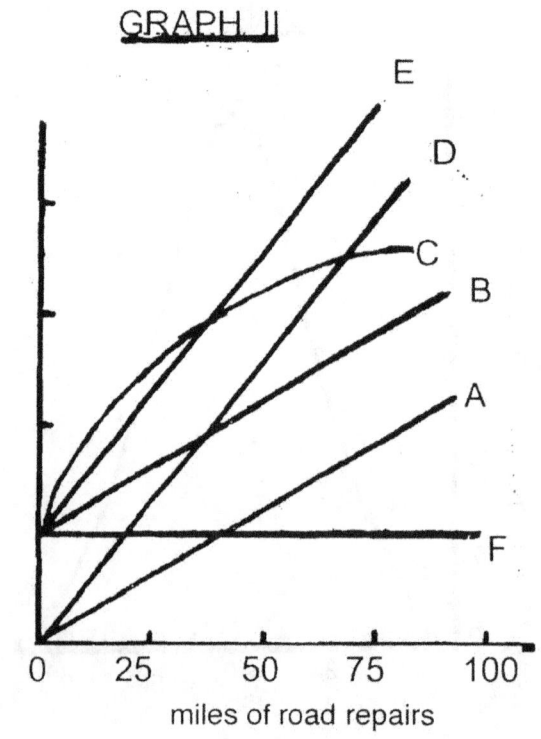
GRAPH II

20. Fiscal experts in municipal affairs have contended that the most acute problem facing the city today seems to be the growth of the city's short-term debt.
    Of the following, the LEAST likely reason for the city to engage in short-term borrowing is that the city

    A. expects money from long-term borrowing that it plans to undertake
    B. needs to be tided over until funds due from the Federal or State government arrive
    C. needs money to finance big construction outlays
    D. anticipates money from future tax collections

21. A MAJOR criticism of the *superagency* has been the

    A. additional layers of control and additional lines of command
    B. merger of departmental functions
    C. political manipulation
    D. professional incompetence in administration

22. The management of a large urban city is different in many ways from the management of other systems, particularly large business organizations.
    The one of the following which does NOT exemplify these differences is:

    A. A mayor, in contrast to a manager of a large business, is often held responsible for services, etc., over which he has little authority.
    B. Top management of a large urban city must deal with a greater number of different pressures from diverse interest groups.
    C. The city government, in contrast to a large business organization, often lacks adequate management controls, and goals are often ill-defined.
    D. The multiplicity of alternatives available to city government as opposed to large businesses, are substantially greater, making decision-making haphazard.

23. The function called internal control applies to those measures taken by a government agency to protect its assets. Internal control has a role to play as an enforcer of administrative edicts as well as for purposes of asset protection.
    Of the following statements relating to internal control, as described above, select the *one* usually considered to be LEAST valid.

    A. Internal control makes auditing by an external agency more difficult.
    B. The function of internal control often involves the auditing process.
    C. That people cannot be trusted to act wisely and honestly seems to be implicit in all the principles of internal control.
    D. Internal control is simply a form of self-audit by the agency itself.

24. In addition to the new effect on workers who are unskilled and undereducated, the severe effect of the high unemployment rate in the city has recently become MOST apparent among

    A. skilled craftsmen in the building trades
    B. clerical employees
    C. middle management personnel
    D. architects and engineers

25. The fact that the city has the second highest jobless rate of any major U.S. city except Detroit is considered particularly significant because, compared to Detroit, unemployment in the city

   A. is caused by city government fiscal measures rather than private business conditions
   B. exists in more than one industry
   C. results in an increase in welfare expenditures to a greater extent
   D. more seriously affects the world-wide economy

25. ___

KEY (CORRECT ANSWERS)

1. D	11. D
2. D	12. D
3. A	13. A
4. A	14. A
5. C	15. B
6. A	16. B
7. D	17. C
8. A	18. A
9. C	19. D
10. A	20. C

21. A
22. D
23. A
24. A
25. B

SUPERVISION, ADMINISTRATION, MANAGEMENT AND ORGANIZATION

EXAMINATION SECTION
TEST 1

DIRECTIONS: Each question or incomplete statement is followed by several suggested answers or completions. Select the one that BEST answers the question or completes the statement. *PRINT THE LETTER OF THE CORRECT ANSWER IN THE SPACE AT THE RIGHT.*

1. One of the responsibilities of the supervisor is to provide top administration with information about clients and their problems that will help in the evaluation of existing policies and indicate the need for modifications.
   In order to fulfill this responsibility, it would be MOST essential for the supervisor to

   A. routinely forward all regularly prepared and recurrent reports from his subordinates to his immediate superior
   B. regularly review agency rules, regulations and policies to make sure that he has sufficient knowledge to make appropriate analyses
   C. note repeated instances of failure of staff to correctly administer a policy and schedule staff conferences for corrective training
   D. analyze reports on cases submitted by subordinates, in order to select relevant trend material to be forwarded to his superiors

2. You find that your division has a serious problem because of unusually long delays in filing reports and overdue approvals to private agencies under contract for services.
   The MOST appropriate step to take FIRST in this situation would be to

   A. request additional staff to work on reports and approvals
   B. order staff to work overtime until the backlog is eliminated
   C. impress staff with the importance of expeditious handling of reports and approvals
   D. analyze present procedures for handling reports and approvals

3. When a supervisor finds that he must communicate orally information that is significant enough to affect the entire staff, it would be MOST important to

   A. distribute a written summary of the information to his staff before discussing it orally
   B. tell his subordinate supervisors to discuss this information at individual conferences with their subordinates
   C. call a follow-up meeting of absentees as soon as they return
   D. restate and summarize the information in order to make sure that everyone understands its meaning and implications

4. Of the following, the BEST way for a supervisor to assist a subordinate who has unusually heavy work pressures is to

   A. point out that such pressures go with the job and must be tolerated
   B. suggest to him that the pressures probably result from poor handling of his workload
   C. help him to be selective in deciding on priorities during the period of pressure
   D. ask him to work overtime until the period of pressure is over

5. Leadership is a basic responsibility of the supervisor. The one of the following which would be the LEAST appropriate way to fulfill this role is for the supervisor to

   A. help staff to work up to their capacities in every possible way
   B. encourage independent judgment and actions by staff members
   C. allow staff to participate in decisions within policy limits
   D. take over certain tasks in which he is more competent than his subordinates

6. Assume that you have assigned a very difficult administrative task to one of your best subordinate supervisors, but he is reluctant to take it on because he fears that he will fail in it. It is your judgment, however, that he is quite capable of performing this task.
   The one of the following which is the MOST desirable way for you to handle this situation is to

   A. reassure him that he has enough skill to perform the task and that he will not be penalized if he fails
   B. reassign the task to another supervisor who is more achievement-oriented and more confident of his skills
   C. minimize the importance of the task so that he will feel it is safe for him to attempt it
   D. stress the importance of the task and the dependence of the other staff members on his succeeding in it

7. Assume that a member of your professional staff deliberately misinterprets a new state directive because he fears that its enforcement will have an adverse effect on clients. Although you consider him to be a good supervisor and basically agree with him, you should direct him to comply.
   Of the following, the MOST desirable way for you to handle this situation would be to

   A. avoid a confrontation with him by transferring responsibility for carrying out the directive to another member of your staff
   B. explain to him that you are in a better position than he to assess the implications of the new directive
   C. discuss with him the basic reasons for his misinterpretation and explain why he must comply with the directive
   D. allow him to interpret the directive in his own way as long as he assumes full responsibility for his actions

8. Of the following, the MAIN reason it is important for an administrator in a large organization to properly coordinate the work delegated to subordinates is that such coordination

   A. makes it unnecessary to hold frequent staff meetings and conferences with key staff members
   B. reduces the necessity for regular evaluation of procedures and programs, production and performance of personnel
   C. results in greater economy and stricter accountability for the organization's resources
   D. facilitates integration of the contributions of the numerous staff members who are responsible for specific parts of the total workload

9. The one of the following which would NOT be an appropriate reason for the formulation of an entirely NEW policy is that it would

   A. serve as a positive affirmation of the agency's function and how it is to be carried out
   B. give focus and direction to the work of the staff, particularly in decision-making
   C. inform the public of the precise conditions under which services will be rendered
   D. provide procedures which constitute uniform methods of carrying out operations

10. Of the following, it is MOST difficult to formulate policy in an organization where

    A. work assignments are narrowly specialized by units
    B. staff members have varied backgrounds and a wide range of competency
    C. units implementing the same policy are in the same geographic location
    D. staff is experienced and fully trained

11. For a supervisor to feel that he is responsible for influencing the attitudes of his staff members is GENERALLY considered

    A. *undesirable;* attitudes of adults are emotional factors which usually cannot be changed
    B. *desirable;* certain attitudes can be obstructive and should be modified in order to provide effective service to clients
    C. *undesirable;* the supervisor should be nonjudgmental and accepting of widely different attitudes and social patterns of staff members
    D. *desirable;* influencing attitudes is a teaching responsibility which the supervisor shares with the training specialist

12. The one of the following which is NOT generally a function of the higher-level supervisor is

    A. projecting the budget and obtaining financial resources
    B. providing conditions conducive to optimum employee production
    C. maintaining records and reports as a basis for accountability and evaluation
    D. evaluating program achievements and personnel effectiveness in accordance with goals and standards

13. As a supervisor in a recently decentralized services center offering multiple services, you are given responsibility for an orientation program for professional staff on the recent reorganization of the Department.
    Of the following, the MOST appropriate step to take FIRST would be to

    A. organize a series of workshops for subordinate supervisors
    B. arrange a tour of the new geographic area of service
    C. review supervisors' reports, statistical data and other relevant material
    D. develop a resource manual for staff on the reorganized center

14. Experts generally agree that the content of training sessions should be closely related to workers' practice.
    Of the following, the BEST method of achieving this aim is for the training conference leader to

    A. encourage group discussion of problems that concern staff in their practice
    B. develop closer working relationships with top administration

C. coordinate with central office to obtain feedback on problems that concern staff
D. observe workers in order to develop a pattern of problems for class discussion

15. The one of the following which is generally the MOST useful teaching tool for professional staff development is

    A. visual aids and tape recordings
    B. professional literature
    C. agency case material
    D. lectures by experts

16. The one of the following which is NOT a good reason for using group conferences as a method of supervision is to

    A. give workers a feeling of mutual support through sharing common problems
    B. save time by eliminating the need for individual conferences
    C. encourage discussion of certain problems that are not as likely to come up in individual conferences
    D. provide an opportunity for developing positive identification with the department and its programs

17. The supervisor, in his role as teacher, applies his teaching in line with his understanding of people and realizes that teaching is a highly individualized process, based on understanding of the worker as a person and as a learner. This statement implies, MOST NEARLY, that the supervisor must help the worker to

    A. overcome his biases
    B. develop his own ways of working
    C. gain confidence in his ability
    D. develop the will to work

18. Of the following, the circumstance under which it would be MOST appropriate to divide a training conference for professional staff into small workshops is when

    A. some of the trainees are not aware of the effect of their attitudes and behavior on others
    B. the trainees need to look at human relations problems from different perspectives
    C. the trainees are faced with several substantially different types of problems in their job assignments
    D. the trainees need to know how to function in many different capacities

19. Of the following, the MAIN reason why it is important to systemically evaluate a specific training program while it is in progress is to

    A. collect data that will serve as a valid basis for improving the agency's overall training program and maintaining control over its components
    B. insure that instruction by training specialists is conducted in a manner consistent with the planned design of the training program
    C. identify areas in which additional or remedial training for the training specialists can be planned and implemented
    D. provide data which are usable in effecting revisions of specific components of the training program

5 (#1)

20. Staff development has been defined as an educational process which seeks to provide agency staff with knowledge about specific job responsibilities and to effect changes in staff attitudes and behavior patterns. Assume that you are assigned to define the educational objectives of a specific training program.
In accordance with the above concept, the MOST helpful formulation would be a statement of the

   A. purpose and goals of each training session
   B. generalized patterns of behavior to be developed in the trainees
   C. content material to be presented in the training sessions
   D. kind of behavior to be developed in the trainees and the situations in which this behavior will be applied

20._____

21. In teaching personnel under your supervision how to gather and analyze facts before attempting to solve a problem, the one of the following training methods which would be MOST effective is

   A. case study
   B. role playing
   C. programmed learning
   D. planned experience'

21._____

22. The importance of analyzing functions traditionally included in the position of caseworker, with a view toward identifying and separating those activities to be performed by the most highly skilled personnel, has been widely discussed.
Of the following, an IMPORTANT *secondary* gain which can result from such differential use of staff is that

   A. supporting job assignments can be given to persons unable to meet the demands of casework, to the satisfaction of all concerned
   B. documentation will be provided on workers who are not suited for all the duties now part of the caseworker's job
   C. caseworkers with a high level of competence in working with people can be rewarded through promotion or merit increases
   D. incompetent workers can be identified and categorized, as a basis for transfer or separation from the service

22._____

23. Of the following, a serious DISADVANTAGE of a performance evaluation system based on standardized evaluation factors is that such a system tends to

   A. exacerbate the anxieties of those supervisors who are apprehensive about determining what happens to another person
   B. subject the supervisor to psychological stress by emphasizing the incompatibility of his dual role as both judge and counselor
   C. create organizational conflict by encouraging personnel who wish to enhance their standing to become too aggressive in the performance of their duties
   D. lead many staff members to concentrate on measuring up in terms of the evaluation factors and to disregard other aspects of their work

23._____

24. Which of the following would contribute MOST to the achievement of conformity of staff activities and goals to the intent of agency policies and procedures?

   A. Effective communications and organizational discipline
   B. Changing nature of the underlying principles and desired purpose of the policies and procedures

24._____

C. Formulation of specific criteria for implementing the policies and procedures
D. Continuous monitoring of the essential effectiveness of agency operations

25. Job enlargement, a management device used by large organizations to counteract the adverse effects of specialization on employee performance, is LEAST likely to improve employee motivation if it is accomplished by

A. lengthening the job cycle and adding a large number of similar tasks
B. allowing the employee to use a greater variety of skills
C. increasing the scope and complexity of the employee's job
D. giving the employee more opportunities to make decisions

KEY (CORRECT ANSWERS)

1. D	11. B
2. D	12. A
3. D	13. A
4. C	14. A
5. D	15. C
6. A	16. B
7. C	17. B
8. D	18. C
9. D	19. A
10. B	20. D

21. A
22. A
23. D
24. A
25. A

TEST 2

DIRECTIONS: Each question or incomplete statement is followed by several suggested answers or completions. Select the one that BEST answers the question or completes the statement. *PRINT THE LETTER OF THE CORRECT ANSWER IN THE SPACE AT THE RIGHT.*

1. When a supervisor requires approval for case action on a higher level, the process used is known as

    A. administrative clearance
    B. going outside channels
    C. administrative consultation
    D. delegation of authority

2. In delegating authority to his subordinates, the one of the following to which a GOOD supervisor should give PRIMARY consideration is the

    A. results expected of them
    B. amount of power to be delegated
    C. amount of responsibility to be delegated
    D. their skill in the performance of present tasks

3. Of the following, the type of decision which could be SAFELY delegated to LOWER-LEVEL staff without undermining basic supervisory responsibility is one which

    A. involves a commitment that can be fulfilled only over a long period of time
    B. has fairly uncertain goals and premises
    C. has the possibility of modification built into it
    D. may generate considerable resistance from those affected by it

4. Of the following, the MOST valuable contribution made by the informal organization in a large public service agency is that such an organization

    A. has goals and values which are usually consistent with and reinforce those of the formal organization
    B. is more flexible than the formal organization and more adaptable to changing conditions
    C. has a communications system which often contributes to the efficiency of the formal organization
    D. represents a sound basis on which to build the formal organizational structure

5. Of the following, the condition under which it would be MOST useful for an agency to develop detailed procedures is when

    A. subordinate supervisory personnel need a structure to help them develop greater independence
    B. employees have little experience or knowledge of how to perform certain assigned tasks
    C. coordination of agency activities is largely dependent upon personal contact
    D. agency activities must continually adjust to changes in local circumstances

6. Assume that a certain administrator has the management philosophy that his agency's responsibility is to routinize existing operations, meet each day's problems as they arise, and resolve problems with a minimum of residual effect upon himself or his agency. The possibility that this official would be able to administer his agency without running into serious difficulties would be MORE likely during a period of

    A. economic change
    B. social change
    C. economic crisis
    D. social and economic stability

7. Some large organizations have adopted the practice of allowing each employee to establish his own performance goals, and then later evaluate himself in an individual conference with his immediate supervisor.
Of the following, a DRAWBACK of this approach is that the employee

   A. may set his goals too low and rate himself too highly
   B. cannot control those variables which may improve his performance
   C. has no guidelines for improving his performance
   D. usually finds it more difficult to criticize himself than to accept criticism from others

8. Decentralization of services cannot completely eliminate the requirement of central office approval for certain case actions. The MOST valid reason for complaint about this requirement is that

   A. unavoidable delay created by referral to central office may cause serious problems for the client
   B. it may lower morale of supervisors who are not given the authority to take final action on urgent cases
   C. the concept of role responsibility is minimized
   D. the objective of delegated responsibility tends to be negated

9. Which of the following would be the MOST useful administrative tool for the purpose of showing the sequence of operations and staff involved? A(n)

   A. organization chart
   B. flow chart
   C. manual of operating procedures
   D. statistical review

10. The prevailing pattern of organization in large public agencies consists of a limited span of control and organization by function or, at lower levels, process.
Of the following, the PRINCIPAL effect which this pattern of organization has on the management of work is that it

    A. reduces the management burden in significant ways
    B. creates a time lag between the perception of a problem and action on it
    C. makes it difficult to direct and observe employee performance
    D. facilitates the development of employees with managerial ability

11. The one of the following which would be the MOST appropriate way to reduce tensions between line and staff personnel in public service agencies is to

    A. provide in-service training that will increase the sensitivity of line and staff personnel to their respective roles
    B. assign to staff personnel the role of providing assistance only when requested by line personnel
    C. separate staff from line personnel and provide staff with its own independent reward structure
    D. give line and staff personnel equal status in making decisions

12. In determining the appropriate span of control for subordinate supervisors, which of the following principles should be followed? The more

    A. complex the work, the broader the effective span of control
    B. similar the jobs being supervised, the more narrow the effective span of control

C. interdependent the jobs being supervised, the more narrow the effective span of control
D. unpredictable the work, the broader the effective span of control

13. A method sometimes used in public service agencies to improve upward communication is to require subordinate supervisory staff to submit to top management monthly narrative reports of any problems which they deem important for consideration.
Of the following, a major DISADVANTAGE of this method is that it may

   A. enable subordinate supervisors to avoid thinking about their problems by simply referring such matters to their superiors
   B. obscure important issues so that they are not given appropriate attention
   C. create a need for numerous staff conferences in order to handle all of the reported problems
   D. encourage some subordinate supervisors to focus on irrelevant matters and compete with each other in the length and content of their reports

13._____

14. The use of a committee as an approach to the problem of coordinating interdepartmental activities can present difficulties if the committee functions PRIMARILY as a(n)

   A. means of achieving personal objectives and goals
   B. instrument for coordinating activities that flow across departmental lines
   C. device for involving subordinate personnel in the decision-making process
   D. means of giving representation to competing interest groups

14._____

15. A study was recently made of the attitudes and perceptions of a sample of workers who had experienced a major organizational change and redefinition of their jobs as a result of separation of certain functions.
Questionnaires administered to these workers indicated that a disproportionate number of workers in the larger agencies were dissatisfied with the reorganization and their new assignments.
Of the following, the MOST plausible reason for this dissatisfaction is that workers in larger agencies are

   A. less likely to be known to management and to be personally disciplined if they expressed dissatisfaction with their new roles
   B. less likely to have the opportunity to participate in planning a reorganization and to be given consideration for the assignments they preferred
   C. given a shorter lead period to implement the changes and therefore had insufficient time to plan the reorganization and carry it out efficiently
   D. usually made up of more older members who have had routinized their work according to habit and find it more difficult to adjust to change

15._____

16. An article which recently appeared in a professional journal presents a proposal for participatory leadership, in which the goal of supervision would be development of subordinates' self-reliance, with the premise that each staff member is held accountable for his own performance.
The one of the following which would NOT be a desirable outcome of this type of supervision is the

   A. necessity for subordinates to critically examine their performance
   B. development by some subordinates of skills not possessed by the supervisor

16._____

C. establishment of a quality control unit for sample checking and identification of errors
D. relaxation of demands made on the supervisor

17. The "management by objectives" concept is a major development in the administration of services organizations. The purpose of this approach is to establish a system for

    A. reduction of waiting time
    B. planning and controlling work output
    C. consolidation of organizational units
    D. work measurement

18. Assume that you encounter a serious administrative problem in implementing a new program. After consulting with the members of your staff individually, you come up with several alternate solutions.
Of the following, the procedure which would be MOST appropriate for evaluating the relative merits of each solution would be to

    A. try all of them on a limited experimental basis
    B. break the problem down into its component parts and analyze the effect of each solution on each component in terms of costs and benefits
    C. break the problem down into its component parts, eliminate all intangibles, and measure the effect of the tangible aspects of each solution on each component in terms of costs and benefits
    D. bring the matter before your weekly staff conference, discuss the relative merits of each alternate solution, and then choose the one favored by the majority of the conference

19. When establishing planning objectives for a service program under your supervision, the one of the following principles which should be followed is that objectives

    A. are rarely verifiable if they are qualitative
    B. should be few in number and of equal importance
    C. should cover as many of the activities of the program as possible
    D. should be set in the light of assumptions about future funding

20. Assume that you have been assigned responsibility for coordinating various aspects of a program in a community services center. Which of the following administrative concepts would NOT be applicable to this assignment?

    A. Functional job analysis   B. Peer group supervision
    C. Differential use of staff   D. Systems design

21. Good administrative practice includes the use of outside consultants as an effective technique in achieving agency objectives. However, the one of the following which would NOT be an appropriate role for the consultant is

    A. provision of technical or professional expertise not otherwise available in the agency
    B. administrative direction of a new program activity
    C. facilitating coordination and communication among agency staff
    D. objective measurement of the effectiveness of agency services

22. Of the following, the MOST common fault of research projects attempting to measure the effectiveness of social programs has been their

    A. questionable methodology
    B. inaccurate findings
    C. unrealistic expectations
    D. lack of objectivity

23. One of the most difficult tasks of supervision in a modern public agency is teaching workers to cope with the hostile reactions of clients. In order to help the disconcerted worker analyze and understand a client's hostile behavior, the supervisor should FIRST

    A. encourage the worker to identify with the client's frustrations and deprivations
    B. give the worker a chance to express and accept his feelings about the client
    C. ask the worker to review his knowledge of the client and his circumstances
    D. explain to the worker that the client's anger is not directed at the worker personally

24. Determination of the level of participation, or how much of the public should participate in a given project, is a vital step in community organization.
    In order to make this determination, the FIRST action that should be taken is to

    A. develop the participants
    B. fix the goals of the project
    C. evaluate community interest in the project
    D. enlist the cooperation of community leaders

25. The one of the following which would be the MOST critical factor for SUCCESSFUL operation of a decentralized system of programs and services is

    A. periodic review and evaluation of services delivered at the community level
    B. transfer of decision-making authority to the community level wherever feasible
    C. participation of indigenous non-professionals in service delivery
    D. formulation of quantitative plans for dealing with community problems wherever feasible

KEY (CORRECT ANSWERS)

1.	A	11.	A
2.	A	12.	C
3.	C	13.	D
4.	C	14.	A
5.	B	15.	B
6.	D	16.	D
7.	A	17.	B
8.	A	18.	C
9.	B	19.	D
10.	B	20.	B

21. B
22. C
23. B
24. B
25. B

TEST 3

DIRECTIONS: Each question or incomplete statement is followed by several suggested answers or completions. Select the one that BEST answers the question or completes the statement. *PRINT THE LETTER OF THE CORRECT ANSWER IN THE SPACE AT THE RIGHT.*

1. Douglas McGregor's theory of human motivation classifies worker behavior into two distinct categories: Theory X and Theory Y. Theory X, the traditional view, states that the average man dislikes to work and will avoid work if he can, unless coerced. Theory Y holds essentially the opposite view. The executive can apply both of these theories to worker behavior BEST if he

    A. follows an "open-door" policy only with respect to his immediate subordinates
    B. recognizes his subordinates' mental and social needs as well as agency needs
    C. recognizes that executive responsibility is primarily limited to fulfillment of agency productivity goals
    D. directs his subordinate managers to follow a policy of close supervision

2. In interpersonal communications it is of paramount importance to determine whether or not what has been said has been understood by others. One of the MOST important sources of such information is known as

    A. the halo effect   B. evaluation
    C. feedback   D. quantitative analysis

3. The grapevine most often provides a USEFUL service by

    A. correcting some of the deficiencies of the formal communication system
    B. rapidly conveying a true picture of events
    C. involving staff in current organizational changes
    D. interfering with the operation of the formal communication system

4. People who are in favor of a leadership style in which the subordinates help make decisions, contend that it produces favorable effects in a work unit. According to these people, which of the following is NOT likely to be an effect of such "participative management"?

    A. Reduced turnover
    B. Accelerated learning of duties
    C. Greater acceptance of change
    D. Reduced acceptance of the work unit's goals

5. Employees of a public service agency will be MOST likely to develop meaningful goals for both the agency and the employee and become committed to attaining them if supervisors

    A. allow them unilaterally to set their own goals
    B. provide them with a clear understanding of the premises underlying the agency's goals
    C. encourage them to concentrate on setting only short-range goals for themselves
    D. periodically review the agency's goals in order to suggest changes in accordance with current conditions

6. The insights of Chester Barnard have influenced the development of management thought in significant ways. He is MOST closely identified with a position that has become known as the

   A. acceptance theory of authority
   B. principle of the manager's or executive's span of control
   C. "Theory X" and "Theory Y" dichotomy
   D. unity of command principle

7. If a manager believes that man is primarily motivated by economic incentives and, above all, seeks security, he MOST usually should operate on the assumption that his subordinates

   A. need to be closely directed and have relatively little ambition
   B. are more responsive to the social forces of their peer group than to the incentives of management
   C. are capable of learning not only to accept but to seek responsibility
   D. are capable of responding favorably to many different kinds of managerial strategies

8. Of the following, the MOST important reason why it is in the interest of public service agencies to involve subordinate personnel in setting goals is that the more committed employees are to the goals of their agency the

   A. *more* likely they are to develop a desire for the agency's achievement of success
   B. *more* likely they are to prefer difficult rather than easy tasks
   C. *more* likely they are to perceive their individual performance as a reliable indicator of the agency's performance
   D. *less* likely they are to choose unreasonably difficult goals

9. As a result of gaining more recent knowledge about motivation, modern executives have had to rethink their notions about what motivates their subordinate managers. Which of the following factors is GENERALLY considered MOST important in modern motivation theory?

   A. Fringe benefits
   B. Working conditions
   C. Recognition of good work performance
   D. Education and experience required for the job

10. Of the following, the MAIN reason why cooperative interrelationships among personnel are more likely than competitive interrelationships to promote efficiency in the operation of a public service agency is that cooperation

    A. allows for a greater degree of specialization by function
    B. increases the opportunities for employees to check on each others' work
    C. provides a feeling of identification with the organization and enhances the desire for accomplishment
    D. improves the capacity of employees to acquire knowledge and learn new skills

11. Four statements are given below. Three of them describe approaches which are desirable in developing a program of employee motivation. The one which does NOT describe such an approach is:

    A. "Establish attainable goals to give employees a sense of achievement."
    B. "Largely discount the self-interest motive because it is impractical to consider it."
    C. "Allow for the participation of persons included in the plans."
    D. "Base plans on group considerations as well as individual considerations."

12. It is GENERALLY acknowledged that certain conditions should exist to insure that a subordinate will decide to accept a communication as being authoritative. Which of the following is LEAST valid as a condition which should exist?

    A. The subordinate understands the communication
    B. At the time of the subordinate's decision, he views the communication as consistent with the organization's purpose and his personal interest
    C. At the time of the subordinate's decision, he views the communication as more consistent with his personal purpose than with the organization's interests
    D. The subordinate is mentally and physically able to comply with the communication

13. In exploring the effects that employee participation has on putting changes in work methods into effect, certain relationships have been established between participation and productivity. It has MOST generally been found that HIGHEST productivity occurs in groups that are given

    A. participation in the process of change only through representatives of their group
    B. no participation in the change process
    C. full participation in the change process
    D. intermittent participation in the process of change

14. Of the following statements, the one which represents a trend LEAST likely to occur in the area of employee-management relations is that:

    A. Employees will exert more influence on decisions affecting their interests.
    B. Technological change will have a stronger impact on organizations' human resources.
    C. Labor will judge management according to company profits.
    D. Government will play a larger role in balancing the interests of the parties in labor-management affairs.

15. Members of an organization must satisfy several fundamental psychological needs in order to be happy and productive. The broadest and MOST basic needs are

    A. achievement, recognition and acceptance
    B. competition, recognition and accomplishment
    C. salary increments and recognition
    D. acceptance of competition and economic reward

16. Morale has been defined as the capacity of a group of people to pull together steadily for a common purpose. Morale thus defined is MOST generally dependent on which one of the following conditions?

    A. Job security
    B. Group and individual self-confidence
    C. Organizational efficiency
    D. Physical health of the individuals

17. Assume that consideration is being given to forming a committee for the purpose of getting a new program under way which requires the coordination of several organizational units. Which one of the following would be a MAJOR weakness of using the "committee" approach in this situation?

    A. Its inappropriateness for decision-making
    B. The necessity to include line and staff employees
    C. The difficulty of achieving proper representation
    D. Its independence from the formal organization

18. Which of the following techniques is NOT used as an approach to encourage communication between individuals at the same level?

    A. The informal organization
    B. The chain of command
    C. Committee meetings
    D. Distribution of written reports

19. In everyday actual operations, downward communications MOST often concern

    A. specific directives about job performance
    B. information about worker performance
    C. information about the rationale of the job
    D. information to indoctrinate the organization's staff on goals to be achieved

20. Communication has been thought of for a long time as a vital process in a formal organization system. Of the following, the MOST accurate statement that can be made concerning this process is that

    A. decision-making depends on communication and organizational structure
    B. communication does not interact but is interdependent with organizational structure and decision-making
    C. effective decision-making is dependent on organizational structure but not on communication
    D. communication is dependent on the decision-making process but not on organizational structure

21. In coaching a subordinate manager in the use of the type of management in which subordinate employees participate, an executive would be MOST accurate in emphasizing that participative management

    A. uses consultative as opposed to democratic techniques
    B. uses democratic as opposed to consultative techniques
    C. requires the involvement of subordinates while reserving for the superior the right to make decisions
    D. requires involving subordinates and giving them the right to make most decisions

22. In most work situations, employees tend to form informal groups and relationships. The BEST way for a supervisor interested in high productivity to deal with such groups and relationships is to

    A. take them into account as much as possible when making work assignments and schedules
    B. ignore them, since such relationships and groups usually have no effect on work productivity

C. attempt to destroy such groups and relationships since they are usually counter-productive
D. ignore them, even though they are usually counterproductive, since nothing can be done about them

23. Assume that in an office an entirely new method has been introduced in the handling of applications for service and related information. Employees USUALLY approach such a sudden change in their work routine with an attitude of

A. *apprehension,* chiefly because such a change makes them uncertain of their position
B. *indifference,* chiefly because most people don't care what they are doing, as long as they are paid
C. *approval,* chiefly because such a change provides a welcome change of pace in their work
D. *acceptance,* mainly because most people prefer changes to the same routines

24. In what order should the following steps be taken when revising office procedure?
   I. To develop the improved method as determined by time and motion studies and effective workplace layout
   II. To find out how the task is now performed
   III. To apply the new method
   IV. To analyze the current method

The CORRECT order is:

A. IV, II, I, III
B. II, I, III, IV
C. I, II, IV, III
D. II, IV, I, III

25. In contrast to broad spans of control, narrow spans of control are MOST likely to

A. provide opportunity for more personal contact between superior and subordinate
B. encourage decentralization
C. stress individual initiative
D. foster group or team effort

KEY (CORRECT ANSWERS)

1.	B	11.	B
2.	C	12.	C
3.	A	13.	C
4.	D	14.	C
5.	B	15.	A
6.	A	16.	B
7.	A	17.	A
8.	A	18.	B
9.	C	19.	A
10.	C	20.	A

21. C
22. A
23. A
24. D
25. A

REPORT WRITING
EXAMINATION SECTION
TEST 1

DIRECTIONS: Each question or incomplete statement is followed by several suggested answers or completions. Select the one that BEST answers the question or completes the statement. *PRINT THE LETTER OF THE CORRECT ANSWER IN THE SPACE AT THE RIGHT.*

Questions 1-4.

DIRECTIONS: Answer Questions 1 through 4 on the basis of the following report which was prepared by a supervisor for inclusion in his agency's annual report.

Line #
1 On Oct. 13, I was assigned to study the salaries paid.
2 to clerical employees in various titles by the city and by
3 private industry in the area.
4 In order to get the data I needed, I called Mr. Johnson at
5 the Bureau of the Budget and the payroll officers at X Corp.—
6 a brokerage house, Y Co. —an insurance company, and Z Inc. —
7 a publishing firm. None of them was available and I had to call
8 all of them again the next day.
9 When I finally got the information I needed, I drew up a
10 chart, which is attached. Note that not all of the companies I
11 contacted employed people at all the different levels used in the
12 city service.
13 The conclusions I draw from analyzing this information is
14 as follows: The city's entry-level salary is about average for
15 the region; middle-level salaries are generally higher in the
16 city government plan than in private industry; but salaries at the
17 highest levels in private industry are better than city em-
18 ployees' pay.

1. Which of the following criticisms about the style in which this report is written is MOST valid?
   A. It is too informal.
   B. It is too concise.
   C. It is too choppy.
   D. The syntax is too complex.

1.____

2. Judging from the statements made in the report, the method followed by this employee in performing his research was
   A. *good*; he contacted a representative sample of businesses in the area
   B. *poor*; he should have drawn more definite conclusions
   C. *good*; he was persistent in collecting information
   D. *poor*; he did not make a thorough study

2.____

151

3. One sentence in this report contains a grammatical error. This sentence begins on line number
   A. 4   B. 7   C. 10   D. 14

4. The type of information given in this report which should be presented in footnotes or in an appendix is the
   A. purpose of the study
   B. specifics about the businesses contacted
   C. reference to the chart
   D. conclusions drawn by the author

5. The use of a graph to show statistical data in a report is SUPERIOR to a table because it
   A. features approximations
   B. emphasizes facts and relationships more dramatically
   C. presents data more accurately
   D. is easily understood by the average reader

6. Of the following, the degree of formality required of a written report in tone is MOST likely to depend on the
   A. subject matter of the report
   B. frequency of its occurrence
   C. amount of time available for its preparation
   D. audience for whom the report is intended

7. Of the following, a distinguishing characteristic of a written report intended for the head of your agency as compared to a report prepared for a lower-echelon staff member is that the report for the agency head should USUALLY include
   A. considerably more detail, especially statistical data
   B. the essential details in an abbreviated form
   C. all available source material
   D. an annotated bibliography

8. Assume that you are asked to write a lengthy report for use by the administrator of your agency, the subject of which is "The Impact of Proposed New Data Processing Operation on Line Personnel" in your agency. You decide that the *most* appropriate type of report for you to prepare is an analytical report, including recommendations.
   The MAIN reason for your decision is that
   A. the subject of the report is extremely complex
   B. large sums of money are involved
   C. the report is being prepared for the administrator
   D. you intend to include charts and graphs

9. Assume that you are preparing a report based on a survey dealing with the attitudes of employees in Division X regarding proposed new changes in compensating employees for working overtime. Three percent of the respondents to the survey voluntarily offer an unfavorable opinion on the method of assigning overtime work, a question not specifically asked of the employees.
On the basis of this information, the MOST appropriate and significant of the following comments for you to make in the report with regard to employees' attitudes on assigning overtime work is that
   A. an insignificant percentage of employees dislike the method of assigning overtime work
   B. three percent of the employees in Division X dislike the method of assigning overtime work
   C. three percent of the sample selected for the survey voiced an unfavorable opinion on the method of assigning overtime work
   D. some employees voluntarily voiced negative feelings about the method of assigning overtime work, making it impossible to determine the extent of this attitude

10. A supervisor should be able to prepare a report that is well-written and unambiguous.
Of the following sentences that might appear in a report, select the one which communicates MOST clearly the intent of its author.
   A. When your subordinates speak to a group of people, they should be well-informed.
   B. When he asked him to leave, SanMan King told him that he would refuse the request.
   C. Because he is a good worker, Foreman Jefferson assigned Assistant Foreman D'Agostino to replace him.
   D. Each of us is responsible for the actions of our subordinates.

11. In some reports, especially longer ones, a list of the resources (books, papers, magazines, etc.) used to prepare it is included. This list is called the
   A. accreditation   B. bibliography
   C. summary   D. glossary

12. Reports are usually divided into several sections, some of which are more necessary than others.
Of the following, the section which is ABSOLUTELY necessary to include in a report is
   A. a table of contents   B. the body
   C. an index   D. a bibliography

13. Suppose you are writing a report on an interview you have just completed with a particularly hostile applicant.
Which of the following BEST describes what you should include in this report?
   A. What you think caused the applicant's hostile attitude during the interview
   B. Specific examples of the applicant's hostile remarks and behavior
   C. The relevant information uncovered during the interview
   D. A recommendation that the applicant's request be denied because of his hostility

14. When including recommendations in a report to your supervisor, which of the following is MOST important for you to do?
   A. Provide several alternative courses of action for each recommendation
   B. First present the supporting evidence, then the recommendations
   C. First present the recommendations, then the supporting evidence
   D. Make sure the recommendations arise logically out of the information in the report

15. It is often necessary that the writer of a report present facts and sufficient arguments to gain acceptance of the points, conclusions, or recommendations set forth in the report.
Of the following, the LEAST advisable step to take in organizing a report, when such argumentation is the important factor, is a(n)
   A. elaborate expression of personal belief
   B. businesslike discussion of the problem as a whole
   C. orderly arrangement of convincing data
   D. reasonable explanation of the primary issues

16. In some types of reports, visual aids add interest, meaning, and support. They also provide an essential means of effectively communicating the message of the report.
Of the following, the selection of the suitable visual aids to use with a report is LEAST dependent on the
   A. nature and scope of the report
   B. way in which the aid is to be used
   C. aid used in other reports
   D. prospective readers of the report

17. Visual aids used in a report may be placed either in the text material or in the appendix.
Deciding where to put a chart, table, or any such aid should depend on the
   A. title of the report   B. purpose of the visual aid
   C. title of the visual aid   D. length of the report

18. A report is often revised several times before final preparation and distribution in an effort to make certain the report meets the needs of the situation for which it is designed.
Which of the following is the BEST way for the author to be sure that a report covers the areas he intended?

A. Obtain a coworker's opinion
B. Compare it with a content checklist
C. Test it on a subordinate
D. Check his bibliography

19. In which of the following situations is an oral report preferable to a written report? When a(n)
    A. recommendation is being made for a future plan of action
    B. department head requests immediate information
    C. long-standing policy change is made
    D. analysis of complicated statistical data is involved

19.____

20. When an applicant is approved, the supervisor must fill in standard forms with certain information.
    The GREATEST advantage of using standard forms in this situation rather than having the supervisor write the report as he sees fit is that
    A. the report can be acted on quickly
    B. the report can be written without directions from a supervisor
    C. needed information is less likely to be left out of the report
    D. information that is written up this way is more likely to be verified

20.____

21. Assume that it is part of your job to prepare a monthly report for your unit head that eventually goes to the director. The report contains information on the number of applicants you have interviewed that have been approved and the number of applicants you have interviewed that have been turned down.
    Errors on such reports are serious because
    A. you are expected to be able to prove how many applicants you have interviewed each month
    B. accurate statistics are needed for effective management of the department
    C. they may not be discovered before the report is transmitted to the director
    D. they may result in loss to the applicants left out of the report

21.____

22. The frequency with which job reports are submitted should depend MAINLY on
    A. how comprehensive the report has to be
    B. the amount of information in the report
    C. the availability of an experienced man to write the report
    D. the importance of changes in the information included in the report

22.____

23. The CHIEF purpose in preparing an outline for a report is usually to insure that
    A. the report will be grammatically correct
    B. every point will be given equal emphasis
    C. principal and secondary points will be properly integrated
    D. the language of the report will be of the same level and include the same technical terms

23.____

24. The MAIN reason for requiring written job reports is to 24.____
    A. avoid the necessity of oral orders
    B. develop better methods of doing the work
    C. provide a permanent record of what was done
    D. increase the amount of work that can be done

25. Assume you are recommending in a report to your supervisor that a radical 25.____
    change in a standard maintenance procedure should be adopted.
    Of the following, the MOST important information to be included in this report is
    A. a list of the reasons for making this change
    B. the names of others who favor the change
    C. a complete description of the present procedure
    D. amount of training time needed for the new procedure

KEY (CORRECT ANSWERS)

1.	A	11.	B
2.	D	12.	B
3.	D	13.	C
4.	B	14.	D
5.	B	15.	A
6.	D	16.	C
7.	B	17.	B
8.	A	18.	B
9.	D	19.	B
10.	D	20.	C

21.	B
22.	D
23.	C
24.	C
25.	A

TEST 2

DIRECTIONS: Each question or incomplete statement is followed by several suggested answers or completions. Select the one that BEST answers the question or completes the statement. *PRINT THE LETTER OF THE CORRECT ANSWER IN THE SPACE AT THE RIGHT.*

1. It is often necessary that the writer of a report present facts and sufficient arguments to gain acceptance of the points, conclusions, or recommendations set forth in the report.
   Of the following, the LEAST advisable step to take in organizing a report, when such argumentation is the important factor, is a(n)
   A. elaborate expression of personal belief
   B. businesslike discussion of the problem as a whole
   C. orderly arrangement of convincing data
   D. reasonable explanation of the primary issues

   1._____

2. Of the following, the factor which is generally considered to be LEAST characteristic of a good control report is that it
   A. stresses performance that adheres to standard rather than emphasizing the exception
   B. supplies information intended to serve as the basis for corrective action
   C. provides feedback for the planning process
   D. includes data that reflect trends as well as current status

   2._____

3. An administrative assistant has been asked by his superior to write a concise, factual report with objective conclusions and recommendations based on facts assembled by other researchers.
   Of the following factors, the administrative assistant should give LEAST consideration to
   A. the educational level of the person or persons for whom the report is being prepared
   B. the use to be made of the report
   C. the complexity of the problem
   D. his own feelings about the importance of the problem

   3._____

4. When making a written report, it is often recommended that the findings or conclusions be presented near the beginning of the report.
   Of the following, the MOST important reason for doing this is that it
   A. facilitates organizing the material clearly
   B. assures that all the topics will be covered
   C. avoids unnecessary repetition of ideas
   D. prepares the reader for the facts that will follow

   4._____

5. You have been asked to write a report on methods of hiring and training new employees. Your report is going to be about ten pages long.
   For the convenience of your readers, a brief summary of your findings should
   A. appear at the beginning of your report
   B. be appended to the report as a postscript
   C. be circulated in a separate memo
   D. be inserted in tabular form in the middle of your report

6. In preparing a report, the MAIN reason for writing an outline is usually to
   A. help organize thoughts in a logical sequence
   B. provide a guide for the typing of the report
   C. allow the ultimate user to review the report in advance
   D. ensure that the report is being prepared on schedule

7. The one of the following which is MOST appropriate as a reason for including footnotes in a report is to
   A. correct capitalization
   B. delete passages
   C. improve punctuation
   D. cite references

8. A completed formal report may contain all of the following EXCEPT
   A. a synopsis
   B. a preface
   C. marginal notes
   D. bibliographical references

9. Of the following, the MAIN use of proofreaders' marks is to
   A. explain corrections to be made
   B. indicate that a manuscript has been read and approved
   C. let the reader know who proofread the report
   D. indicate the format of the report

10. Informative, readable, and concise reports have been found to observe the following rules:
    Rule I.   Keep the report short and easy to understand
    Rule II. Vary the length of sentences.
    Rule III. Vary the style of sentences so that, for example, they are not all just subject-verb, subject-verb.
    Consider this hospital laboratory report: The experiment was started in January. The apparatus was put together in six weeks. At that time, the synthesizing process was begun. The synthetic chemicals were separated. Then they were used in tests on patients.
    Which one of the following choices MOST accurately classifies the above rules into those which are violated by this report ad those which are not?
    A. II is violated, but I and III are not.
    B. III is violated, but I and II are not.
    C. II and III are violated, but I is not.
    D. I, II, and III are violated,

Questions 11-13.

DIRECTIONS: Questions 11 through 13 are based on the following example of a report. The report consists of eight numbered sentences, some of which are not consistent with the principles of good report writing.

(1) I interviewed Mrs. Loretta Crawford in Room 424 of County Hospital. (2) She had collapsed on the street and been brought into emergency. (3) She is an attractive woman with many friends judging by the cards she had received. (4) She did not know what her husband's last job had been, or what their present income was. (5) The first thing that Mrs. Crawford said was that she had never worked and that her husband was presently unemployed. (6) She did not know if they had any medical coverage or if they could pay the bill. (7) She said that her husband could not be reached by telephone but that he would be in to see her that afternoon. (8) I left word at the nursing station to be called when he arrived.

11. A good report should be arranged in logical order.
    Which of the following sentences from the report does NOT appear in its proper sequence in the report?
    A. 1   B. 4   C. 7   D. 8

12. Only material that is relevant to the main thought of a report should be included. Which of the following sentences from the report contains material which is LEAST relevant to this report? Sentence
    A. 3   B. 4   C. 6   D. 8

13. Reports should include all essential information.
    Of the following, the MOST important fact that is missing from this report is:
    A. Who was involved in the interview
    B. What was discovered at the interview
    C. When the interview took place
    D. Where the interview took place

Questions 14-15.

DIRECTIONS: Each of Questions 14 and 15 consists of four numbered sentences which constitute a paragraph in a report. They are not in the right order. Choose the numbered arrangement appearing after letter A, B, C, or D which is MOST logical and which BEST expresses the thought of the paragraph.

14. I. Congress made the commitment explicit in the Housing Act of 1949, establishing as a national goal the realization of a decent home and suitable environment for every American family.
    II. The result has been that the goal of decent home and suitable environment is still as far distant as ever for the disadvantaged urban family
    III. In spite of this action by Congress, federal housing programs have continued to be fragmented and grossly under-funded.
    IV. The passage of the National Housing Act signaled a new federal commitment to provide housing for the nation's citizens.

The CORRECT answer is:
A. I, IV, III, II   B. IV, I, III, II   C. IV, I, III, II   D. II, IV, I, III

15.
   I. The greater expense does not necessarily involve "exploitation," but it is often perceived as exploitative and unfair by those who are aware of the price differences involved, but unaware of operating costs.
   II. Ghetto residents believe they are "exploited" by local merchants, and evidence substantiates some of these beliefs.
   III. However, stores in low-income areas were more likely to be small independents, which could not achieve the economies available to supermarket chains and were, therefore, more likely to charge higher prices, and the customers were more likely to buy smaller-sized packages which are more expensive per unit of measure.
   IV. A study conducted in one city showed that distinctly higher prices were charged for goods sold in ghetto stores than in other areas.

   The CORRECT answer is:
   A. IV, II, I, III   B. IV, I, III, II   C. II, IV, III, I   D. II, III, IV, I

16. In organizing data to be presented in a formal report, the FIRST of the following steps should be
    A. determining the conclusions to be drawn
    B. establishing the time sequence of the data
    C. sorting and arranging like data into groups
    D. evaluating how consistently the data support the recommendations

17. All reports should be prepared with at least one copy so that
    A. there is one copy for your file
    B. there is a copy for your supervisor
    C. the report can be sent to more than one person
    D. the person getting the report can forward a copy to someone else

18. Before turning in a report of an investigation he has made, a supervisor discovers some additional information he did not include in this report. Whether he rewrites this report to include this additional information should PRIMARILY depend on the
    A. importance of the report itself
    B. number of people who will eventually review this report
    C. established policy covering the subject matter of the report
    D. bearing this new information has on the conclusions of the report

KEY (CORRECT ANSWERS)

1.	A	11.	B
2.	A	12.	A
3.	D	13.	C
4.	D	14.	B
5.	A	15.	C
6.	A	16.	C
7.	D	17.	A
8.	C	18.	D
9.	A		
10.	C		

DOCUMENTS AND FORMS
PREPARING WRITTEN MATERIALS
EXAMINATION SECTION
TEST 1

DIRECTIONS: Each question or incomplete statement is followed by several suggested answers or completions. Select the one that BEST answers the question or completes the statement. *PRINT THE LETTER OF THE CORRECT ANSWER IN THE SPACE AT THE RIGHT.*

1. Of the following types of documents, it is MOST important to retain and file
   A. working drafts of reports that have been submitted in final form
   B. copies of letters of good will which conveyed a message that could not be handled by phone
   C. interoffice orders for materials which have been received and verified
   D. interoffice memoranda regarding the routine of standard forms

   1.____

2. The MAXIMUM number of 2¾" x 4¼" size forms which may be obtained from one ream of 17" x 22" paper is
   A. 4,000   B. 8,000   C. 12,000   D. 16,000

   2.____

3. On a general organization chart, staff positions NORMALLY should be pictured
   A. directly above the line positions to which they report
   B. to the sides of the main flow lines
   C. within the box of the highest level subordinate positions pictured
   D. directly below the line positions which report to them

   3.____

4. When an administrator is diagramming an office layout, of the following, his PRIMARY job generally should be to indicate the
   A. lighting intensities that will be required by each operator
   B. noise level that will be produced by the various equipment employed in the office
   C. direction of the work flow and the distance involved in each transfer
   D. durability of major pieces of office equipment currently in use or to be utilized

   4.____

5. One common guideline or rule-of-thumb ratio for evaluating the efficiency of files is the number of records requested divided by the number of records filed. Generally, if this ratio is very low, it would point MOST directly to the need for
   A. improving the indexing and coding systems
   B. improving the charge-out procedures
   C. exploring the need for transferring records from active storage to the archives
   D. exploring the need to encourage employees to keep more records in their private files

   5.____

6. The GREATEST percentage of money spent on preparing and keeping the usual records in an office generally is expended for which one of the following?
   A. Renting space in which to place the record-keeping equipment
   B. Paying salaries of record-preparing and record-keeping personnel
   C. Depreciation of purchased record-preparation and record-keeping machines
   D. Paper and forms upon which to place the records

7. In a certain office, file folders are constantly being removed from the files for use by administrators. At the same time, new material is coming in to be filed in some of these folders.
   Of the following, the BEST way to avoid delays in filing of the new material and to keep track of the removed folders is to
   A. keep a sheet listing all folders removed from the file, who has them, and a follow-update to check on their return; attach to this list new material received for filing
   B. put an "out" slip in the place of any file folder removed, telling what folder is missing, date removed, and who has it; file new material received at front of files
   C. put a temporary "out" folder in place of the one removed, giving title or subject, date removed, and who has it; put into this temporary folder any new material received
   D. keep a list of all folders removed and who has them; forward any new material received for filing while a folder is out to the person who has it

8. Folders labeled "Miscellaneous" should be used in an alphabetic filing system MAINLY to
   A. provide quick access to recent material
   B. avoid setting up individual folders for infrequent correspondence
   C. provide temporary storage for less important documents
   D. temporarily hold papers which will not fit into already crowded individual folders

9. Out-of-date and seldom-used records should be removed periodically from the files because
   A. overall responsibility for records will be transferred to the person in charge of the central storage files
   B. duplicate copies of every record are not needed
   C. valuable filing space will be regained and the time needed to find a current record will be cut down
   D. worthwhile suggestions on improving the filing system will result whenever this is done

10. Of the following, the BEST reason for discarding certain material from office files would be that the
    A. files are crowded
    B. material in the files is old
    C. material duplicates information obtainable from other sources in the files
    D. material is referred to most often by employees in an adjoining office

11. Of the following, the MAIN factor contributing to the expense of maintaining an office procedure manual would be the
    A. infrequent use of the manual
    B. need to revise it regularly
    C. cost of loose-leaf binders
    D. high cost of printing

11._____

12. The suggestion that memos or directives which circulate among subordinates be initialed by each employee is a
    A. *poor* one, because, with modern copying machines, it would be possible to supply every subordinate with a copy of each message for his personal use
    B. *good* one, because it relieves the supervisor of blame for the action of subordinates who have read and initialed the messages
    C. *poor* one, because initialing the memo or directive is no guarantee that the subordinate has read the material
    D. *good* one, because it can be used as a record by the supervisor to show that his subordinates have received the message and were responsible for reading it

12._____

13. Of the following, the MOST important reason for microfilming office records is to
    A. save storage space needed to keep records
    B. make it easier to get records when needed
    C. speed up the classification of information
    D. shorten the time which records must be kept

13._____

14. Your office filing cabinets have become so overcrowded that it is difficult to use the files.
    Of the following, the MOST desirable step for you to take FIRST to relieve this situation would be to
    A. assign your assistant to spend some time each day reviewing the material in the files and to give you his recommendations as to what material may be discarded
    B. discard all material which has been in the files more than a given number of years
    C. submit a request for additional filing cabinets in your next budget request
    D. transfer enough material to the central storage room of your agency to give you the amount of additional filing space needed

14._____

15. In indexing names of business firms and other organizations, one of the rules to be followed is:
    A. The word "and" is considered an indexing unit
    B. When a firm name includes the full name of a person who is not well known, the person's first name is considered as the first indexing unit
    C. Usually, the units in a firm name are indexed in the order in which they are written
    D. When a firm's name is made up of single letters (such as ABC Corp.), the letters taken together are considered as more than one indexing unit

15._____

16. Assume that your unit processes confidential forms which are submitted by persons seeking financial assistance. An individual comes to your office, gives you his name, and states that he would like to look over a form which he sent in about a week ago because he believes he omitted some important information.
Of the following, the BEST thing for you to do FIRST is to
    A. locate the proper form
    B. call the individual's home telephone number to verify his identity
    C. ask the individual if he has proof of his identity
    D. call the security office

17. An employee has been assigned to open her division head's mail and place it on his desk. One day, the employee opens a letter which she then notices is marked "Personal."
Of the following, the BEST action for her to take is to
    A. write "Personal" on the letter and staple the envelope to the back of the letter
    B. ignore the matter and treat the letter the same way as the others
    C. give it to another division head to hold until her own division head comes into the office
    D. leave the letter in the envelope and write "Sorry-opened by mistake" on the envelope, and initial it

18. The MOST important reason for having a filing system is to
    A. get papers out of the way
    B. have a record of everything that has happened
    C. retain information to justify your actions
    D. enable rapid retrieval of information

19. The system of filing which is used MOST frequently is called _____ filing.
    A. alphabetic
    B. alphanumeric
    C. geographic
    D. numeric

20. In judging the adequacy of a standard office form, which of the following is LEAST important?
    A. Date of the form
    B. Legibility of the form
    C. Size of the form
    D. Design of the form

21. Assume that the letters and reports which are dictated to you fall into a few distinct subject-matter areas.
The practice of trying to familiarize yourself with the terminology in these areas is
    A. *good*, because you will have a basis for commenting on the dictated material
    B. *good*, because it will be easier to take the dictation at the rate at which it is given
    C. *poor*, because the functions and policies of an office are not of your concern
    D. *poor*, because it will take too much time away from your assigned work

22. A letter was dictated on June 9 and was ready to be typed on June 12. The letter was typed on June 13, signed on June 14, and mailed on June 14. The date that, ORDINARILY, should have appeared on the letter is June
    A. 9 B. 12 C. 13 D. 14

23. Of the following, the BEST reason for putting the "key point" at the beginning of a letter is that it
    A. may save time for the reader
    B. is standard practice in writing letters
    C. will more likely to be typed correctly
    D. cannot logically be placed elsewhere

24. As a supervisor, you have been asked to attend committee meetings and take the minutes.
    The body of such minutes GENERALLY consists of
    A. the date and place of the meeting and the list of persons present
    B. an exact verbatim report of everything that was said by each person who spoke
    C. a clear description of each matter discussed and the action decided on
    D. the agenda of the meeting

25. When typing a rough draft from a recorded transcription, a stenographer under your supervision reaches a spot on the recording that is virtually inaudible.
    Of the following, the MOST advisable action that you should recommend to her is to
    A. guess what the dictator intended to say based on what he said in the parts that are clear
    B. ask the dictator to listen to his unsatisfactory recording
    C. leave an appropriate amount of space for that portion that is inaudible
    D. stop typing the draft and send a note to the dictator identifying the item that could not be completed

KEY (CORRECT ANSWERS)

1.	D	11.	B
2.	D	12.	D
3.	B	13.	A
4.	C	14.	A
5.	C	15.	C
6.	B	16.	C
7.	C	17.	D
8.	B	18.	D
9.	C	19.	A
10.	C	20.	A

21.	B
22.	D
23.	A
24.	C
25.	C

TEST 2

DIRECTIONS: Each question or incomplete statement is followed by several suggested answers or completions. Select the one that BEST answers the question or completes the statement. *PRINT THE LETTER OF THE CORRECT ANSWER IN THE SPACE AT THE RIGHT.*

1. To tell a newly employed clerk to fill a top drawer of a four-drawer cabinet with heavy binders which will be often used and to keep lower drawers only partly filled is
   A. *good*, because a tall person would have to bend unnecessarily if he had to use a lower drawer
   B. *bad*, because the file cabinet may tip over when the top drawer is opened
   C. *good*, because it is the most easily reachable drawer for the average person
   D. *bad*, because a person bending down at another drawer may accidentally bang his head on the bottom of the drawer when he straightens up

1.____

2. If you have requisitioned a "ream" of paper in order to duplicate a single page office announcement, how many announcements can be printed from the one package of paper?
   A. 200   B. 500   C. 700   D. 1,000

2.____

3. In the operations of a government agency, a voucher is ORDINARILY used to
   A. refer someone to the agency for a position or assignment
   B. certify that an agency's records of financial transactions are accurate
   C. order payment from agency funds of a stated amount to an individual
   D. enter a statement of official opinion in the records of the agency

3.____

4. Of the following types of cards used in filing systems, the one which is generally MOST helpful in locating records which might be filed under more than one subject is the _____ card.
   A. out   B. tickler
   C. cross-reference   D. visible index

4.____

5. The type of filing system in which one does NOT need to refer to a card index in order to find the folder is called
   A. alphabetic   B. geographic   C. subject   D. locational

5.____

6. Of the following, records management is LEAST concerned with
   A. the development of the best method for retrieving important information
   B. deciding what records should be kept
   C. deciding the number of appointments a client will need
   D. determining the types of folders to be used

6.____

7. If records are continually removed from a set of files without "charging" them to the borrower, the filing system will soon become ineffective.
Of the following terms, the one which is NOT applied to a form used in the charge-out system is a
   A. requisition card
   B. out-folder
   C. record retrieval form
   D. substitution card

8. A new clerk has been told to put 500 cards in alphabetical order. Another clerk suggests that she divide the cards into four groups, such as A to F, G to L, M to R, and S to Z, and then alphabetize these four smaller groups.
The suggested method is
   A. *poor*, because the clerk will have to handle the sheets more than once and will waste time
   B. *good*, because it saves time, is more accurate, and is less tiring
   C. *good*, because she will not have to concentrate on it so much when it is in smaller groups
   D. *poor*, because this method is much more tiring than straight alphabetizing

9. In Microsoft Excel, data and records are entered into
   A. pages   B. forms   C. cells   D. contracts

10. Suppose a clerk has been given pads of pre-printed forms to use when taking phone messages for others in her office. The clerk is then observed using scraps of paper and not the forms for writing her messages.
It should be explained that the BEST reason for using the forms is that
   A. they act as a checklist to make sure that the important information is taken
   B. she is expected to do her work in the same way as others in the office
   C. they make sure that unassigned paper is not wasted on phone messages
   D. learning to use these forms will help train her to use more difficult forms

11. The high-speed printing process used for producing large quantities of superior quality copy and cost efficiency is called
   A. photocopying
   B. laser printing
   C. inkjet printing
   D. word processing

12. Of the following, the MAIN reason a stock clerk keeps a perpetual inventory of supplies in the storeroom is that such an inventory will
   A. eliminate the need for a physical inventory
   B. provide a continuous record of supplies on hand
   C. indicate whether a shipment of supplies is satisfactory
   D. dictate the terms of the purchase order

13. As a supervisor, you may be required to handle different types of correspondence.
Of the following types of letters, it would be MOST important to promptly seal which kind of letter?
    A. One marked "confidential"
    B. Those containing enclosures
    C. Any letter to be sent airmail
    D. Those in which copies will be sent along with the original

13._____

14. While opening incoming mail, you notice that one letter indicates that an enclosure was to be included but, even after careful inspection, you are not able to find the information to which this refers.
Of the following, the thing that you should do FIRST is
    A. replace the letter in its envelope and return it to the sender
    B. file the letter until the sender's office mails the missing information
    C. type out a letter to the sender informing him of his error
    D. make a notation in the margin of the letter that the enclosure was omitted

14._____

15. You have been given a checklist and assigned the responsibility of inspecting certain equipment in the various offices of your agency.
Which of the following is the GREATEST advantage of the checklist?
    A. It indicates which equipment is in greatest demand.
    B. Each piece of equipment on the checklist will be checked only once.
    C. It helps to insure that the equipment listed will not be overlooked.
    D. The equipment listed suggests other equipment you should look for.

15._____

16. The BEST way to evaluate the overall state of completion of a construction project is to check the progress estimate against the
    A. inspection worksheet   B. construction schedule
    C. inspector's checklist   D. equipment maintenance schedule

16._____

17. The usual contract for agency work includes a section entitled "Instructions to Bidders," which states that the
    A. contractor agrees that he has made his own examination and will make no claim for damages on account of errors or omissions
    B. contractor shall not make claims for damages of any discrepancy, error, or omission in any plans
    C. estimates of quantities and calculations are guaranteed by the agency to be correct and are deemed to be a representation of the conditions affecting the work
    D. plans, measurements, dimensions, and conditions under which the work is to be performed are guaranteed by the agency

17._____

18. In order to avoid disputes over payments for extra work in a contract for construction, the BEST procedure to follow would be to
    A. have contractor submit work progress reports daily
    B. insert a special clause in the contract specifications
    C. have a representative on the job at all times to verify conditions
    D. allocate a certain percentage of the cost of the job to cover such expenses

18._____

19. Prior to the installation of equipment called for in the specifications, the contractor is USUALLY required to submit for approval
    A. sets of shop drawings
    B. a set of revised specifications
    C. a detailed description of the methods of work to be used
    D. a complete list of skilled and unskilled tradesmen he proposes to use

20. During the actual construction work, the CHIEF value of a construction schedule is to
    A. insure that the work will be done on time
    B. reveal whether production is falling behind
    C. show how much equipment and material is required for the project
    D. furnish data as to the methods and techniques of construction operations

KEY (CORRECT ANSWERS)

1.	B	11.	B
2.	B	12.	B
3.	C	13.	A
4.	C	14.	D
5.	A	15.	C
6.	C	16.	B
7.	C	17.	A
8.	B	18.	C
9.	C	19.	A
10.	A	20.	B

EXAMINATION SECTION
TEST 1

DIRECTIONS: Each question or incomplete statement is followed by several suggested answers or completions. Select the one that BEST answers the question or completes the statement. *PRINT THE LETTER OF THE CORRECT ANSWER IN THE SPACE AT THE RIGHT.*

1. A significant difference between ordinary contract law and construction contract law is that under most construction contracts,

    A. *breach of contract* is interpreted more widely
    B. a prime contractor's bid proposal is normally considered to be irrevocable after the bid opening and during the acceptance period prescribed in the bidding documents
    C. a subcontractor's bid is normally considered to be irrevocable even if the acceptance period is extended without his knowledge or consent
    D. an owner is not bound by oral agreements regarding the materials or workmanship of a project

    1.____

2. Most negotiated construction contracts are on a _____ basis.

    A. cost-plus-fee   B. lump-sum
    C. unit-price   D. fee simple

    2.____

3. When a specifier states outright the actual make, model, and catalog number of a product or the installation instructions of a manufacturer, he has written a _____ specification into the contract.

    A. reference   B. descriptive
    C. proprietary   D. performance

    3.____

4. The written documents in a construction contract that describe the work to be done — including materials, equipment, construction systems, standards, and workmanship — requirements are commonly referred to as

    A. reference documents   B. drawings
    C. general conditions   D. specifications

    4.____

5. According to the CSI Masterformat for specifications, each of the following would be listed in the General Requirements division of the specifications EXCEPT

    A. alternates   B. bonds and certificates
    C. maintenance   D. summary of work

    5.____

6. In construction contract documents, invitations to bid are typically bound in the

    A. agreement   B. general conditions
    C. specifications   D. addenda

    6.____

7. When substantial completion of a project has been achieved, it is customary for an inspection to be held to determine items that require completion or correction. The record of these items is known as a(n)

    A. supplementary condition   B. punch list
    C. escalator clause   D. change order

    7.____

8. The manner in which construction contracts are most commonly terminated is by

   A. full and satisfactory performance by both parties
   B. proving impossibility of performance
   C. breach of contract by either party
   D. mutual agreement of both parties

9. On a unit-price project, a bid in which each bid item includes its own direct project cost plus its pro rata share of the project overhead, markup, bond, and tax is referred to as

   A. balanced
   B. bonded
   C. weighted
   D. cost-plus-percentage

10. Extensions of time in construction contracts are typically formalized by an instrument known as a(n)

    A. change order
    B. squinter
    C. supplementary condition
    D. easement

11. Under the terms of most cost-plus contracts, a common contract provision is for

    A. weekly or biweekly reimbursement of payrolls, and monthly reimbursement of all other costs, including a pro rata share of the contractor's fee
    B. monthly reimbursement of all costs including payroll and a pro rata share of the fee
    C. weekly reimbursement of all costs including payroll, and a monthly pro rata installment of the contractor's fee
    D. weekly or biweekly reimbursement of payrolls, and monthly reimbursement of all other costs except any portion of the contractor's fee, which is paid in full upon substantial completion

12. When open bidding is being used, it is necessary to include a prepared proposal form with the contract documents, because it

    A. helps in itemizing unbalanced bids
    B. exposes the different unit prices used by competing bidders
    C. is required by law
    D. ensures that all bids will be prepared and evaluated on the same basis

13. Where several different kinds or classes of similar materials are used, they should be described in a manner that permits some materials to be specified for every part of the building. This technique is a system known as the

    A. residuary legatee
    B. subdivision
    C. criterion reference
    D. variable proviso

14. A physical aspect of a construction site that differs materially from that indicated by the contract documents, or that is of an unusual nature and differs materially from the environment normally encountered, is described in the contract as a(n)

    A. supplementary condition
    B. bid point
    C. changed condition
    D. estoppel

15. Which of the following is a performance specification?

    A. Ceilings will be 2' x 2' lay-in acoustical panels.
    B. The heating system shall use #6 oil and shall be a hot water system.

C. Doors and other interior woodwork will have a natural finish.
D. Contractors shall install four inch ceramic tile throughout bathroom floor area.

16. Which of the following are generally TRUE of construction contract documents?
    I. Specific provisions prevail over general provisions.
    II. The handwritten version prevails over the typewritten version.
    III. In the event that inconsistencies exist where numbers are expressed in words and figures, the numbers govern.
    IV. If a conflict exists between drawings and specifications, the drawings usually take precedence.

    The CORRECT answer is:

    A. I, II
    B. III, IV
    C. I, II, IV
    D. II, III, IV

17. For very large construction projects, an insurance program is sometimes used which combines all the interests involved in a construction project for insurance purposes with one insurer chosen by either the owner or the contractor. This type of arrangement is known as

    A. comprehensive general liability insurance
    B. umbrella excess liability coverage
    C. wrap-up insurance policy
    D. subrogation

18. In a cost-incentive contract, the most common share of savings awarded to a contractor is _____ percent.

    A. 40
    B. 50
    C. 60
    D. 75

19. In the CSI Masterformat for specifications, which of the following items would be described and listed in Division 9?

    A. Carpet
    B. Insulation
    C. Rough carpentry
    D. Pest control

20. The submission of a complimentary bid by a contractor is generally thought to be an acceptable practice when it is done for any of the following reasons EXCEPT to

    A. fix prices and make the bidding process less competitive
    B. keep the goodwill of the owner or engineer who solicits the bid
    C. please an owner-client
    D. obtain the refund of plan deposits

21. Which of the following specifications is most effectively written?

    A. Each joint must be filled solid with mortar.
    B. Each joint is to be filled solid with mortar.
    C. Each joint shall be filled solid with mortar.
    D. Fill each joint solid with mortar.

22. Which of the following is a duty of an architect-engineer under the terms of a typical construction contract?

    A. Authorizing a contractor's periodic payments
    B. Ensuring that workmanship and materials fulfill the requirements of drawings and specifications
    C. Issuing direct instructions as to the method or procedures used in construction operations
    D. Conducting property surveys that describe the project site

23. In a technical section of a construction contract, tests for soil compaction would be described in a subparagraph under the heading of

    A. materials/equipment
    B. fabrication
    C. field quality control
    D. project/site conditions

24. Which of the following is a form that authorizes a contractor to proceed with work until a formal change order can be processed?

    A. Writ of mandamus
    B. Field order
    C. Presentment
    D. Letter of intent

25. When included in a construction contract, completed operations insurance is a liability contract that covers which of the following damages?
    I. Injuries to persons
    II. Damage to property attributed to the operation
    III. Damage to the completed work itself
    The CORRECT answer is:

    A. I only
    B. III only
    C. I, II
    D. II, III

KEY (CORRECT ANSWERS)

1. B		11. A	
2. A		12. D	
3. C		13. A	
4. D		14. C	
5. B		15. B	
6. C		16. A	
7. B		17. C	
8. A		18. B	
9. A		19. A	
10. A		20. A	

21. D
22. B
23. C
24. B
25. C

TEST 2

DIRECTIONS: Each question or incomplete statement is followed by several suggested answers or completions. Select the one that BEST answers the question or completes the statement. *PRINT THE LETTER OF THE CORRECT ANSWER IN THE SPACE AT THE RIGHT.*

1. Design decisions and special project requirements recorded at the end of the design-development phase of document preparation are included in the

   A. addendum
   B. project manual
   C. outline specification
   D. supplementary conditions

2. The greatest apparent drawback to using product approval standards in the bidding of a construction project is that

   A. competition is limited
   B. the bidding period is extended
   C. bidders assume a greater risk in accepting products other than those specified
   D. relatively less flexibility

3. The general clauses of a construction contract are composed of each of the following EXCEPT

   A. specifications
   B. supplementary conditions
   C. provisions of the agreement
   D. general conditions

4. In specifications writing, the most common form of duplication is the use of a heading titled

   A. Work of Other Sections
   B. Scope of Work
   C. Work Not Included
   D. Duplication-Repetition

5. A common provision of construction contracts is that final payment is due the contractor

   A. 30 days after substantial completion
   B. at the end of the warranty period
   C. at the stated end of the contract period
   D. upon final completion

6. The MAIN advantage of the bidder's choice specification over the base bid specification is that

   A. product selection rests entirely with the architect or engineer
   B. greater competition is invited
   C. bid shopping is eliminated
   D. specifications are generally shorter

7. Sometimes, an owner will require that a contractor include in his bid a listing of the sub-contractors whose bids were used in the preparation of the prime contractor's proposal. The subcontractor listing requirement is primarily used by the owner for the purpose of

   A. estimating unit prices
   B. keeping the subcontractors subject to the owners' approval
   C. determining the percentage for a cost-plus-percentage contract
   D. discouraging bid shopping by the prime contractor

8. Special warranties that are written into construction contracts typically extend a term to

   A. 1 to 5 years
   B. 5 to 10 years
   C. 2 to 20 years
   D. 2 to lifetime

9. Of the following, which most clearly is considered a general release in full by a contractor of all claims against the owner arising out of or in consequence of the work?

   A. Agreement to terminate the contract
   B. Submission to binding arbitration
   C. Acceptance of final payment
   D. Completion of the work specified in the contract

10. A project manual is typically recorded toward the final review of the _____ phase of document preparation.

    A. construction documents
    B. schematic design
    C. design-development
    D. evaluation

11. Which of the following Division headings appears EARLIEST in the CSI Masterformat of specifications?

    A. Wood and plastics
    B. Thermal and moisture protection
    C. Sitework
    D. Concrete

12. In a typical technical section, the criteria by which the subcontractor determines that the substrates to receive his work are sound, proper, and free of defects are included in the subparagraphs under the heading of

    A. examination
    B. preparation
    C. field quality control
    D. mixes

13. For a contractor, each of the following is a potential disadvantage associated with granting an extension for the owner's acceptance period EXCEPT

    A. the potential for rises in labor wages
    B. the forfeiture of bid bonds
    C. the delaying of material orders by price advances
    D. a subcontractor or supplier's unwillingness to stand by earlier price quotes

14. What is the term for bidding requirements, contract forms, contract conditions, and specifications all bound collectively?

    A. Project manual
    B. Conditions
    C. Contract forms
    D. Master documents

15. Which of the following descriptions would NOT appear in Part 1 of a technical section that follows the CSI standard format?

    A. Submittals
    B. Equipment
    C. Delivery, storage, and handling
    D. Schedules

16. Which of the following is a disadvantage associated with the cost-plus-percentage contract?

    A. There are no direct incentives for the contractor to minimize construction costs.
    B. It is not suitable for work whose scope and nature are poorly defined at the outset of operations.
    C. It is considered unsuitable for public projects.
    D. It does not offer much flexibility in handling emergency situations.

17. In construction contracts, the term of the general warranty typically does not exceed

    A. 90 days   B. 6 months   C. 1 year   D. 2 years

18. In a construction contract, what is the term for a word description of a basic trade or material installation which outlines the quality of material to be used and the quality of workmanship to be practiced in its installation?

    A. Annotated drawing   B. Technical section
    C. Standard reference   D. Specification division

19. When an addendum is added to a construction contract, which of the following elements is typically included FIRST?

    A. Date of addendum
    B. Opening remarks and instructions
    C. Addendum and addendum number
    D. Name of architect/engineer or issuing agency

20. The main DISADVANTAGE associated with the use of alternates in the bidding process is that they

    A. decrease the security of individual bids
    B. complicate the bidding process and may increase inaccuracies
    C. are only effective when they are subtractive, rather than additive
    D. do not give the owner a clear idea of how to minimize costs

21. In a technical section written to conform to the CSI standard format, Part 2 would include descriptions of

    A. preparation   B. references
    C. field quality control   D. materials

22. In a typical project manual, which of the following elements appears FIRST?

    A. Bid bond   B. Schedule of drawings
    C. Agreement   D. General conditions

23. The insurance considerations of a construction contract, especially those governing liability, are typically incorporated into the

    A. agreement   B. general conditions
    C. specifications   D. addenda

24. Written or graphic instruments issued after the execution of a contract, which alter contract documents by additions, deletions, or corrections, are known specifically as

    A. contract modifications
    B. change orders
    C. addenda
    D. supplementary conditions

25. When a progress payments are part of a construction contract, it is common for a contractor to apply for a payment
    I. when a prescribed amount of quantified construction costs have been expended
    II. on completion of designated phases of the work
    III. a prescribed number of days before it is due under the payment schedule written into the contract

    The CORRECT answer is:

    A. II only
    B. I or III
    C. II or III
    D. I, II, or III

KEY (CORRECT ANSWERS)

1.	C	11.	C
2.	B	12.	A
3.	A	13.	B
4.	B	14.	A
5.	A	15.	D
6.	B	16.	A
7.	D	17.	C
8.	C	18.	B
9.	C	19.	D
10.	A	20.	B

21.	D
22.	C
23.	B
24.	A
25.	C

READING COMPREHENSION
UNDERSTANDING AND INTERPRETING WRITTEN MATERIAL
EXAMINATION SECTION
TEST 1

DIRECTIONS: Each question or incomplete statement is followed by several suggested answers or completions. Select the one that BEST answers the question or completes the statement. *PRINT THE LETTER OF THE CORRECT ANSWER IN THE SPACE AT THE RIGHT.*

Questions 1-3.

DIRECTIONS: Questions 1 through 3, inclusive, are to be answered in accordance with the following paragraph.

All cement work contracts, more or less, in setting. The contraction in concrete walls and other structures causes fine cracks to develop at regular intervals. The tendency to contract increases in direct proportion to the quantity of cement in the concrete. A rich mixture will contract more than a lean mixture. A concrete wall which has been made of a very lean mixture and which has been built by filling only about one foot in depth of concrete in the form each day will frequently require close inspection to reveal the cracks.

1. According to the above paragraph,

    A. shrinkage seldom occurs in concrete
    B. shrinkage occurs only in certain types of concrete
    C. by placing concrete at regular intervals, shrinkage may be avoided
    D. it is impossible to prevent shrinkage

1.____

2. According to the above paragraph, the one of the factors which reduces shrinkage in concrete is the

    A. volume of concrete in wall
    B. height of each day's pour
    C. length of wall
    D. length and height of wall

2.____

3. According to the above paragraph, a rich mixture

    A. pours the easiest
    B. shows the largest amount of cracks
    C. is low in cement content
    D. need not be inspected since cracks are few

3.____

Questions 4-6.

DIRECTIONS: Questions 4 through 6, inclusive, are to be answered SOLELY on the basis of the following paragraph.

It is best to avoid surface water on freshly poured concrete in the first place. However, when there is a very small amount present, the recommended procedure is to allow it to evaporate before finishing. If there is considerable water, it is removed with a broom, belt, float, or by other convenient means. It is never good practice to sprinkle dry cement, or a mixture of cement and fine aggregate, on concrete to take up surface water. Such fine materials form a layer on the surface that is likely to dust or hair check when the concrete hardens.

4. The MAIN subject of the above passage is

   A. surface cracking of concrete
   B. evaporation of water from freshly poured concrete
   C. removing surface water from concrete
   D. final adjustments of ingredients in the concrete mix

5. According to the above passage, the sprinkling of dry cement on the surface of a concrete mix would MOST LIKELY

   A. prevent the mix from setting
   B. cause discoloration on the surface of the concrete
   C. cause the coarse aggregate to settle out too quickly
   D. cause powdering and small cracks on the surface of the concrete

6. According to the above passage, the thing to do when considerable surface water is present on the freshly poured concrete is to

   A. dump the concrete back into the mixer and drain the water
   B. allow the water to evaporate before finishing
   C. remove the water with a broom, belt, or float
   D. add more fine aggregate but not cement

Questions 7-9.

DIRECTIONS: Questions 7 through 9, inclusive, are to be answered ONLY in accordance with the information given in the paragraph below.

Before placing the concrete, check that the forms are rigid and well braced and place the concrete within 45 minutes after mixing it. Fill the forms to the top with the wearing-course concrete. Level off the surfaces with a strieboard. When the concrete becomes stiff but still workable (in a few hours), finish the surface with a wood float. This fills the hollows and compacts the concrete and produces a smooth but gritty finish. For a non-gritty and smoother surface (but one that is more slippery when wet), follow up with a steel trowel after the water sheen from the wood-troweling starts to disappear. If you wish, slant the tread forward a fraction of an inch so that it will shed rain water.

7. Slanting the tread a fraction of an inch gives a surface that will

   A. have added strength
   B. not be slippery when wet
   C. shed rain water
   D. not have hollows

8. In addition to giving a smooth but gritty finish, the use of a wood float will tend to

   A. give a finish that is slippery when wet
   B. compact the concrete
   C. give a better wearing course
   D. provide hollows to retain rain water

9. Which one of the following statements is most nearly correct?

   A. Having checked the forms, one may place the concrete immediately after mixing same.
   B. One must wait at least 15 minutes after mixing the concrete before it may be placed in the forms.
   C. A gritty compact finish and one which is more slippery when wet will result with the use of a wood float.
   D. A steel trowel used promptly after a wood float will tend to give a non-gritty smooth finish.

Questions 10-11.

DIRECTIONS: Questions 10 and 11 are to be answered SOLELY on the basis of information contained in the following paragraph.

Tools and plastering methods have changed very little over the years. Most of the changes are mere improvements of the basic tools. The tools formerly made by hand are now machine-made and are *rigidly* constructed of light, but strong, materials in contrast to the clumsy constructions of the early types. The power-driven mixers and hoisting equipment used on large plastering jobs today produce better mortars and lighten the tasks involved.

10. According to the above paragraph, present day tools used for plastering

    A. have made plastering much more complicated than it used to be
    B. are heavier than the old-fashioned tools they replaced
    C. produce poorer results but speed up the job
    D. are lighter and stronger than the hand-made tools of the past

11. As used in the above paragraph, the word *rigidly* means MOST NEARLY

    A. feeble   B. weakly   C. firmly   D. flexibly

Questions 12-18.

DIRECTIONS: Questions 12 through 18 are to be answered in accordance with the following paragraphs.

SURFACE RENEWING OVERLAYS

A surface renewing overlay should consist of material which can be constructed in very thin layers. The material must fill surface voids and provide an impervious skid-resistant surface. It must also be sufficiently resistant to traffic abrasion to provide an economical service life.

Materials meeting these requirements are:
- a. Asphalt concrete having small particle size
- b. Hot sand asphalts
- c. Surface seal coats

Fine-graded asphalt concrete or hot sand asphalt can be constructed in layers as thin as one-half inch and fulfill all requirements for surface renewing overlays. They are recommended for thin resurfacing of pavements having high traffic volumes, as their service lives are relatively long when constructed properly. They can be used for minor leveling, they are quiet riding, and their appearance is exceptionally pleasing. Seal coats or slurry seals may fulfill surface requirements for low traffic pavements.

12. A surface renewing overlay must fill surface voids, provide an impervious skid-resistant surface, and

    A. be resistant to traffic abrasion
    B. have small particle size
    C. be exceptionally pleasing in appearance
    D. be constructed in half-inch layers

13. An *impervious skid-resistant surface* means a surface that is

    A. rough to the touch and fixed firmly in place
    B. waterproof and provides good gripping for tires
    C. not damaged by skidding vehicles
    D. smooth to the touch and quiet riding

14. The number of types of materials that can be constructed in very thin layers and are also suitable for surface renewing overlays is

    A. 1   B. 2   C. 3   D. 4

15. The SMALLEST thickness of asphalt concrete or hot sand asphalt that can fulfill all requirements for surface renewing overlays is _____ inch(es).

    A. ¼   B. ½   C. 1   D. 2

16. The materials that are recommended for thin resurfacing of pavements having high traffic volumes are

    A. those that have relatively long service lives
    B. asphalt concretes with maximum particle size
    C. surface seal coats
    D. slurry seals with voids

17. Fine-graded asphalt concrete and hot sand asphalt are quiet riding and are also

    A. recommended for low traffic pavements
    B. used as slurry seal coats
    C. suitable for major leveling
    D. exceptionally pleasing in appearance

18. The materials that may fulfill surface requirements for low traffic pavements are 18.____

    A. fine-graded asphalt concretes
    B. hot sand asphalts
    C. seal coats or slurry seals
    D. those that can be used for minor leveling

Questions 19-25.

DIRECTIONS: Questions 19 through 25 are to be answered SOLELY on the basis of the paragraphs below.

OPEN-END WRENCHES

Solid, non-adjustable wrenches with openings in one or both ends are called open-end wrenches. Wrenches with small openings are usually shorter than wrenches with large openings. This proportions the lever advantage of the wrench to the bolt or stud and helps prevent wrench breakage or damage to the bolt or stud.

Open-end wrenches may have their jaws parallel to the handle or at angles anywhere up to 90 degrees. The average angle is 15 degrees. This angular displacement variation permits selection of a wrench suited for places where there is room to make only a part of a complete turn of a nut or bolt. Handles are usually straight, but may be curved. Those with curved handles are called S-wrenches. Other open-end wrenches may have offset handles. This allows the head to reach nut or bolt heads that are sunk below the surface.

There are a few basic rules that you should keep in mind when using wrenches. They are:

    I. ALWAYS use a wrench that fits the nut properly. Otherwise, the wrench may slip, or the nut may be damaged.
    II. Keep wrenches clean and free from oil. Otherwise, they may slip, resulting in possible serious injury to you or damage to the work.
    III. Do NOT increase the leverage of a wrench by placing a pipe over the handle. Increased leverage may damage the wrench or the work.

19. Open-end wrenches 19.____

    A. are adjustable
    B. are solid
    C. always have openings at both ends
    D. are always S-shaped

20. Wrench proportions are such that wrenches with _____ openings have _____ handles. 20.____

    A. larger; shorter   B. smaller; longer
    C. larger; longer   D. smaller; thicker

21. The average angle between the jaws and the handle of a wrench is _____ degrees. 21.____

    A. 0   B. 15   C. 22   D. 90

22. Offset handles are intended for use MAINLY with

   A. offset nuts
   B. bolts having fine threads
   C. nuts sunk below the surface
   D. bolts that permit limited swing

23. The wrench which is selected should fit the nut properly because this

   A. prevents distorting the wrench
   B. insures use of all wrench sizes
   C. avoids damaging the nut
   D. overstresses the bolt

24. Oil on wrenches is

   A. *good* because it prevents rust
   B. *good* because it permits easier turning
   C. *bad* because the wrench may slip off the nut
   D. *bad* because the oil may spoil the work

25. Extending the handle of a wrench by slipping a piece of pipe over it is considered

   A. *good* because it insures a tight nut
   B. *good* because less effort is needed to loosen a nut
   C. *bad* because the wrench may be damaged
   D. *bad* because the amount of tightening can not be controlled

KEY (CORRECT ANSWERS)

1.	D	11.	C
2.	B	12.	A
3.	B	13.	B
4.	C	14.	C
5.	D	15.	B
6.	C	16.	A
7.	C	17.	D
8.	B	18.	C
9.	A	19.	B
10.	D	20.	C

21. B
22. C
23. C
24. C
25. C

TEST 2

DIRECTIONS: Each question or incomplete statement is followed by several suggested answers or completions. Select the one that BEST answers the question or completes the statement. *PRINT THE LETTER OF THE CORRECT ANSWER IN THE SPACE AT THE RIGHT.*

Questions 1-3.

DIRECTIONS: Questions 1 through 3 are to be answered SOLELY on the basis of the following passage.

    A utility plan is a floor plan which shows the layout of a heating, electrical, plumbing, or other utility system. Utility plans are used primarily by the persons reponsible for the utilities, but they are important to the craftsman as well. Most utility installations require the leaving of openings in walls, floors, and roofs for the admission or installation of utility features. The craftsman who is, for example, pouring a concrete foundation wall must study the utility plans to determine the number, sizes, and locations of the openings he must leave for piping, electric lines, and the like.

1. The one of the following items of information which is LEAST likely to be provided by a utility plan is the 1.____

    A. location of the joists and frame members around stairwells
    B. location of the hot water supply and return piping
    C. location of light fixtures
    D. number of openings in the floor for radiators

2. According to the passage, the persons who will *most likely* have the GREATEST need for the information included in a utility plan of a building are those who 2.____

    A. maintain and repair the heating system
    B. clean the premises
    C. paint housing exteriors
    D. advertise property for sale

3. According to the passage, a repair crew member should find it MOST helpful to consult a utility plan when information is needed about the 3.____

    A. thickness of all doors in the structure
    B. number of electrical outlets located throughout the structure
    C. dimensions of each window in the structure
    D. length of a roof rafter

Questions 4-9.

DIRECTIONS: Questions 4 through 9 are to be answered SOLELY on the basis of the following passage.

    The basic hand-operated hoisting device is the tackle or purchase, consisting of a line called a fall, reeved through one or more blocks. To hoist a load of given size, you must set up a rig with a safe working load equal to or in excess of the load to be hoisted. In order to do this, you must be able to calculate the safe working load of a single part of line of given size, the safe working load of a given purchase which contains a line of given size, and the minimum size of hooks or shackles which you must use in a given type of purchase to hoist a given load. You must also be able to calculate the thrust which a given load will exert on a gin pole or a set of shears inclined at a given angle, the safe working load which a spar of a given size used as a gin pole or as one of a set of shears will sustain, and the stress which a given load will set up in the back guy of a gin pole or in the back guy of a set of shears inclined at a given angle.

4. The above passage refers to the lifting of loads by means of

   A. erected scaffolds
   B. manual rigging devices
   C. power-driven equipment
   D. conveyor belts

5. It can be concluded from the above passage that a set of shears serves to

   A. absorb the force and stress of the working load
   B. operate the tackle
   C. contain the working load
   D. compute the safe working load

6. According to the above passage, a spar can be used for a

   A. back guy   B. block   C. fall   D. gin pole

7. According to the above passage, the rule that a user of hand-operated tackle MUST follow is to make sure that the safe working load is AT LEAST

   A. equal to the weight of the given load
   B. twice the combined weight of the block and falls
   C. one-half the weight of the given load
   D. twice the weight of the given load

8. According to the above passage, the two parts that make up a tackle are

   A. back guys and gin poles
   B. blocks and falls
   C. rigs and shears
   D. spars and shackles

9. According to the above passage, in order to determine whether it is safe to hoist a particular load, you MUST

   A. use the maximum size hooks
   B. time the speed to bring a given load to a desired place
   C. calculate the forces exerted on various types of rigs
   D. repeatedly lift and lower various loads

Questions 10-15.

DIRECTIONS: Questions 10 through 15 are to be answered SOLELY on the basis of the following set of instructions.

3 (#2)

PATCHING SIMPLE CRACKS IN A BUILT-UP ROOF

If there is a visible crack in built-up roofing, the repair is simple and straightforward:

1. With a brush, clean all loose gravel and dust out of the crack, and clean three or four inches around all sides of it.
2. With a trowel or putty knife, fill the crack with asphalt cement and then spread a layer of asphalt cement about 1/8 inch thick over the cleaned area.
3. Place a strip of roofing felt big enough to cover the crack into the wet cement and press it down firmly.
4. Spread a second layer of cement over the strip of felt and well past its edges.
5. Brush gravel back over the patch.

10. According to the above passage, in order to patch simple cracks in a built-up roof, it is necessary to use a

    A. putty knife and a drill
    B. knife and pliers
    C. tack hammer and a punch
    D. brush and a trowel

11. According to the above passage, the size of the area that should be clear of loose gravel and dust before the asphalt cement is first applied should

    A. be the exact size of the crack itself
    B. extend three or four inches on all sides of the crack
    C. be 1/8 inch greater than the size of the crack itself
    D. extend the length of the roofing strip

12. According to the above passage, loose gravel and dust in the crack should be removed with a

    A. brush   B. felt pad   C. trowel   D. dust mop

13. Assume that both layers of asphalt cement needed to patch the crack are of the same thickness.
    The total thickness of asphalt cement used in the patch should be MOST NEARLY _____ inch.

    A. 1/2   B. 1/3   C. 1/4   D. 1/8

14. According to the instructions in the above passage, how large should the strip of roofing felt be cut?

    A. Three of four inches square
    B. Smaller than the crack and small enough to be surrounded by cement on all sides of the strip
    C. Exactly the same size and shape of the area covered by the wet cement
    D. Large enough to completely cover the crack

15. The final or finishing action to be taken in patching a simple crack in a built-up roof is to

    A. clean out the inside of the crack
    B. spread a layer of asphalt a second time
    C. cover the crack with roofing felt
    D. cover the patch of roofing felt and cement with gravel

Questions 16-17.

DIRECTIONS: Questions 16 and 17 are to be answered SOLELY on the basis of the information given in the following paragraph.

Supplies are to be ordered from the stockroom once a week. The standard requisition form, Form SP21, is to be used for ordering all supplies. The form is prepared in triplicate, one white original and two green copies. The white and one green copy are sent to the stockroom, and the remaining green copy is to be kept by the orderer until the supplies are received.

16. According to the above paragraph, there is a limit on the

    A. amount of supplies that may be ordered
    B. day on which supplies may be ordered
    C. different kinds of supplies that may be ordered
    D. number of times supplies may be ordered in one year

17. According to the above paragraph, when the standard requisition form for supplies is prepared,

    A. a total of four requisition blanks is used
    B. a white form is the original
    C. each copy is printed in two colors
    D. one copy is kept by the stock clerk

Questions 18-21.

DIRECTION: Questions 18 through 21 are to be answered SOLELY on the basis of the following passage.

The Oil Pollution Act for U. S. waters defines an *oily mixture* as 100 parts or more of oil in one million parts of mixture. This mixture is not allowed to be discharged into the prohibited zone. The prohibited zone may, in special cases, be extended 100 miles out to sea but, in general, remains at 50 miles offshore. The United States Coast Guard must be contacted to report all *oily mixture* spills. The Federal Water Pollution Control Act provides for a fine of $10,000 for failure to notify the United States Coast Guard. An employer may take action against an employee if the employee causes an *oily mixture* spill. The law holds your employer responsible for either cleaning up or paying for the removal of the oil spillage.

18. According to the Oil Pollution Act, an *oily mixture* is defined as one in which there are _____ parts or more of oil in _____ parts of mixture.

    A. 50; 10,000
    B. 100; 10,000
    C. 100; 1,000,000
    D. 10,000; 1,000,000

19. Failure to notify the proper authorities of an *oily mixture* spill is punishable by a fine. Such fine is provided for by the

    A. United States Coast Guard
    B. Federal Water Pollution Control Act
    C. Oil Pollution Act
    D. United States Department of Environmental Protection

20. According to the law, the one responsible for the removal of an *oily mixture* spilled into U.S. waters is the

    A. employer
    B. employee
    C. U.S. Coast Guard
    D. U.S. Pollution Control Board

21. The *prohibited zone,* in general, is the body of water

    A. within 50 miles offshore
    B. beyond 100 miles offshore
    C. within 10,000 yards of the coastline
    D. beyond 10,000 yards from the coastline

Questions 22-25.

DIRECTIONS: Questions 22 through 25 are to be answered SOLELY on the basis of the following paragraph.

Synthetic detergents are materials produced from petroleum products or from animal or vegetable oils and fats. One of their advantages is the fact that they can be made to meet a particular cleaning problem by altering the foaming, wetting, and emulsifying properties of a cleaner. They are added to commonly used cleaning materials such as solvents, water, and alkalies to improve their cleaning performance. The adequate wetting of the surface to be cleaned is paramount in good cleaning performance. Because of the relatively high surface tension of water, it has poor wetting ability, unless its surface tension is decreased by addition of a detergent or soap. This allows water to flow into crevices and around small particles of soil, thus loosening them.

22. According to the above paragraph, synthetic detergents are made from all of the following EXCEPT

    A. petroleum products   B. vegetable oils
    C. surface tension oils   D. animal fats

23. According to the above paragraph, water's poor wetting ability is related to

    A. its low surface tension
    B. its high surface tension
    C. its vegetable oil content
    D. the amount of dirt on the surface to be cleaned

24. According to the above paragraph, synthetic detergents are added to all of the following EXCEPT

    A. alkalines   B. water   C. acids   D. solvents

25. According to the above paragraph, altering a property of a cleaner can give an advantage in meeting a certain cleaning problem.
The one of the following that is NOT a property altered by synthetic detergents is the cleaner's

   A. flow ability
   B. foaming property
   C. emulsifying property
   D. wetting ability

KEY (CORRECT ANSWERS)

1. A
2. A
3. B
4. B
5. A

6. D
7. A
8. B
9. C
10. D

11. B
12. A
13. C
14. D
15. D

16. D
17. B
18. C
19. B
20. A

21. A
22. C
23. B
24. C
25. A

ARITHMETICAL REASONING

EXAMINATION SECTION
TEST 1

DIRECTIONS: Each question or incomplete statement is followed by several suggested answers or completions. Select the one that BEST answers the question or completes the statement. *PRINT THE LETTER OF THE CORRECT ANSWER IN THE SPACE AT THE RIGHT.*

1. If it takes 2 men 9 days to do a job, how many men are needed to do the same job in 3 days?

    A. 4   B. 5   C. 6   D. 7

2. Suppose that a department operates 1,644 buildings. If one employee is needed for every 2 buildings, and one foreman is needed for every 18 employees, the number of foremen needed is CLOSEST to

    A. 45   B. 50   C. 55   D. 60

3. If 60 bars of soap cost the same as 2 gallons of wax, how many bars of soap can be bought for the price of 5 gallons of wax?

    A. 120   B. 150   C. 180   D. 300

4. An employee waxes 275 sq.ft. of floor on Monday, 352 sq.ft. on Tuesday, 179 sq.ft. on Wednesday, and 302 sq.ft. on Thursday.
In order to average 280 sq.ft. of floor waxed a day, how many square feet of floor must he wax on Friday?

    A. 264   B. 278   C. 292   D. 358

5. A project covers 35 acres altogether. Lawns, playgrounds, and walks take up 28 acres and the rest is given over to buildings.
What percentage of the total area is given over to buildings?

    A. 7%   B. 20%   C. 25%   D. 28%

6. When preparing for a mopping operation, fill the standard 16 quart bucket to the 3/4 full mark with warm water. Then add detergent at the rate of 2 oz. per gallon of water and disinfectant at the rate of 1 oz. to 3 gallons of water. According to these directions, the amount of detergent and disinfectant to add to 3/4 of a bucket of warm water is _____ oz. detergent and _____ oz. disinfectant.

    A. 4; 1/2   B. 5; 3/4   C. 6; 1   D. 8; 1 1/4

7. If corn brooms weigh 32 lbs. a dozen, the average weight of one corn broom is CLOSEST to _____ lbs. _____ oz.

    A. 2; 14   B. 2; 11   C. 2; 9   D. 2; 6

8. At the beginning of the year, a foreman has 7 dozen electric bulbs in stock. During the year, he receives a shipment of 14 dozen bulbs, and also replaces 5 burned out bulbs a month in each of 3 buildings in his area. How many electric bulbs does he have on hand at the end of the year? _____ dozen.

   A. 3   B. 6   C. 8   D. 12

9. A project has 4 buildings, each 14 floors high. Each floor has 10 apartments. If 35% of the apartments in the project have 3 rooms or less, how many apartments have 4 or more rooms?

   A. 196   B. 210   C. 364   D. 406

10. An employee takes 1 hour and 30 minutes a day to sweep 30 flights of stairs. How many flights of stairs does he sweep in a month if he spends a total of 30 hours doing this job and works at the same rate?

    A. 200   B. 300   C. 600   D. 900

11. During a month, Employee A washed 30 windows, Employee B washed 4 times as many windows as Employee A, and Employee C washed half as many windows as Employee B. The TOTAL number of windows washed by all three men together during this month is

    A. 180   B. 210   C. 240   D. 330

12. How much would it cost to completely fence in the playground area shown at the right with fencing costing $7.50 a foot?
    A. $615.00
    B. $820.00
    C. $885.00
    D. $960.00

13. A drill bit measures .625 inches. The fractional equivalent, in inches, is

    A. 9/16   B. 5/8   C. 11/16   D. 3/4

14. The number of cubic yards of sand required to fill a bin measuring 12 feet by 6 feet by 4 feet is MOST NEARLY

    A. 8   B. 11   C. 48   D. 96

15. Assume that you are assigned to put down floor tiles in a room measuring 8 feet by 10 feet. Individual tiles measure 9 inches by 9 inches.
    The total number of floor tiles required to cover the entire floor is MOST NEARLY

    A. 107   B. 121   C. 142   D. 160

16. Lumber is usually sold by the board foot, and a board foot is defined as a board one foot square and one inch thick.
    If the price of one board foot of lumber is 90 cents and you need 20 feet of lumber 6 inches wide and 1 inch thick, the cost of the 20 feet of lumber is

    A. $9.00   B. $12.00   C. $18.00   D. $24.00

17. For a certain plumbing repair job, you need three lengths of pipe, 12 1/4 inches, 6 1/2 inches, and 8 5/8 inches.
    If you cut these three lengths from the same piece of pipe, which is 36 inches long, and each cut consumes 1/8 inch of pipe, the length of pipe REMAINING after you have cut out your three pieces should be _____ inches.

    A. 7 1/4   B. 7 7/8   C. 8 1/4   D. 8 7/8

18. A maintenance bond for a roadway pavement is in an amount of 10% of the estimated cost.
    If the estimated cost is $8,000,000, the maintenance bond is

    A. $8,000   B. $80,000   C. $800,000   D. $8,000,000

19. Specifications require that a core be taken every 700 square yards of paved roadway or fraction thereof. A 100 foot by 200 foot rectangular area would require _____ core(s).

    A. 1   B. 2   C. 3   D. 4

20. An applicant must file a map at a scale of 1" = 40'. Six inches on the map represents _____ feet on the ground.

    A. 600   B. 240   C. 120   D. 60

21. A 100' x 110' lot has an area of MOST NEARLY _____ acre.

    A. 1/8   B. 1/4   C. 3/8   D. 1/2

22. 1 inch is MOST NEARLY equal to _____ feet.

    A. .02   B. .04   C. .06   D. .08

23. The area of the triangle EFG shown at the right is MOST NEARLY _____ sq. ft.

    A. 36   B. 42   C. 48   D. 54

24. Specifications state: As further security for the faithful performance of this contract, the Comptroller shall deduct, and retain until the final payment, 10% of the value of the work certified for payment in each partial payment voucher, until the amount so deducted and retained shall equal 5% of the contract price or in the case of a unit price contract, 5% of the estimated amount to be paid to the Contractor under the contract.
    For a $300,000 contract, the amount to be retained at the end of the contract is

    A. $5,000   B. $10,000   C. $15,000   D. $20,000

25. Asphalt was laid for a length of 210 feet on the entire width of a street whose curb-to-curb distance is 30 feet. The number of square yards covered with asphalt is MOST NEARLY

    A. 210   B. 700   C. 2,100   D. 6,300

KEY (CORRECT ANSWERS)

1.	C	11.	B
2.	A	12.	C
3.	B	13.	B
4.	C	14.	B
5.	B	15.	C
6.	C	16.	A
7.	B	17.	C
8.	B	18.	C
9.	C	19.	D
10.	C	20.	B

21. B
22. D
23. A
24. C
25. B

SOLUTIONS TO PROBLEMS

1. (2)(9) = 18 man-days. Then, 18 ÷ 3 = 6 men

2. The number of employees = 1644 ÷ 2 = 822. The number of foremen needed = 822 ÷ 18 ≈ 45

3. 1 gallon of wax costs the same as 60 ÷ 2 = 30 bars of soap. Thus, 5 gallons of wax costs the same as (5)(30) = 150 bars of soap.

4. To average 280 sq.ft. for five days means a total of (5)(280) = 1400 sq.ft. for all five days. The number of square feet to be waxed on Friday = 1400 - (275+352+179+302) = 292

5. The acreage for buildings is 35 - 28 = 7. Then, 7/35 = 20%

6. (16)(3/4) = 12 quarts = 3 gallons. The amount of detergent, in ounces, is (2)(3) = 6. The amount of disinfectant is 1 oz.

7. One corn broom weighs 32 ÷ 12 = 2 2/3 lbs. ≈ 2 lbs. 11 oz.

8. Number of bulbs at the beginning of the year = (7)(12) + (14)(12) = 252. Number of bulbs replaced over an entire year = (5)(3)(12) = 180. The number of unused bulbs = 252 - 180 = 72 = 6 dozen.

9. Total number of apartments = (4)(14)(10) = 560. The number of apartments with at least 4 rooms = (.65)(560) = 364.

10. 30 ÷ 1 1/2 = 20. Then, (20)(30) = 600 flights of stairs

11. The number of windows washed by A, B, C were 30, 120, and 60. Their total is 210.

12. The two missing dimensions are 26 - 14 = 12 ft. and 33 - 9 = 24 ft. Perimeter = 9 + 12 + 33 + 26 + 24 + 14 = 118 ft. Thus, total cost of fencing = (118)($7.50) = $885.00

13. $.625 = \dfrac{625}{1000} = \dfrac{5}{8}$

14. (12)(6)(4) = 288 cu.ft. Now, 1 cu.yd. = 27 cu.ft.; 288 cu.ft. is equivalent to 10 2/3 or about 11 cu.yds.

15. 144 sq.in. = 1 sq.ft. The room measures (8 ft.)x(10 ft.) = 80 sq.ft. = 11,520 sq.in. Each tile measures (9)(9) = 81 sq.in. The number of tiles needed = 11,520 ÷ 81 = 142.2 or about 142.

16. 20 ft. by 6 in. = (20 ft.)(1/2 ft.) = 10 sq.ft. Then, (10X.90) = $9.00

17. There will be 3 cuts in making 3 lengths of pipe, and these 3 cuts will use (3)(1/8) = 3/8 in. of pipe. The amount of pipe remaining after the 3 pieces are removed = 36 - 12 1/4 - 6 1/2 - 8 5/8 - 3/8 = 8 1/4 in.

18. The maintenance bond = (.10)($8,000,000) = $800,000

19. $(100)(200) = 20,000$ sq.ft. $= 20,000 \div 9 \approx 2222$ sq.yds. Then, $2222 \div 700 \approx 3.17$. Since a core must be taken for each 700 sq.yds. plus any left over fraction, 4 cores will be needed.

20. Six inches means $(6)(40) = 240$ ft. of actual length.

21. $(100 \text{ ft.})(110 \text{ ft.}) = 11,000$ sq.ft. ≈ 1222 sq.yds. Then, since 1 acre = 4840 sq.yds., 1222 sq.yds. is equivalent to about 1/4 acre.

22. 1 in. = 1/12 ft. $\approx$ .08 ft.

23. Area of $\triangle$ EFG = $(1/2)(8)(6) + (1/2)(4)(6) = 36$ sq.ft.

24. The amount to be retained = $(.05)(\$300,000) = \$15,000$

25. $(210)(30) = 6300$ sq.ft. Since 1 sq.yd. = 9 sq.ft., 6300 sq.ft. equals 700 sq.yds.

TEST 2

DIRECTIONS: Each question or incomplete statement is followed by several suggested answers or completions. Select the one that BEST answers the question or completes the statement. *PRINT THE LETTER OF THE CORRECT ANSWER IN THE SPACE AT THE RIGHT.*

1. The TOTAL length of four pieces of 2" pipe, whose lengths are 7'3 1/2", 4'2 3/16", 5'7 5/16", and 8'5 7/8", respectively, is

    A. 24'6 3/4"
    B. 24'7 15/16"
    C. 25'5 13/16"
    D. 25'6 7/8"

2. Under the same conditions, the group of pipes that gives the SAME flow as one 6" pipe is (neglecting friction) _____ pipes.

    A. 3 3" B. 4 3" C. 2 4" D. 3 4"

3. A water storage tank measures 5' long, 4' wide, and 6' deep and is filled to the 5 1/2' mark with water.
   If one cubic foot of water weighs 62 pounds, the number of pounds of water required to COMPLETELY fill the tank is

    A. 7,440 B. 6,200 C. 1,240 D. 620

4. A hot water line made of copper has a straight horizontal run of 150 feet and, when installed, is at a temperature of 45°F. In use, its temperature rises to 190°F.
   If the coefficient of expansion for copper is 0.0000095" per foot per degree F, the total expansion, in inches, in the run of pipe is given by the product of 150 multiplied by 0.0000095 by

    A. 145
    B. 145 x 12
    C. 145 divided by 12
    D. 145 x 12 x 12

5. To dig a trench 3'0" wide, 50'0" long, and 5'6" deep, the total number of cubic yards of earth to be removed is MOST NEARLY

    A. 30 B. 90 C. 140 D. 825

6. If it costs $65 for 20 feet of subway rail, the cost of 150 feet of this rail will be

    A. $487.50 B. $512.00 C. $589.50 D. $650.00

7. The number of cubic feet of concrete it takes to fill a form 10 feet long, 3 feet wide, and 6 inches deep is

    A. 12 B. 15 C. 20 D. 180

8. The sum of 4 1/16, 5 1/4, 3 5/8, and 4 7/16 is

    A. 17 3/16 B. 17 1/4 C. 17 5/16 D. 17 3/8

9. If you earn $10.20 per hour and time and one-half for working over 40 hours, your gross salary for a week in which you worked 42 hours would be

    A. $408.00 B. $428.40 C. $438.60 D. $770.80

10. A drill bit, used to drill holes in track ties, has a diameter of 0.75 inches. When expressed as a fraction, the diameter of this drill bit is

    A. 1/4"   B. 3/8"   C. 1/2"   D. 3/4"

11. Three dozen shovels were purchased for use.
    If the shovels were used at the rate of nine a week, the number of weeks that the three dozen lasted was

    A. 3   B. 4   C. 9   D. 12

12. Assume that you earn $20,000 per year.
    If twenty percent of your pay is deducted for taxes, social security, and pension, your weekly take-home pay will be MOST NEARLY

    A. $280   B. $308   C. $328   D. $344

13. If a measurement scaled from a drawing is one inch, and the scale of the drawing is 1/8 inch to the foot, then the one inch measurement would represent an ACTUAL length of

    A. 8 feet
    C. 1/8 of a foot
    B. 2 feet
    D. 8 inches

14. Tiles 12" x 12" are used to lay a floor having the dimensions 10'0" x 12'0".
    The MINIMUM number of tiles needed to completely cover the floor is

    A. 60   B. 96   C. 120   D. 144

15. The volume of concrete in a strip of sidewalk 30 feet long by 4 feet wide by 3 inches thick is _____ cubic feet.

    A. 30   B. 120   C. 240   D. 360

16. To change a quantity of cubic feet into an equivalent quantity of cubic yards, _____ the quantity by _____.

    A. multiply; 9
    C. multiply; 27
    B. divide; 9
    D. divide; 27

17. If a pump can deliver 50 gallons of water per minute, then the time needed for this pump to empty an excavation containing 5,800 gallons of water is _____ hour(s) _____ minutes.

    A. 2; 12   B. 1; 56   C. 1; 44   D. 1; 32

18. The sum of 3 1/6", 4 1/4", 3 5/8", and 5 7/16" is

    A. 15 9/16"   B. 16 1/8"   C. 16 23/48"   D. 16 3/4"

19. If a measurement scaled from a drawing is 2 inches, and the scale of the drawing is 1/8 inch to the foot, then the two inch measurement would represent an ACTUAL length of

    A. 8 feet
    C. 1/4 of a foot
    B. 4 feet
    D. 16 feet

20. A room is 7'6" wide by 9'0" long with a ceiling height of 8'0". One gallon of flat paint will cover approximately 400 square feet of wall.
    The number of gallons of this paint required to paint the walls of this room, making no deductions for windows or doors, is MOST NEARLY

    A. 1/4   B. 1/2   C. 2/3   D. 1

    20._____

21. The cost of a certain job is broken down as follows:

    Materials $3,750
    Rental of equipment 1,200
    Labor   3,150

    The percentage of the total cost of the job that can be charged to materials is MOST NEARLY

    A. 40%   B. 42%   C. 44%   D. 46%

    21._____

22. By trial, it is found that by using two cubic feet of sand, a 5 cubic foot batch of concrete is produced. Using the same proportions, the amount of sand required to produce 2 cubic yards of concrete is MOST NEARLY _____ cubic feet.

    A. 20   B. 22   C. 24   D. 26

    22._____

23. It takes 4 men 6 days to do a certain job.
    Working at the same speed, the number of days it will take 3 men to do this job is

    A. 7   B. 8   C. 9   D. 10

    23._____

24. The cost of rawl plugs is $27.50 per gross. The cost of 2,448 rawl plugs is

    A. $467.50   B. $472.50   C. $477.50   D. $482.50

    24._____

25. In a certain district, the area of a building may be no longer than 55% of the area of the lot on which it stands. On a rectangular lot 75 ft. by 125 ft., the maximum permissible area of building is, in square feet, MOST NEARLY

    A. 5,148   B. 5,152   C. 5,156   D. 5,160

    25._____

KEY (CORRECT ANSWERS)

1. D
2. B
3. D
4. A
5. A

6. A
7. B
8. D
9. C
10. D

11. B
12. B
13. A
14. C
15. A

16. D
17. B
18. C
19. D
20. C

21. D
22. B
23. B
24. A
25. C

SOLUTIONS TO PROBLEMS

1. $3\frac{1}{6}" + 4\frac{1}{4}" + 3\frac{5}{8}" + 5\frac{7}{16}" = 3\frac{8}{48}" + 4\frac{12}{48}" + 3\frac{30}{48}" + 5\frac{21}{48}" = 15\frac{71}{48}" = 16\frac{23}{48}"$

2. The flow of a 6" pipe is measured by the cross-sectional area. Since diameter = 6", radius = 3", and so area = 9 π sq.in. A single 3" pipe would have a cross-sectional area of (3/2) π sq.in. = 2.25 π sq.in. Now, 9 ÷ / 2.25 = 4. Thus, four 3" pipes is equivalent, in flow, to one 6" pipe.

3. (5x4x6) - (5x4x5 1/2) = 10. Then, (10)(62) = 620 pounds.

4. The total expansion = (150')(.0000095"/1 ft.)(190°-45°). So, the last factor is 145.

5. (3')(50')(5 1/2') = 825 cu.ft. Since 1 cu.yd. = 27 cu.ft., 825 cu.ft. cu.yds.

6. 150 ÷ 20 = 7.5. Then, (7.5)($65) = $487.50

7. (10')(3')(1/2') = 15 cu.ft.

8. $4\frac{1}{16} + 5\frac{4}{16} + 3\frac{10}{16} + 4\frac{7}{16} = 16\frac{22}{16} = 17\frac{3}{8}$

9. Gross salary = ($10.20)(40) + ($15.30)(2) = $438.60

10. $75" = \frac{75}{100}" = \frac{3}{4}"$

11. 3 dozen = 36 shovels. Then, 36 ÷ 9 = 4 weeks

12. Since 20% is deducted, the take-home pay = ($20,000)(.80) = $16,000 for the year, which is $16,000 ÷ 52 ≈ $308 per week.

13. A scale drawing where 1/8" means an actual size of 1 ft. implies that a scale drawing of 1" means an actual size of (1')(8) = 8'

14. (10')(12') = 120 sq.ft. Since each tile is 1 sq.ft., a total of 120 tiles will be used.

15. (30')(4')(1/4') = 30 cu.ft.

16. To convert a given number of cubic feet into an equivalent number of cubic yards, divide by 27.

17. 5800 ÷ 50 = 116 min. = 1 hour 56 minutes

18. $3\frac{1}{6}" + 4\frac{1}{4}" + 3\frac{5}{8}" + 5\frac{7}{16}" = 3\frac{8}{48}" + 4\frac{12}{48}" + 3\frac{30}{48}" + 5\frac{21}{48}" = 15\frac{71}{48}" = 16\frac{23}{48}"$

19. 2 ÷ 1/8 = 16, so a 2" drawing represents an actual length of 16 feet.

20. The area of the 4 walls = 2(7 1/2')(8') + 2(9')(8') = 264 sq.ft. Then, 264 ÷ 400 = .66 or about 2/3 gallon of paint.

21. $3750 + $1200 + $3150 = $8100. Then, $3750/$8100 ≈ 46%

22. 2 cu.yds. ÷ 5 cu.ft. = 54 ÷ 5 = 10.8. Now, (10.8)(2 cu.ft.) ≈ 22 cu.ft. Note: 2 cu.yds. = 54 cu.ft.

23. (4)(6) = 24 man-days. Then, 24 ÷ 3 = 8 days

24. 2448 ÷ 144 = 17. Then, (17)($27.50) = $467.50

25. (75')(125') = 9375 sq.ft. The maximum area of the building = (.55)(9375 sq.ft.) * 5156 sq.ft.

TEST 3

DIRECTIONS: Each question or incomplete statement is followed by several suggested answers or completions. Select the one that BEST answers the question or completes the statement. *PRINT THE LETTER OF THE CORRECT ANSWER IN THE SPACE AT THE RIGHT.*

1. A steak weighed 2 pounds, 4 ounces. How much did it cost at $4.60 per pound?
    A. $7.80   B. $8.75   C. $9.90   D. $10.35

2. twenty pints of water just fill a pail. the capacity of the pail, in gallons, is
    A. 2   B. 2 1/4   C. 2 1/2   D. 2 3/4

3. The sum of 5/12 and 1/4 is
    A. 7/12   B. 2/3   C. 3/4   D. 5/6

4. The volume of earth, in cubic yards, excavated from a trench 4'0" wide by 5'6" deep by 18'6" long is MOST NEARLY
    A. 14.7   B. 15.1   C. 15.5   D. 15.9

5. 5/8 written as a decimal is
    A. 62.5   B. 6.25   C. .625   D. .0625

6. The number of cubic feet in a cubic yard is
    A. 9   B. 12   C. 27   D. 36

7. If it costs $16.20 to lay one square yard of asphalt, to lay a patch 15' by 15', it will cost MOST NEARLY
    A. $405.00   B. $3,645.00   C. $134.50   D. $243.00

8. You are assigned thirty (30) asphalt workers to be divided into two crews so that one crew will have 2/3 as many men as the other.
The number of men you would put into the SMALLER crew is
    A. 10   B. 12   C. 14   D. 20

9. It takes 12 asphalt workers, working 6 hours a day, 5 days to complete a certain job. The number of days it will take 10 men, working 8 hours a day, to do the same job, assuming all work at the same rate, is
    A. 2 1/2   B. 3   C. 4 1/2   D. 6

10. A street is laid to a 3% grade.
This means that in 150 ft., the street grade will rise
    A. 4 1/2 inches   B. 45 inches
    C. 4 1/2 feet   D. 45 feet

11. The sum of the following dimensions, 3 4/8, 4 1/8, 5 1/8, and 6 1/4, is

    A. 19   B. 19 1/8   C. 19 1/4   D. 19 1/2

12. A worker is paid $9.30 per hour.
    If he works 8 hours each day on Monday, Tuesday, and Wednesday, 3 1/2 hours on Thursday, and 3 hours on Friday, the TOTAL amount due him is

    A. $283.65   B. $289.15   C. $276.20   D. $285.35

13. The price of metal lath is $395.00 per 100 square yards. The cost of 527 square yards of this lath is MOST NEARLY

    A. $2,076.50   B. $2,079.10   C. $2,081.70   D. $2,084.30

14. The total cost of applying 221 square yards of plaster board is $3,430.
    The cost per square yard is MOST NEARLY

    A. $14.00   B. $14.50   C. $15.00   D. $15.50

15. In a three-coat plaster job, the scratch coat is 1/8 in. thick in front of the lath, the brown coat is 3/16 in. thick, and the finish coat is 1/8 in. thick.
    The TOTAL thickness of this plaster job, measured from the face of the lath, is

    A. 7/16"   B. 1/2"   C. 9/16"   D. 5/8"

16. If an asphalt worker earns $38,070 per year, his wages per month are MOST NEARLY

    A. $380.70   B. $735.00   C. $3,170.00   D. $3,807.00

17. The sum of 4 1/2 inches, 3 1/4 inches, and 7 1/2 inches is 1 foot _____ inches.

    A. 3   B. 3 1/4   C. 3 1/2   D. 4

18. The area of a rectangular asphalt patch, 9 ft. 3 in. by 6 ft. 9 in., is _____ square feet.

    A. 54   B. 54 1/4   C. 54 1/2   D. 62 7/16

19. The number of cubic feet in a cubic yard is

    A. 3   B. 9   C. 16   D. 27

20. A 450 ft. long street with a grade of 2% will have one end of the street higher than the other end by _____ feet.

    A. 2   B. 44   C. 9   D. 20

21. If the drive wheel of a roller is 6 ft. in diameter and the tiller wheel is 4 ft. in diameter, whenever the drive wheel makes a complete revolution on a straight pass, the tiller wheel makes _____ revolution(s).

    A. 1   B. 1 1/4   C. 1 1/2   D. 2

22. A point on the centerline of a street is marked: Station 42 + 51. Another point on the centerline 30 feet from the first is marked Station 42+81.
    A third should be marked Station

    A. 12+51   B. 42+21   C. 45+51   D. 72+51

23. In twenty minutes, a truck moving with a speed of 30 miles an hour will cover a distance   23.____
    of _____ miles.

    A. 3   B. 5   C. 10   D. 30

24. The number of pounds in a ton is   24.____

    A. 500   B. 1,000   C. 2,000   D. 5,000

25. During his summer vacation, a boy earned $45.00 per day and saved 60% of his earn-   25.____
    ings.
    If he worked 45 days, how much did he save during his vacation?

    A. $15.00   B. $18.00   C. $1,215.00   D. $22.50

KEY (CORRECT ANSWERS)

1. D   11. A
2. C   12. A
3. B   13. C
4. B   14. D
5. C   15. A

6. C   16. C
7. A   17. B
8. B   18. D
9. C   19. D
10. C   20. C

21. C
22. B
23. C
24. C
25. C

SOLUTIONS TO PROBLEMS

1. ($4.60)(2 1/4 lbs.) = $10.35

2. 1 gallon = 8 pints, so 20 pints = 20/8 = 2 1/2 gallons

3. $\dfrac{5}{12}+\dfrac{1}{4}=\dfrac{5}{12}+\dfrac{3}{12}=\dfrac{8}{12}=\dfrac{2}{3}$

4. (4')(5 1/2')(18 1/2') = 407 cu.ft. Since 1 cu.yd. = 27 cu.ft., 407 cu.ft. ≈ 15.1 cu.yds.

5. 5/8 = 5 ÷ 8.000 = .625

6. There are (3)(3)(3) = 27 cu.ft. in a cu.yd.

7. (15')(15') = 225 sq.ft. = 25 sq.yds. Then, ($16.20)(25) = $405.00

8. Let 2x = size of smaller crew and 3x = size of larger crew. Then, 2x + 3x = 30. Solving, x = 6. Thus, the smaller crew consists of 12 workers.

9. (12)(6)(5) = 360 worker-days. Then, 360 ÷ [(10)(8)] = 4 1/2 days

10. (.03)(150') = 4 1/2 ft.

11. $3\dfrac{4}{8}+4\dfrac{1}{8}+5\dfrac{1}{8}+6\dfrac{2}{8}=18\dfrac{8}{8}=19$

12. ($9.30)(8+8+8+3 1/2+3) = ($9.30)(30 1/2) = $283.65

13. The cost of 527 sq.yds. = (5.27)($395.00) = $2081.65 ≈ $2081.70

14. $3430 ÷ 221 ≈ $15.50

15. $\dfrac{1}{8}"+\dfrac{3}{16}"+\dfrac{1}{8}"=\dfrac{2}{16}"+\dfrac{3}{16}"+\dfrac{2}{16}"=\dfrac{7}{16}"$

16. $38,070 ÷ 12 = $3172.50 ≈ $3170.00 per month

17. 4 1/2" + 3 1/4" + 7 1/2" = 15 1/4" = 1 ft. 3 1/4 in.

18. 9 ft. 3 in. = 9 1/4 ft., 6 ft. 9 in. = 6 3/4 ft. Area = (9 1/4)(6 3/4) = 62 7/16 sq.ft.

19. A cubic yard = (3)(3)(3) = 27 cubic feet

20. (450')(.02) = 9 ft.

21. 6/4 = 1 1/2 revolutions

22. Station 42 + 51
    30 ft away would be 51 + 30 = 81 OR 51 - 30 = 21
    Station 42 + 81 or 42 + 21 (ANSWER: B)

23. 30 miles in 60 minutes means 10 miles in 20 minutes.

24. There are 2000 pounds in a ton.

25. ($45.00)(.60) = $27.00 savings per day. For 45 days, his savings is (45)($27.00) = $1215.00

PROGRAM EVALUATION

Table of Contents

	Pages
Program Evaluation Strategy	1
Managing for Success	1
Types of Program Evaluation	1
Judging vs. Coaching	1
Conducting a Program Evaluation	3
The Need for Planning	3
Stage 1 - Evaluability Assessment	3
Performance Measurement	4
Mission, Goals and Objectives	4
Performance Indicators	5
Stage 2 - Designing the Evaluation	6
Stage 3 - Conducting the Study	8
Developing Data Measurement System	8
Determine Data Availability	9
Collecting Data	9
Analyzing Data	10
Data Presentation	10
Refining Measures	10
Stage 4 - Reporting Evaluation Findings	11
Stage 5 - Program Offices Implement Improvement Activities	12
Stage 6 - On-Going Consultation	13

212

PROGRAM EVALUATION

Program Evaluation Strategy

MANAGING FOR SUCCESS

An essential component of any successful organization is its ability to continually assess and evaluate its performance. To establish effective and efficient programs, managers need fundamental information regarding the position and progress of their programs, and what improvements can be made to enhance the overall quality of their operations.

In identifying this need, the PTO's Office of Planning and Evaluation (P&E) has developed an evaluation strategy for the Patent and Trademark Office. Our goal is to support PTO in planning, assessing, and improving its program activities, so that managers have the information and support they need to continually develop and advance their programs.

TYPES OF PROGRAM EVALUATION

Program evaluation is based on the fundamental idea that programs should have a demonstrable benefit.

In its simplest terms, program evaluation is defined as a systematic approach to assessing the performance of a program or service. Program evaluations are most commonly referred to as either summative or formative in nature. Summative evaluations make a judgment about a program's operations and usefulness, whereas formative evaluations describe a program's operations in order to improve the way in which it functions.

In recent years, the formative approach to evaluating has evolved into what has come to be called "evaluation research."

Evaluation research includes:
- Design of programs
- Ongoing monitoring of how well programs are functioning
- Assessment of program impact
- Analysis of benefits relative to costs.

This approach seems to be the most productive. As internal evaluators, our goal is not only to report to managers on their program's current situation, but also assist them in developing and enhancing the resources they need for continual operational improvement.

JUDGING VS. COACHING

In conducting formative evaluations, the goal is not to judge a program's worth or usefulness, rather the goal is to provide recommendations for program improvements in addition to assessing impacts and results.

A program evaluation trainer, uses the example of a world-class figure-skating champion to differentiate the roles of a coach and judge. As a skater performs, both the judge and the coach are meticulously assessing the skaters every move; however, each has a different motive for evaluating the performance. The judge looks at the performance and impassively scores the skater against the competition, providing little, if any, feedback to the skater. The coach on the other hand, goes a step beyond assessing the performance by actually working with the skater to improve his or her performance. The judge's objective is to score the skater's single performance, whereas the coach's objective is to help the skater achieve his or her fullest potential for future performances.

The coaching perspective helps programs become as efficient and effective as possible, while reaching their fullest potential. Using the example, the coach can work with and recommend improvements to the skater, but it is the skater who is responsible for making the improvements and for eventually becoming a guide and example for others that follow. By diagnosing, consulting and informing programs on their performance, we not only help programs gain a better understanding of what works well within their organization, we also maintain PTO's strategic goal of providing our customers with the highest level of quality and service in all aspects of PTO operations.

Conducting a Program Evaluation

In order to be effective, every evaluation must be tailored to the individual program or organization.

The following are stages in conducting a program evaluation. These stages are designed to adapt to individual needs, interests and the stage of development of the organization or program being evaluated.

THE NEED FOR PLANNING

Ideally, a successful evaluation will provide the best information possible on all key issues within a given set of constraints, such as available time, staff and budget resources. This makes it important to consider at the outset that the design of the evaluation needs to be done carefully, since criticism of the findings will likely focus on the methodology used.

Given the constraints we are all under these days, you may very well ask why you should spend precious resources on planning and designing your evaluation. The answer is precisely because of those constraints. In addition to increasing credibility in the product, a careful and sound design:

- increases overall quality,
- contains costs,
- ensures timeliness of findings,
- increases the strength and specificity of findings and recommendations,
- decreases criticism of methodology,
- improves customer satisfaction, and
- results in less resources required to carry out the evaluation.

STAGE 1: EVALUABILITY ASSESSMENT

Program evaluation is essentially a process in which questions are asked about a program or activity and answers are actively sought. In order to have an effective evaluation--which will result in improved program performance--first, the right questions must be asked, and second, the evaluation team must assure that the questions can be accurately answered.

Before conducting any formal evaluation, an evaluability assessment is conducted. The purpose of the evaluability assessment is to identify the program's goals, performance indicators and data sources, which will be used to conduct the evaluation. The evaluability assessment not only answers the question of whether a program can be meaningfully evaluated, but whether the evaluation is likely to contribute to improved program performance.

During the evaluability assessment there is usually a clear indication of whether a program is ready to be evaluated. If the necessary information (goals, objectives, performance measurements, etc.) is available and is identified by the evaluators and intended users as clear, concise and realistic (given resource allocations and restrictions), the evaluation can proceed. However, if the goals, objectives and performance indicators are found to be either underdeveloped or undefined, the program office is advised to first focus on developing or redefining their performance measurements before continuing with the evaluation.

The foremost question is whether or not the program can be evaluated in a meaningful way based on what currently exists.

Program evaluations are generally concerned with whether a program or policy is achieving its intended goal or purpose. Frequently though, the goals and purposes were to attract as much support as possible for the proposed project, but may lack consistency or be too ambitious given the realities of program functions. Programs and policies that do not have clear and consistent goals can not be evaluated for their effectiveness. Thus, uncovering those goals and purposes is generally the starting point of most evaluations. This first stage of an evaluation is necessary to determine whether they can be evaluated.

Program Evaluation Criteria

- Program goals and objectives, important side effects, and priority information needs are well defined.
- Program goals and objectives are plausible.
- Relevant performance data can be obtained.
- The intended users of the evaluation results have agreed on how they will use the information.

Performance Measurement

Performance measurement is a process by which a program objectively measures how it is accomplishing its mission through the delivery of its products, services, or processes. It is a self-assessment, goal-setting, and progress monitoring tool, which provides on-going performance feedback to both management and staff. A good performance measurement system is designed to provide information which helps clarify goals and motivates performance, solves problems, and corrects deviations or alters planned directions.

Performance Measurement is crucial to the overall management of programs because of one basic principle: "What gets measured, gets done."

Mission, Goals and Objectives

The first step in performance measurement is identifying the mission, goals and objectives. The following is a brief description of each:

The mission is the purpose for which a program or organization was created. A mission answers the following questions:

- Who are we?
- What do we do?
- For whom do we do it?
- Why do we do it?

Goals are statements, usually general and abstract, about how the program expects to accomplish its mission. Goals may be quantitative ("Increase production") or qualitative ("Improve worker morale").

> **Tips on Goal Setting**
>
> - Goals may be general or specific and may encompass time spans ranging from a few months to several years.
> - Goals may be set for the entire organization, programs, and individuals.
> - Goals at the various organizational levels must be coordinated if the organization is to achieve its intended overall purpose.
> - There must be coordination of the long-term goals of the organization with the short term goals of departments and programs, and of both of these with the personal goals of workers
> - Involve both management and staff when developing goals.

Objectives are the means for accomplishing goals. They must be quantifiable containing specific statements detailing the desired accomplishments of a program's goals.

> **Rules for Writing Objectives**
>
> - Use a single issue per objective.
>
> - Define measurable objectives using a verb-noun structure ("Increase productivity by 15 percent by fiscal year 2015").
>
> - Specify an expected time for achievement.

Performance Indicators

Once goals and objectives have been established, performance indicators are developed. Performance indicators track and measure whether the goals and objectives have been reached, or how well the program is progressing toward achieving them.

In the classical sense, a performance indicator is defined as a ratio where the output of an effort is divided by the inputs (labor, energy, time, etc.) required to produce it. . For example:

$$\frac{\text{\# of customers helped}}{\text{\# of service reps}}$$

$$\frac{\text{\# of acceptable documents produced}}{\text{hours expanded for documents}}$$

> **Customer Requirements and Stakeholder Requirements** are the Building Blocks for Measurement Ratios. When designing indicators ask the question: How Do We Know We Met Customer Requirements?

Two integral components of performance indicators are effectiveness and efficiency. Effective production is defined as producing the desired results, whereas efficient production is defined as producing the desired outputs with a minimum level of input. Simply stated, effectiveness is doing the right things, and efficiency is doing things right.

Effectiveness and efficiency are both critical measures of performance and success. Organizations can temporarily survive without perfect efficiency, but would most likely die if they were ineffective. When designing performance measurements, it is essential that an organization considers both effectiveness and efficiency. Omitting either would result in performance measurements that provide inaccurate and often costly productivity information.

It bears repeating that if a program has not clearly identified its goals and objectives and set effectiveness and efficiency measures, it will be difficult to evaluate.

Four Criteria for Measurement Effectiveness and Efficiency

1. **Quality-** The measure must define and reflect quality of production or services as well as quantity. A measure that assesses only quantity outputs can lead to reduced productivity.

2. **Mission and goals-** The measure must define and assess only outputs and services that are integrated with the organizational mission and strategic goals. Measures directed to products and services that are not consistent with mission and goals threaten productivity.

3. **Rewards and Incentives-** Measures must be integrated with performance incentives, reward systems and practices. Measures that have no important contingencies will not work to improve productivity.

4. **Employee Involvement-** There must be involvement of employees and other direct stakeholders in the definition and construction of productivity measures. When lack of involvement has not resulted in commitment and buy-in, results from the measures are not likely to be received favorably or to have any impact on future productivity.

STAGE 2: DESIGNING THE EVALUATION

What's worth knowing?
How will we get it?
How will it be used?

By the time you have an idea of the evaluation capacity of your program, you may have the answers to many of the questions that lead to the design. Every question asked by an evaluation can be looked at with varying levels of intensity and thoroughness. When great precision is needed and resources are available, the most powerful of evaluations may be conducted, on the other hand when time and resources are limited and only approximate answers are needed, the level of the evaluation will differ. Given the diversity of programs, policies and projects to be evaluated, the number of questions to be answered, and the differing availability of resources, there can be no single recipe for a successful evaluation. However, these simple guidelines, once tailored, should provide a solid framework for conducting an evaluation.

In determining the design of an evaluation, the following questions are answered and an Evaluation Design Proposal is drafted.

1. Why are we doing this evaluation?

Clarify what the overall purpose of the evaluation is and what specific objectives will be accomplished. Focus not only on what the evaluation will do, but also identify what the evaluation will NOT do.

2. For whom are we doing this evaluation?

It is essential to identify who the audience is so that their needs, perspectives and constraints can be assessed. Identify both the primary audience and secondary audiences.

Who is sponsoring the evaluation? Who is authorizing the expenditure of funds and human resources? Who will be approving the report?

3. What are we evaluating?

Discuss the issues of the evaluation. Are we studying the need for a program or activity? The operations of a program or activity? The effects of a program or activity? Define the specific questions to be answered during the evaluation.

4. How are we doing this evaluation?

Make a list of the information needed to conduct the evaluation. Once the information needs are defined, identify the data collection techniques. Examples of Data Collection Techniques:

- Surveys
- Interviews
- Focus Group Sessions
- Case Studies
- Tests
- Observations
- Document Reviews
- Production Reports
- Computerized databases

5. When are we doing this evaluation?

Establish both the beginning and completion dates and interim deadlines. It may be helpful to set up a project plan to track the dates and resources.

6. Where are we doing this evaluation?

Determine the location of the evaluation. Will a special staff be pulled together? Will they need space for meetings? For working? For storage of files?

7. Who is doing this evaluation?

Assess the skills and resources needed to conduct the evaluation. Identify possible training needs and establish roles and responsibilities for each team member (Hendricks, 1994).

> **Tips on Building an Effective Study Team**
> - Keep teams small.
> - Acknowledge team members' need for high performance.
> - Reward both team leaders and team members.
> - Focus on people, not methodology.
> - Keep a skills inventory of team members.
> - Make use of project management tools to create benchmarks of success.
> - Form a policy group and a work group to involve policy makers, managers, and key staff in the evaluation.

Consider whether the skills and resources are available internally, or whether it might be more economical or beneficial to hire an external contractor to conduct the evaluation. Depending on the nature of the program or project, it may be critical that the results of the evaluation come from an outside, objective source.

One More Thing

After the design is completed, it is helpful to take an overall look at the design.

A well-designed evaluation can usually be recognized by the way it has:

1. Defined and posed questions for study.
2. Developed the methodological strategies for answering those questions.
3. Formulated a data collection plan that anticipates and addresses problems and obstacles that are likely to be encountered.
4. Provided a detailed analysis plan that will ensure that the questions posed will be answered with the appropriate data in the best possible fashion.
5. Established and maintained focus on the usefulness of the product for the intended user.

A sound design reduces downtime deciding what to do next, reduces time spent on collecting and analyzing irrelevant data and strengthens the relevance of the evaluation.

STAGE 3: CONDUCTING THE STUDY

Once the evaluation proposal is drafted and agreed upon by the evaluation team and the evaluation users, the process of collecting and analyzing the relevant data can begin.

DATA COLLECTION AND ANALYSIS

Developing A Data Measurement System

There are two methods of evaluation studies: qualitative and quantitative. Qualitative data collection systems permit the evaluator to study selected issues, cases, or events in depth and detail; data collection is not constrained by predetermined categories of analysis. Quantitative methods use standardized measures that fit diverse opinions and experiences into predetermined response categories. Considering evaluation design alternatives leads directly to consideration of the relative strengths and weaknesses of qualitative and quantitative studies, and the time and resources available for the study.

The advantage of the quantitative approach is that it measures the reactions of a great many people to a limited set of questions, thus facilitating comparison and statistical aggregation of the data. It gives a broad, generalized set of findings. Qualitative methods typically produce a wealth of detailed data about a much smaller number of people and cases. Qualitative data provide depth and detail through direct quotation and careful description of program situations, events, people, interactions, and observed behaviors.

Purposes and functions of qualitative and quantitative data are different, yet can be complementary. The statistics from standardized items make summaries, comparisons, and generalizations quite easy and precise. The narrative comments from open-ended questions are typically meant to provide a forum for elaboration, explanations, meanings, and new ideas.

It is recommended that an evaluation team engage stakeholders early because they have a different perspective, have data the evaluator needs, and can influence the evaluation positively if they are engaged, or negatively if they are ignored or threatened.

Categorizing research questions into major categories can help refine the research agenda of almost any study. Time spent in developing a detailed research design, data collection and analysis plan may improve the quality of the overall results.

Stakeholders include potential users of evaluation information and those with an investment in the organization or unit involved in the study.

Determine Data Availability

Once it has been established what to measure, it must be determined if the data for those measures is available and how to get it. If data is not available, alternative indicators must be identified.

The evaluation team should try to keep its indicators simple and use existing data whenever possible. However, do not compromise the evaluation by discarding indicators the team thinks are meaningful and important before weighing their obtainability.

    Data Availability Concerns

1. Does the data currently exist ? If not, can it be developed, and at what effort and cost?
2. If the data exists, what will it cost to retrieve the data?
3. What will it take to get the data converted into the established measurement values?
4. Will a system investment be required? At what cost?
5. Will management support this level of cost? Can a limited version be used?
6. When will data be produced?

Collecting Data

The collection of data addresses the critical issues of making sure the correct data is identified, and a baseline is collected. The baseline data reflects the initial status of the program or process. During this phase, in addition to documenting the method of collection of the data, document any problems with the process, and work to resolve any process problems regularly. Meet with management at the end of an established trial period to evaluate results.

Analyzing Data

Once we have collected the data and before we meet with management, we must analyze the data to make sure that it will provide us with enough information and the right type of information on which to base an evaluation. We must ensure that the data fits the indicators identified to analyze. Agree to finalize the current indicators or revise them as needed, and analyze the baseline data collected for the purpose of setting goals.

DATA PRESENTATION

Once the data has been collected and analyzed, it must be decided how the data and results will be presented. Numbers by themselves are often difficult to understand, they cannot explain circumstances, and they may not easily lead to conclusions. Therefore, it is important to present the information in ways that make it easy to understand, that show relationships to other data, and that allow the information to be used to support decision-making processes. Whenever possible, use graphical tools to present data.

Measures must be shown in context. The most frequent evaluation contexts are: (1) goals compared to actual results, (2) trends in relation to previous periodic results, and (3) comparison of results to other relevant data. Using one or more of these contexts, meaningful conclusions should be drawn about the measurement result with little or no explanation.

REFINING MEASURES

Indicators may need some slight modifications or adjustment to better meet performance information needs of program or executive management. Continually check the usefulness of measurement data and adjust data collection methods if necessary.

Adjusting Measures

Are the measures working well?
What are the measures indicating?
Are additional indicators necessary?
Is data not really available (too difficult or expensive to acquire)?
Is data too difficult to use?

Balance Types Of Measures

One consideration of performance indicator development is that measures are interrelated and cannot be viewed in isolation. Timeliness, quality and cost are always in contention with each other, and the impact of improving any one or two must be weighed in relation to the expense of the third. A balance must be reached between the effectiveness and the economy and efficiency.

Consider Weighting Measures

Not all indicators are equally important. To reflect importance or priorities within measures or categories of measures, weight or index the measures. Weighting or indexing measures is an involved and advanced process and may not be necessary or appropriate for every program. However, weighting measures can provide some valuable insights into program outcomes.

Integrating with Management Process

Once performance results become available, the challenge shifts to presenting and using them effectively.

Establish Goals

Goals should be established based on: (1) policy or administrative priorities, (2) mission (3) customer feedback, (4) past history, (5) forecasted demand and (6) benchmark information.

Determine What The Measurements Say

It is extremely important to understand what the measurements say, as well as what they do not say. The measurements must be compared to performance goals, benchmarks, or past performance. Then variances or changes must be analyzed, and subsequent actions must be planned. In addition to program performance evaluation, the measurement results in the evaluation process can be used for external reporting, planning and budgeting activities and performance appraisal evaluation.

STAGE 4: REPORTING EVALUATION RESULTS

Reporting evaluation results is more of a process than a stage. Beginning on the first day of the evaluation, the evaluators should be continually reporting and discussing their findings with the evaluation users. It is not only important to keep them updated on the evaluation's progress, but also, it is important to keep them informed of any findings and recommendations that can be implemented before the full completion of the evaluation. Remember, the reason for doing an evaluation is to help an organization or program become as effective and efficient as possible. The sooner an organization can implement changes or improvements, the better.

Action-Oriented Reporting

As stated previously, the purpose of an evaluation is to improve a program or an organization's performance. The way in which evaluators do this is by providing recommendations for improvement to management and staff.

The majority of an evaluation report should be devoted to communicating the findings and specific recommendations. Reports should be action-oriented, centered mostly around the findings, but also around the recommendations and suggestions for implementation.

Action-oriented reports are often structured as a series of short reports targeted to specific audiences, rather than one all inclusive document.

Findings and recommendations should be presented clearly and concisely, in a way that meets the informational needs of the audience. In order for recommendations to be accepted by an organization, it must first understand what is being recommended and why it is relevant to their concerns. Evaluation studies are only useful if they are used.

Program Evaluation Report

Generally, an evaluation report should include:
- Executive Summary
  Purpose of Evaluation
  Program Background
  Evaluation Methodology
- Analysis of the Findings
- Recommendations

Tips for Reporting Evaluation Results

- Remember that the burden for effectively reporting results is on the evaluators, not the audience.
- Be aggressive. Instead of waiting for audiences to request information, actively look for opportunities to report results. Report regularly and frequently, appear in person if at all possible, and target multiple reports and briefings to specific audiences and /or issues.

- Simplify, simplify! Audiences are usually busy and their interest is pulled in different directions, so determine and report on the key points. If the core message creates interest, quickly follow up with more details.

- Study the audience. Learn about their backgrounds, interests, concerns, plans, pet peeves, etc.

- Focus on actions. Audiences are rarely interested in general information; they usually want guidance that will help them decide what to do next.

- Report in many different ways. Rather than using only one reporting technique or another, produce several different types of reports. Use written reports, personal briefings, screen show presentations, etc.

STAGE 5: PROGRAM OFFICES IMPLEMENT IMPROVEMENT ACTIVITIES

In this phase of the evaluation process, program office managers implement and monitor the recommendations and action plans originating from the evaluation study. The program manager facilitates the solution of problems by motivating staff and providing technical support. Particular attention must be given to customer and stakeholder requirements.

All employees should be trained in the process improvement recommendations so that they will possess the skills needed to recommend solutions to future problems. Decisions made closer to the customer and occurrence of events save time, reduce errors, and improve morale and service.

STAGE 6: ON-GOING CONSULTATION

Program evaluation is a continuous process of measuring, analyzing and refining an organization or program's performance.

A program evaluation is not an end in itself, rather it is the beginning of a continuous self-evaluation mechanism. With an effective evaluation comes additional data, refined measurements and new initiatives. In order to remain effective, organizations must continually evaluate this information to ensure the achievement of their mission, goals, and objectives.

PHILOSOPHY, PRINCIPLES, PRACTICES, AND TECHNICS OF SUPERVISION, ADMINISTRATION, MANAGEMENT, AND ORGANIZATION

TABLE OF CONTENTS

	Page
MEANING OF SUPERVISION	1
THE OLD AND THE NEW SUPERVISION	1
THE EIGHT (8) BASIC PRINCIPLES OF THE NEW SUPERVISION	1
I. Principle of Responsibility	1
II. Principle of Authority	2
III. Principle of Self-Growth	2
IV. Principle of Individual Worth	2
V. Principle of Creative Leadership	2
VI. Principle of Success and Failure	2
VII. Principle of Science	3
VIII. Principle of Cooperation	3
WHAT IS ADMINISTRATION?	3
I. Practices Commonly Classed as "Supervisory"	3
II. Practices Commonly Classed as "Administrative"	3
III. Practices Commonly Classed as Both "Supervisory" and "Administrative"	4
RESPONSIBILITIES OF THE SUPERVISOR	4
COMPETENCIES OF THE SUPERVISOR	4
THE PROFESSIONAL SUPERVISOR-EMPLOYEE RELATIONSHIP	4
MINI-TEXT IN SUPERVISION, ADMINISTRATION, MANAGEMENT, AND ORGANIZATION	5
I. Brief Highlights	5
A. Levels of Management	6
B. What the Supervisor Must Learn	6
C. A Definition of Supervision	6
D. Elements of the Team Concept	6
E. Principles of Organization	6
F. The Four Important Parts of Every Job	7
G. Principles of Delegation	7
H. Principles of Effective Communications	7
I. Principles of Work Improvement	7
J. Areas of Job Improvement	7
K. Seven Key Points in Making Improvements	8

L.	Corrective Techniques for Job Improvement	8
M.	A Planning Checklist	8
N.	Five Characteristics of Good Directions	9
O.	Types of Directions	9
P.	Controls	9
Q.	Orienting the New Employee	9
R.	Checklist for Orienting New Employees	9
S.	Principles of Learning	10
T.	Causes of Poor Performance	10
U.	Four Major Steps in On-the-Job Instructions	10
V.	Employees Want Five Things	10
W.	Some Don'ts in Regard to Praise	11
X.	How to Gain Your Workers' Confidence	11
Y.	Sources of Employee Problems	11
Z.	The Supervisor's Key to Discipline	11
AA.	Five Important Processes of Management	12
BB.	When the Supervisor Fails to Plan	12
CC.	Fourteen General Principles of Management	12
DD.	Change	12

II. Brief Topical Summaries 13
    A. Who/What is the Supervisor?   13
    B. The Sociology of Work   13
    C. Principles and Practices of Supervision   14
    D. Dynamic Leadership   14
    E. Processes for Solving Problems   15
    F. Training for Results   15
    G. Health, Safety, and Accident Prevention   16
    H. Equal Employment Opportunity   16
    I. Improving Communications   16
    J. Self-Development   17
    K. Teaching and Training   17
        1. The Teaching Process   17
            a. Preparation   17
            b. Presentation   18
            c. Summary   18
            d. Application   18
            e. Evaluation   18
        2. Teaching Methods   18
            a. Lecture   18
            b. Discussion   18
            c. Demonstration   19
            d. Performance   19
            e. Which Method to Use   19

PHILOSOPHY, PRINCIPLES, PRACTICES, AND TECHNICS
OF
SUPERVISION, ADMINISTRATION, MANAGEMENT, AND ORGANIZATION

MEANING OF SUPERVISION

The extension of the democratic philosophy has been accompanied by an extension in the scope of supervision. Modern leaders and supervisors no longer think of supervision in the narrow sense of being confined chiefly to visiting employees, supplying materials, or rating the staff. They regard supervision as being intimately related to all the concerned agencies of society, they speak of the supervisor's function in terms of "growth," rather than the "improvement" of employees.

This modern concept of supervision may be defined as follows: Supervision is leadership and the development of leadership within groups which are cooperatively engaged in inspection, research, training, guidance, and evaluation.

THE OLD AND THE NEW SUPERVISION

TRADITIONAL
1. Inspection
2. Focused on the employee
3. Visitation
4. Random and haphazard
5. Imposed and authoritarian
6. One person usually

MODERN
1. Study and analysis
2. Focused on aims, materials, methods, supervisors, employees, environment
3. Demonstrations, intervisitation, workshops, directed reading, bulletins, etc.
4. Definitely organized and planned (scientific)
5. Cooperative and democratic
6. Many persons involved (creative)

THE EIGHT (8) BASIC PRINCIPLES OF THE NEW SUPERVISION

I. Principle of Responsibility
   Authority to act and responsibility for acting must be joined.
   A. If you give responsibility, give authority.
   B. Define employee duties clearly.
   C. Protect employees from criticism by others.
   D. Recognize the rights as well as obligations of employees.
   E. Achieve the aims of a democratic society insofar as it is possible within the area of your work.
   F. Establish a situation favorable to training and learning.
   G. Accept ultimate responsibility for everything done in your section, unit, office, division, department.
   H. Good administration and good supervision are inseparable.

II. Principle of Authority
The success of the supervisor is measured by the extent to which the power of authority is not used.
   A. Exercise simplicity and informality in supervision
   B. Use the simplest machinery of supervision
   C. If it is good for the organization as a whole, it is probably justified.
   D. Seldom be arbitrary or authoritative.
   E. Do not base your work on the power of position or of personality.
   F. Permit and encourage the free expression of opinions.

III. Principle of Self-Growth
The success of the supervisor is measured by the extent to which, and the speed with which, he is no longer needed.
   A. Base criticism on principles, not on specifics.
   B. Point out higher activities to employees.
   C. Train for self-thinking by employees to meet new situations.
   D. Stimulate initiative, self-reliance, and individual responsibility
   E. Concentrate on stimulating the growth of employees rather than on removing defects.

IV. Principle of Individual Worth
Respect for the individual is a paramount consideration in supervision.
   A. Be human and sympathetic in dealing with employees.
   B. Don't nag about things to be done.
   C. Recognize the individual differences among employees and seek opportunities to permit best expression of each personality.

V. Principle of Creative Leadership
The best supervision is that which is not apparent to the employee.
   A. Stimulate, don't drive employees to creative action.
   B. Emphasize doing good things.
   C. Encourage employees to do what they do best.
   D. Do not be too greatly concerned with details of subject or method.
   E. Do not be concerned exclusively with immediate problems and activities.
   F. Reveal higher activities and make them both desired and maximally possible.
   G. Determine procedures in the light of each situation but see that these are derived from a sound basic philosophy.
   H. Aid, inspire, and lead so as to liberate the creative spirit latent in all good employees.

VI. Principle of Success and Failure
There are no unsuccessful employees, only unsuccessful supervisors who have failed to give proper leadership.
   A. Adapt suggestions to the capacities, attitudes, and prejudices of employees.
   B. Be gradual, be progressive, be persistent.
   C. Help the employee find the general principle; have the employee apply his own problem to the general principle.
   D. Give adequate appreciation for good work and honest effort.
   E. Anticipate employee difficulties and help to prevent them.
   F. Encourage employees to do the desirable things they will do anyway.
   G. Judge your supervision by the results it secures.

VII. Principle of Science
Successful supervision is scientific, objective, and experimental. It is based on facts, not on prejudices.
- A. Be cumulative in results.
- B. Never divorce your suggestions from the goals of training.
- C. Don't be impatient of results.
- D. Keep all matters on a professional, not a personal, level.
- E. Do not be concerned exclusively with immediate problems and activities.
- F. Use objective means of determining achievement and rating where possible.

VIII. Principle of Cooperation
Supervision is a cooperative enterprise between supervisor and employee.
- A. Begin with conditions as they are.
- B. Ask opinions of all involved when formulating policies.
- C. Organization is as good as its weakest link.
- D. Let employees help to determine policies and department programs.
- E. Be approachable and accessible—physically and mentally.
- F. Develop pleasant social relationships.

WHAT IS ADMINISTRATION

Administration is concerned with providing the environment, the material facilities, and the operational procedures that will promote the maximum growth and development of supervisors and employees. (Organization is an aspect and a concomitant of administration.)

There is no sharp line of demarcation between supervision and administration; these functions are intimately interrelated and, often, overlapping. They are complementary activities.

I. Practices Commonly Classed as "Supervisory"
- A. Conducting employees' conferences
- B. Visiting sections, units, offices, divisions, departments
- C. Arranging for demonstrations
- D. Examining plans
- E. Suggesting professional reading
- F. Interpreting bulletins
- G. Recommending in-service training courses
- H. Encouraging experimentation
- I. Appraising employee morale
- J. Providing for intervisitation

II. Practices Commonly Classified as "Administrative"
- A. Management of the office
- B. Arrangement of schedules for extra duties
- C. Assignment of rooms or areas
- D. Distribution of supplies
- E. Keeping records and reports
- F. Care of audio-visual materials
- G. Keeping inventory records
- H. Checking record cards and books

I. Programming special activities
J. Checking on the attendance and punctuality of employees

III. Practices Commonly Classified as Both "Supervisory" and "Administrative"
A. Program construction
B. Testing or evaluating outcomes
C. Personnel accounting
D. Ordering instructional materials

RESPONSIBILITIES OF THE SUPERVISOR

A person employed in a supervisory capacity must constantly be able to improve his own efficiency and ability. He represent the employer to the employees and only continuous self-examination can make him a capable supervisor.

Leadership and training are the supervisor's responsibility. An efficient working unit is one in which the employees work with the supervisor. It is his job to bring out the best in his employees. He must always be relaxed, courteous, and calm in his association with his employees. Their feelings are important, and a harsh attitude does not develop the most efficient employees.

COMPETENCES OF THE SUPERVISOR

I. Complete knowledge of the duties and responsibilities of his position.
II. To be able to organize a job, plan ahead, and carry through.
III. To have self-confidence and initiative.
IV. To be able to handle the unexpected situation and make quick decisions.
V. To be able to properly train subordinates in the positions they are best suited for.
VI. To be able to keep good human relations among his subordinates.
VII. To be able to keep good human relations between his subordinates and himself and to earn their respect and trust.

THE PROFESSIONAL SUPERVISOR-EMPLOYEE RELATIONSHIP

There are two kinds of efficiency: one kind is only apparent and is produced in organizations through the exercise of mere discipline; this is but a simulation of the second, or true, efficiency which springs from spontaneous cooperation. If you are a manager, no matter how great or small your responsibility, it is your job, in the final analysis, to create and develop this involuntary cooperation among the people whom you supervise. For, no matter how powerful a combination of money, machines, and materials a company may have, this is a dead and sterile thing without a team of willing, thinking, and articulate people to guide it.

The following 21 points are presented as indicative of the exemplary basic relationship that should exist between supervisor and employee:

1. Each person wants to be liked and respected by his fellow employee and wants to be treated with consideration and respect by his superior.
2. The most competent employee will make an error. However, in a unit where good relations exist between the supervisor and his employees, tenseness and fear do not exist. Thus, errors are not hidden or covered up, and the efficiency of a unit is not impaired.

3. Subordinates resent rules, regulations, or orders that are unreasonable or unexplained.
4. Subordinates are quick to resent unfairness, harshness, injustices, and favoritism.
5. An employee will accept responsibility if he knows that he will be complimented for a job well done, and not too harshly chastised for failure; that his supervisor will check the cause of the failure, and, if it was the supervisor's fault, he will assume the blame therefore. If it was the employee's fault, his supervisor will explain the correct method or means of handling the responsibility.
6. An employee wants to receive credit for a suggestion he has made, that is used. If a suggestion cannot be used, the employee is entitled to an explanation. The supervisor should not say "no" and close the subject.
7. Fear and worry slow up a worker's ability. Poor working environment can impair his physical and mental health. A good supervisor avoids forceful methods, threats, and arguments to get a job done.
8. A forceful supervisor is able to train his employees individually and as a team, and is able to motivate them in the proper channels.
9. A mature supervisor is able to properly evaluate his subordinates and to keep them happy and satisfied.
10. A sensitive supervisor will never patronize his subordinates.
11. A worthy supervisor will respect his employees' confidences.
12. Definite and clear-cut responsibilities should be assigned to each executive.
13. Responsibility should always be coupled with corresponding authority.
14. No change should be made in the scope or responsibilities of a position without a definite understanding to that effect on the part of all persons concerned.
15. No executive or employee, occupying a single position in the organization, should be subject to definite orders from more than one source.
16. Orders should never be given to subordinates over the head of a responsible executive. Rather than do this, the officer in question should be supplanted.
17. Criticisms of subordinates should, whoever possible, be made privately, and in no case should a subordinate be criticized in the presence of executives or employees of equal or lower rank.
18. No dispute or difference between executives or employees as to authority or responsibilities should be considered too trivial for prompt and careful adjudication.
19. Promotions, wage changes, and disciplinary action should always be approved by the executive immediately superior to the one directly responsible.
20. No executive or employee should ever be required, or expected, to be at the same time an assistant to, and critic of, another.
21. Any executive whose work is subject to regular inspection should, wherever practicable, be given the assistance and facilities necessary to enable him to maintain an independent check of the quality of his work.

MINI-TEXT IN SUPERVISION, ADMINISTRATION, MANAGEMENT, AND ORGANIZATION

I. Brief Highlights

Listed concisely and sequentially are major headings and important data in the field for quick recall and review.

A. Levels of Management
Any organization of some size has several levels of management. In terms of a ladder, the levels are:

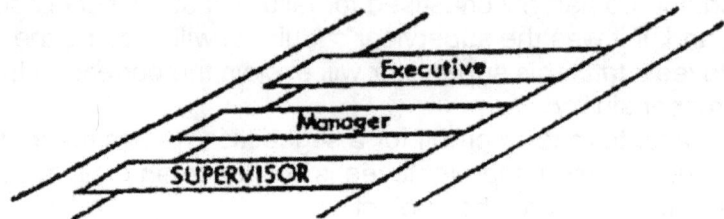

The first level is very important because it is the beginning point of management leadership.

B. What the Supervisor Must Learn
A supervisor must learn to:
1. Deal with people and their differences
2. Get the job done through people
3. Recognize the problems when they exist
4. Overcome obstacles to good performance
5. Evaluate the performance of people
6. Check his own performance in terms of accomplishment

C. A Definition of Supervisor
The term supervisor means any individual having authority, in the interests of the employer, to hire, transfer, suspend, lay-off, recall, promote, discharge, assign, reward, or discipline other employees or responsibility to direct them, or to adjust their grievances, or effectively to recommend such action, if, in connection with the foregoing, exercise of such authority is not of a merely routine or clerical nature but requires the use of independent judgment.

D. Elements of the Team Concept
What is involved in teamwork? The component parts are:
1. Members
2. A leader
3. Goals
4. Plans
5. Cooperation
6. Spirit

E. Principles of Organization
1. A team member must know what his job is.
2. Be sure that the nature and scope of a job are understood.
3. Authority and responsibility should be carefully spelled out.
4. A supervisor should be permitted to make the maximum number of decisions affecting his employees.
5. Employees should report to only one supervisor.
6. A supervisor should direct only as many employees as he can handle effectively.
7. An organization plan should be flexible.

8. Inspection and performance of work should be separate.
9. Organizational problems should receive immediate attention.
10. Assign work in line with ability and experience.

F. The Four Important Parts of Every Job
1. Inherent in every job is the *accountability* for results.
2. A second set of factors in every job is *responsibilities*.
3. Along with duties and responsibilities one must have the *authority* to act within certain limits without obtaining permission to proceed.
4. No job exists in a vacuum. The supervisor is surrounded by key *relationships*.

G. Principles of Delegation
Where work is delegated for the first time, the supervisor should think in terms of these questions:
1. Who is best qualified to do this?
2. Can an employee improve his abilities by doing this?
3. How long should an employee spend on this?
4. Are there any special problems for which he will need guidance?
5. How broad a delegation can I make?

H. Principles of Effective Communications
1. Determine the media.
2. To whom directed?
3. Identification and source authority.
4. Is communication understood?

I. Principles of Work Improvement
1. Most people usually do only the work which is assigned to them.
2. Workers are likely to fit assigned work into the time available to perform it.
3. A good workload usually stimulates output.
4. People usually do their best work when they know that results will be reviewed or inspected.
5. Employees usually feel that someone else is responsible for conditions of work, workplace layout, job methods, type of tools/equipment, and other such factors.
6. Employees are usually defensive about their job security.
7. Employees have natural resistance to change.
8. Employees can support or destroy a supervisor.
9. A supervisor usually earns the respect of his people through his personal example of diligence and efficiency.

J. Areas of Job Improvement
The areas of job improvement are quite numerous, but the most common ones which a supervisor can identify and utilize are:
1. Departmental layout
2. Flow of work
3. Workplace layout
4. Utilization of manpower
5. Work methods
6. Materials handling

7. Utilization
8. Motion economy

K. Seven Key Points in Making Improvements
1. Select the job to be improved
2. Study how it is being done now
3. Question the present method
4. Determine actions to be taken
5. Chart proposed method
6. Get approval and apply
7. Solicit worker participation

L. Corrective Techniques of Job Improvement
Specific Problems
1. Size of workload
2. Inability to meet schedules
3. Strain and fatigue
4. Improper use of men and skills
5. Waste, poor quality, unsafe conditions
6. Bottleneck conditions that hinder output
7. Poor utilization of equipment and machine
8. Efficiency and productivity of labor

General Improvement
1. Departmental layout
2. Flow of work
3. Work plan layout
4. Utilization of manpower
5. Work methods
6. Materials handling
7. Utilization of equipment
8. Motion economy

Corrective Techniques
1. Study with scale model
2. Flow chart study
3. Motion analysis
4. Comparison of units produced to standard allowance
5. Methods analysis
6. Flow chart and equipment study
7. Down time vs. running time
8. Motion analysis

M. A Planning Checklist
1. Objectives
2. Controls
3. Delegations
4. Communications
5. Resources
6. Manpower

7. Equipment
8. Supplies and materials
9. Utilization of time
10. Safety
11. Money
12. Work
13. Timing of improvements

N. Five Characteristics of Good Directions
In order to get results, directions must be:
1. Possible of accomplishment
2. Agreeable with worker interests
3. Related to mission
4. Planned and complete
5. Unmistakably clear

O. Types of Directions
1. Demands or direct orders
2. Requests
3. Suggestion or implication
4. volunteering

P. Controls
A typical listing of the overall areas in which the supervisor should establish controls might be:
1. Manpower
2. Materials
3. Quality of work
4. Quantity of work
5. Time
6. Space
7. Money
8. Methods

Q. Orienting the New Employee
1. Prepare for him
2. Welcome the new employee
3. Orientation for the job
4. Follow-up

R. Checklist for Orienting New Employees   Yes No
1. Do you appreciate the feelings of new employees when they first report for work? ___ ___
2. Are you aware of the fact that the new employee must make a big adjustment to his job? ___ ___
3. Have you given him good reasons for liking the job and the organization? ___ ___
4. Have you prepared for his first day on the job? ___ ___
5. Did you welcome him cordially and make him feel needed? ___ ___

	Yes	No

6. Did you establish rapport with him so that he feels free to talk and discuss matters with you? ___ ___
7. Did you explain his job to him and his relationship to you? ___ ___
8. Does he know that his work will be evaluated periodically on a basis that is fair and objective? ___ ___
9. Did you introduce him to his fellow workers in such a way that they are likely to accept him? ___ ___
10. Does he know what employee benefits he will receive? ___ ___
11. Does he understand the importance of being on the job and what to do if he must leave his duty station? ___ ___
12. Has he been impressed with the importance of accident prevention and safe practice? ___ ___
13. Does he generally know his way around the department? ___ ___
14. Is he under the guidance of a sponsor who will teach the right way of doing things? ___ ___
15. Do you plan to follow-up so that he will continue to adjust successfully to his job? ___ ___

S. Principles of Learning
1. Motivation
2. Demonstration or explanation
3. Practice

T. Causes of Poor Performance
1. Improper training for job
2. Wrong tools
3. Inadequate directions
4. Lack of supervisory follow-up
5. Poor communications
6. Lack of standards of performance
7. Wrong work habits
8. Low morale
9. Other

U. Four Major Steps in On-The-Job Instruction
1. Prepare the worker
2. Present the operation
3. Tryout performance
4. Follow-up

V. Employees Want Five Things
1. Security
2. Opportunity
3. Recognition
4. Inclusion
5. Expression

W. Some Don'ts in Regard to Praise
1. Don't praise a person for something he hasn't done.
2. Don't praise a person unless you can be sincere.
3. Don't be sparing in praise just because your superior withholds it from you.
4. Don't let too much time elapse between good performance and recognition of it

X. How to Gain Your Workers' Confidence
Methods of developing confidence include such things as:
1. Knowing the interests, habits, hobbies of employees
2. Admitting your own inadequacies
3. Sharing and telling of confidence in others
4. Supporting people when they are in trouble
5. Delegating matters that can be well handled
6. Being frank and straightforward about problems and working conditions
7. Encouraging others to bring their problems to you
8. Taking action on problems which impede worker progress

Y. Sources of Employee Problems
On-the-job causes might be such things as:
1. A feeling that favoritism is exercised in assignments
2. Assignment of overtime
3. An undue amount of supervision
4. Changing methods or systems
5. Stealing of ideas or trade secrets
6. Lack of interest in job
7. Threat of reduction in force
8. Ignorance or lack of communications
9. Poor equipment
10. Lack of knowing how supervisor feels toward employee
11. Shift assignments

Off-the-job problems might have to do with:
1. Health
2. Finances
3. Housing
4. Family

Z. The Supervisor's Key to Discipline
There are several key points about discipline which the supervisor should keep in mind:
1. Job discipline is one of the disciplines of life and is directed by the supervisor.
2. It is more important to correct an employee fault than to fix blame for it.
3. Employee performance is affected by problems both on the job and off.
4. Sudden or abrupt changes in behavior can be indications of important employee problems.
5. Problems should be dealt with as soon as possible after they are identified.
6. The attitude of the supervisor may have more to do with solving problems than the techniques of problem solving.
7. Correction of employee behavior should be resorted to only after the supervisor is sure that training or counseling will not be helpful.

8. Be sure to document your disciplinary actions.
9. Make sure that you are disciplining on the basis of facts rather than personal feelings.
10. Take each disciplinary step in order, being careful not to make snap judgments, or decisions based on impatience.

AA. Five Important Processes of Management
1. Planning
2. Organizing
3. Scheduling
4. Controlling
5. Motivating

BB. When the Supervisor Fails to Plan
1. Supervisor creates impression of not knowing his job
2. May lead to excessive overtime
3. Job runs itself—supervisor lacks control
4. Deadlines and appointments missed
5. Parts of the work go undone
6. Work interrupted by emergencies
7. Sets a bad example
8. Uneven workload creates peaks and valleys
9. Too much time on minor details at expense of more important tasks

CC. Fourteen General Principles of Management
1. Division of work
2. Authority and responsibility
3. Discipline
4. Unity of command
5. Unity of direction
6. Subordination of individual interest to general interest
7. Remuneration of personnel
8. Centralization
9. Scalar chain
10. Order
11. Equity
12. Stability of tenure of personnel
13. Initiative
14. Esprit de corps

DD. Change

Bringing about change is perhaps attempted more often, and yet less well understood, than anything else the supervisor does. How do people generally react to change? (People tend to resist change that is imposed upon them by other individuals or circumstances.

Change is characteristic of every situation. It is a part of every real endeavor where the efforts of people are concerned.

13

1. Why do people resist change?
   People may resist change because of:
   a. Fear of the unknown
   b. Implied criticism
   c. Unpleasant experiences in the past
   d. Fear of loss of status
   e. Threat to the ego
   f. Fear of loss of economic stability

2. How can we best overcome the resistance to change?
   In initiating change, take these steps:
   a. Get ready to sell
   b. Identify sources of help
   c. Anticipate objections
   d. Sell benefits
   e. Listen in depth
   f. Follow up

II. Brief Topical Summaries

   A. Who/What is the Supervisor?
      1. The supervisor is often called the "highest level employee and the lowest level manager."
      2. A supervisor is a member of both management and the work group. He acts as a bridge between the two.
      3. Most problems in supervision are in the area of human relations, or people problems.
      4. Employees expect: Respect, opportunity to learn and to advance, and a sense of belonging, and so forth.
      5. Supervisors are responsible for directing people and organizing work. Planning is of paramount importance.
      6. A position description is a set of duties and responsibilities inherent to a given position.
      7. It is important to keep the position description up-to-date and to provide each employee with his own copy.

   B. The Sociology of Work
      1. People are alike in many ways; however, each individual is unique.
      2. The supervisor is challenged in getting to know employee differences. Acquiring skills in evaluating individuals is an asset.
      3. Maintaining meaningful working relationships in the organization is of great importance.
      4. The supervisor has an obligation to help individuals to develop to their fullest potential.
      5. Job rotation on a planned basis helps to build versatility and to maintain interest and enthusiasm in work groups.
      6. Cross training (job rotation) provides backup skills.

7. The supervisor can help reduce tension by maintaining a sense of humor, providing guidance to employees, and by making reasonable and timely decisions. Employees respond favorably to working under reasonably predictable circumstances.
8. Change is characteristic of all managerial behavior. The supervisor must adjust to changes in procedures, new methods, technological changes, and to a number of new and sometimes challenging situations.
9. To overcome the natural tendency for people to resist change, the supervisor should become more skillful in initiating change.

C. Principles and Practices of Supervision
1. Employees should be required to answer to only one superior.
2. A supervisor can effectively direct only a limited number of employees, depending upon the complexity, variety, and proximity of the jobs involved.
3. The organizational chart presents the organization in graphic form. It reflects lines of authority and responsibility as well as interrelationships of units within the organization.
4. Distribution of work can be improved through an analysis using the "Work Distribution Chart."
5. The "Work Distribution Chart" reflects the division of work within a unit in understandable form.
6. When related tasks are given to an employee, he has a better chance of increasing his skills through training.
7. The individual who is given the responsibility for tasks must also be given the appropriate authority to insure adequate results.
8. The supervisor should delegate repetitive, routine work. Preparation of recurring reports, maintaining leave and attendance records are some examples.
9. Good discipline is essential to good task performance. Discipline is reflected in the actions of employees on the job in the absence of supervision.
10. Disciplinary action may have to be taken when the positive aspects of discipline have failed. Reprimand, warning, and suspension are examples of disciplinary action.
11. If a situation calls for a reprimand, be sure it is deserved and remember it is to be done in private.

D. Dynamic Leadership
1. A style is a personal method or manner of exerting influence.
2. Authoritarian leaders often see themselves as the source of power and authority.
3. The democratic leader often perceives the group as the source of authority and power.
4. Supervisors tend to do better when using the pattern of leadership that is most natural for them.
5. Social scientists suggest that the effective supervisor use the leadership style that best fits the problem or circumstances involved.
6. All four styles—telling, selling, consulting, joining—have their place. Using one does not preclude using the other at another time.

7. The theory X point of view assumes that the average person dislikes work, will avoid it whenever possible, and must be coerced to achieve organizational objectives.
8. The theory Y point of view assumes that the average person considers work to be a natural as play, and, when the individual is committed, he requires little supervision or direction to accomplish desired objectives.
9. The leader's basic assumptions concerning human behavior and human nature affect his actions, decisions, and other managerial practices.
10. Dissatisfaction among employees is often present, but difficult to isolate. The supervisor should seek to weaken dissatisfaction by keeping promises, being sincere and considerate, keeping employees informed, and so forth.
11. Constructive suggestions should be encouraged during the natural progress of the work.

E. Processes for Solving Problems
1. People find their daily tasks more meaningful and satisfying when they can improve them.
2. The causes of problems, or the key factors, are often hidden in the background. Ability to solve problems often involves the ability to isolate them from their backgrounds. There is some substance to the cliché that some persons "can't see the forest for the trees."
3. New procedures are often developed from old ones. Problems should be broken down into manageable parts. New ideas can be adapted from old one.
4. People think differently in problem-solving situations. Using a logical, patterned approach is often useful. One approach found to be useful includes these steps:
   a. Define the problem
   b. Establish objectives
   c. Get the facts
   d. Weigh and decide
   e. Take action
   f. Evaluate action

F. Training for Results
1. Participants respond best when they feel training is important to them.
2. The supervisor has responsibility for the training and development of those who report to him.
3. When training is delegated to others, great care must be exercised to insure the trainer has knowledge, aptitude, and interest for his work as a trainer.
4. Training (learning) of some type goes on continually. The most successful supervisor makes certain the learning contributes in a productive manner to operational goals.
5. New employees are particularly susceptible to training. Older employees facing new job situations require specific training, as well as having need for development and growth opportunities.
6. Training needs require continuous monitoring.
7. The training officer of an agency is a professional with a responsibility to assist supervisors in solving training problems.

8. Many of the self-development steps important to the supervisor's own growth are equally important to the development of peers and subordinates. Knowledge of these is important when the supervisor consults with others on development and growth opportunities.

G. Health, Safety, and Accident Prevention
1. Management-minded supervisors take appropriate measures to assist employees in maintaining health and in assuring safe practices in the work environment.
2. Effective safety training and practices help to avoid injury and accidents.
3. Safety should be a management goal. All infractions of safety which are observed should be corrected without exception.
4. Employees' safety attitude, training and instruction, provision of safe tools and equipment, supervision, and leadership are considered highly important factors which contribute to safety and which can be influenced directly by supervisors.
5. When accidents do occur, they should be investigated promptly for very important reasons, including the fact that information which is gained can be used to prevent accidents in the future.

H. Equal Employment Opportunity
1. The supervisor should endeavor to treat all employees fairly, without regard to religion, race, sex, or national origin.
2. Groups tend to reflect the attitude of the leader. Prejudice can be detected even in very subtle form. Supervisors must strive to create a feeling of mutual respect and confidence in every employee.
3. Complete utilization of all human resources is a national goal. Equitable consideration should be accorded women in the work force, minority-group members, the physically and mentally handicapped, and the older employee. The important question is: "Who can do the job?"
4. Training opportunities, recognition for performance, overtime assignments, promotional opportunities, and all other personnel actions are to be handled on an equitable basis.

I. Improving Communications
1. Communications is achieving understanding between the sender and the receiver of a message. It also means sharing information—the creation of understanding.
2. Communication is basic to all human activity. Words are means of conveying meanings; however, real meanings are in people.
3. There are very practical differences in the effectiveness of one-way, impersonal, and two-way communications. Words spoken face-to-face are better understood. Telephone conversations are effective, but lack the rapport of person-to-person exchanges. The whole person communicates.
4. Cooperation and communication in an organization go hand in hand. When there is a mutual respect between people, spelling out rules and procedures for communicating is unnecessary.
5. There are several barriers to effective communications. These include failure to listen with respect and understanding, lack of skill in feedback, and misinterpreting the meanings of words used by the speaker. It is also common

practice to listen to what we want to hear, and tune out things we do not want to hear.
6. Communication is management's chief problem. The supervisor should accept the challenge to communicate more effectively and to improve interagency and intra-agency communications.
7. The supervisor may often plan for and conduct meetings. The planning phase is critical and may determine the success or the failure of a meeting.
8. Speaking before groups usually requires extra effort. Stage fright may never disappear completely, but it can be controlled.

J. Self-Development
1. Every employee is responsible for his own self-development.
2. Toastmaster and toastmistress clubs offer opportunities to improve skills in oral communications.
3. Planning for one's own self-development is of vital importance. Supervisors know their own strengths and limitations better than anyone else.
4. Many opportunities are open to aid the supervisor in his developmental efforts, including job assignments; training opportunities, both governmental and non-governmental—to include universities and professional conferences and seminars.
5. Programmed instruction offers a means of studying at one's own rate.
6. Where difficulties may arise from a supervisor's being away from his work for training, he may participate in televised home study or correspondence courses to meet his self-development needs.

K. Teaching and Training
1. The Teaching Process
Teaching is encouraging and guiding the learning activities of students toward established goals. In most cases this process consists of five steps: preparation, presentation, summarization, evaluation, and application.

   a. Preparation
   Preparation is two-fold in nature; that of the supervisor and the employee. Preparation by the supervisor is absolutely essential to success. He must know what, when, where, how, and whom he will teach. Some of the factors that should be considered are:
   1) The objectives
   2) The materials needed
   3) The methods to be used
   4) Employee participation
   5) Employee interest
   6) Training aids
   7) Evaluation
   8) Summarization

   Employee preparation consists in preparing the employee to receive the material. Probably the most important single factor in the preparation of the employee is arousing and maintaining his interest. He must know the objectives of the training, why he is there, how the material can be used, and its importance to him.

b. Presentation
In presentation, have a carefully designed plan and follow it. The plan should be accurate and complete, yet flexible enough to meet situations as they arise. The method of presentation will be determined by the particular situation and objectives.

c. Summary
A summary should be made at the end of every training unit and program. In addition, there may be internal summaries depending on the nature of the material being taught. The important thing is that the trainee must always be able to understand how each part of the new material relates to the whole.

d. Application
The supervisor must arrange work so the employee will be given a chance to apply new knowledge or skills while the material is still clear in his mind and interest is high. The trainee does not really know whether he has learned the material until he has been given a chance to apply it. If the material is not applied, it loses most of its value.

e. Evaluation
The purpose of all training is to promote learning. To determine whether the training has been a success or failure, the supervisor must evaluate this learning.
In the broadest sense, evaluation includes all the devices, methods, skills, and techniques used by the supervisor to keep himself and the employees informed as to their progress toward the objectives they are pursuing. The extent to which the employee has mastered the knowledge, skills, and abilities, or changed his attitudes, as determined by the program objectives, is the extent to which instruction has succeeded or failed.
Evaluation should not be confined to the end of the lesson, day, or program but should be used continuously. We shall note later the way this relates to the rest of the teaching process.

2. Teaching Methods
A teaching method is a pattern of identifiable student and instructor activity used in presenting training material.
All supervisors are faced with the problem of deciding which method should be used at a given time.

a. Lecture
The lecture is direct oral presentation of material by the supervisor. The present trend is to place less emphasis on the trainer's activity and more on that of the trainee.

b. Discussion
Teaching by discussion or conference involves using questions and other techniques to arouse interest and focus attention upon certain areas, and by doing so creating a learning situation. This can be one of the most

valuable methods because it gives the employees an opportunity to express their ideas and pool their knowledge.

    c. Demonstration
The demonstration is used to teach how something works or how to do something. It can be used to show a principle or what the results of a series of actions will be. A well-staged demonstration is particularly effective because it shows proper methods of performance in a realistic manner.

    d. Performance
Performance is one of the most fundamental of all learning techniques or teaching methods. The trainee may be able to tell how a specific operation should be performed but he cannot be sure he knows how to perform the operation until he has done so.
As with all methods, there are certain advantages and disadvantages to each method.

    e. Which Method to Use
Moreover, there are other methods and techniques of teaching. It is difficult to use any method without other methods entering into it. In any learning situation, a combination of methods is usually more effective than any one method alone.

Finally, evaluation must be integrated into the other aspects of the teaching-learning process.

It must be used in the motivation of the trainees; it must be used to assist in developing understanding during the training; and it must be related to employee application of the results of training.

This is distinctly the role of the supervisor.

www.ingramcontent.com/pod-product-compliance
Lightning Source LLC
Chambersburg PA
CBHW081803300426
44116CB00014B/2226